# GOLF AND THE
# AMERICAN COUNTRY CLUB

SPORT AND SOCIETY

*Series Editors*
Benjamin G. Rader
Randy Roberts

*A list of books in the series appears
at the end of this book.*

# GOLF AND THE
# AMERICAN COUNTRY CLUB

RICHARD J. MOSS

University of Illinois Press
Urbana and Chicago

∞ This book is printed on acid-free paper.

The Library of Congress cataloged the cloth edition
as follows:
Moss, Richard J.
Golf and the American country club / Richard J. Moss.
p.   cm. — (Sport and society)
Includes bibliographical references and index.
ISBN 0-252-02642-X (cloth : alk. paper)
1. Golf—Social aspects—United States. 2. Country clubs—
Social aspects—United States. I. Title. II. Series.
GV979.S63M67      2001
796.352'06'873—dc21      00-010832

Paperback ISBN 978-0-252-07413-4

# CONTENTS

# ACKNOWLEDGMENTS

IN THE COURSE of writing this book I have incurred a number of debts that I happily acknowledge. Peter Levine, Benjamin Rader, Geoffrey S. Cornish, Richard L. Wentworth, and Rand Jerris each read all or part of the manuscript and each offered helpful suggestions. At Colby College I have received aid and comfort from a number of people at crucial points. Peter Westervelt, Tony Corrado, and Dawn DiBlasi provided editing, newspaper clippings, and general manuscript improvement services that were priceless. Sarah P. Ward turned my fountain pen smudges into a modern "processed" manuscript. Her contributions in the last stages of this project were enormous. I must also thank John J. Gibson for the support that he has generously tendered to me and to Colby College.

Several friends have provided spiritual and emotional support. Pearl Rose, Bill and Georgia Katz, Don Roberts, and the Gentlemen of the Scramble have helped in hard-to-define ways. To my wife, Jane, my golf book has been a trial. I dedicate it to her in hopes that I may continue to do golf research, play golf, and buy golf clubs at my present brisk pace.

# INTRODUCTION

IN THE SUMMER of 1968 I had the good fortune to meet a handsome, somewhat eccentric older woman on a flight from Chicago. Dressed in a bright red suit and white blouse, she exuded upper-middle-class respectability. I, however, did not. She must have known that her traveling companion sported nearly all the outward signs of a "counterculture" radical—long hair, frayed jeans, and peace symbols. A few moments after takeoff, however, she turned and asked me what I noticed most when I looked down at the ground from an airplane. In retrospect it seems odd that I told her the truth. I answered, "Golf courses." Her eyes brightened, and she replied, "Exactly, but I see the swimming pools as well." I could literally feel her growing anticipation as the next few moments passed. She grabbed my arm and informed me of our incredible luck; below in the Chicago suburbs stood a magnificent country club in full summer glory.

With childlike intensity she began an informal essay on the unlikely subject of country clubs as seen from the air. As we both viewed the scene from the airliner's tiny window, she pointed out the "clear boundary" that divided the club from the surrounding urban sprawl. The club, she claimed, was like a village, neat and ordered, miraculously preserved amid modern chaos. Indeed, the course and buildings were deeply at odds with their surroundings. Everything within the boundary of the club seemed clear and carefully planned. Even though we had only moments to digest the scene below, we both could trace the course as it left the clubhouse and made its way, in eighteen variable segments, around the bordered parcel and back to the clubhouse. All the elements—roads, auxiliary buildings, parking lots—were precisely placed, organized by some clear but unseen principle. The surrounding area provided a stunning contrast. Here and there some sense of order intruded, but the eye was drawn to other things. I particularly noticed a road that ended in a weed-choked field of rusting oil tanks. In the end, however, my strongest impression was of the difference between the ordered serenity of the club and the general anarchy of the suburb around it.

This airborne encounter left a vivid memory because it so clearly touched my ambivalence, my inability to take clear positions on important issues. The 1960s were decidedly not a good time for golf and country clubs. Members of the counterculture in particular saw golf and country clubs as embodying much that they found wrong with America. To put things in simple terms, by 1968 I had in a half-hearted way capitulated to the critique that condemned golf and country clubs along with almost all the other symbols of American bourgeois life. I say "capitulated" for I had essentially been raised at a country club. Both my parents played and belonged to a club. My father had for several years been president of his club; he loved the place and took pride in being a respected member. My involvement went far beyond being just "a member's kid," however; I worked in the pro shop, caddied, and mowed greens at my parents' club and at another local course. The values I encountered at college challenged and eventually chilled the warm feelings I felt when I remembered all those idyllic days I had spent on the course and at the club.

The country club, it seemed, ran counter to the keystone American value, equality. There was no denying the essentially exclusive nature of these institutions. Nearly everyone could explain the social structure of his or her town by reference to its country clubs. Social classes and ethnic groups seemed to sort themselves out as much by country club as by wage level.

Getting into a club became important not so much because it constituted a positive accomplishment in itself but because it gave the new member the right to participate in the exclusion of the unworthy. Country clubs, many argued, existed to create unequal access, to draw a boundary between the elect and the unwanted.

The negative response to country clubs was rooted in much more than egalitarianism, however. Golf, the dominant sport at such clubs, was (and still is) portrayed as elitist. For example, in a column entitled "What Is It," Dan Jenkins wrote of an African American gentleman who, knowing nothing about golf, found himself at a Masters Tournament. Jenkins pointed out Jack Nicklaus and Johnny Miller walking down the fairway with their black caddies. The black man responded: "Golf? I get it. A couple of blond Nazis walking through the woods with two spades carrying their shit."[1] Responses like this one gave me pause; they made me think that golf and the country clubs where it is played involved much more than a struggle between open, equal access and the personal freedom to exclude undesirables from a private institution. Further complicating matters for me was the often-voiced charge that golf is a "faggot sport," that golfers are unmanly in some sense. Could the game of the upper class, the dominating class, really be effeminate? In the end I was left wondering about the source of all these strong feelings, stereotypes, and compelling images; where and how had the country club and the game of golf taken root in America? How had what is essentially a playing field become a cultural site capable of eliciting the strongest allegiance and the harshest criticism?

This little book is an attempt to answer those questions. It is framed by several important limitations and assumptions. First, the story you will find here is divided into two clearly defined sections. The country club and golf flourished for almost a half a century after their inception in America. In 1930, however, the atmosphere changed. Golf as a sport and the country club as an institution entered a period of radical transformation that continues to this day. Second, I have for the most part emphasized those people who created the country clubs. Over the last century the intentions of these founding fathers and mothers have been lost. Today many may use the term *coun-*

*try clubbers* to mean bewildered, vacuous, slightly hedonistic, and mammothly politically incorrect people in brightly colored clothes. The people who founded and nurtured the clubs between 1880 and 1930 were much more complex than this modern stereotype suggests. One of this book's main purposes is to accurately portray what the elite classes hoped to accomplish by inventing the country club and in many ways by making golf their game. Finally, for reasons that will become clear as you read the book, I take for granted that the country club and golf are inextricably linked. In short, you cannot comprehend one without understanding the other.

## ✻ 1 ✻

# THE COUNTRY CLUB IDEA
# AND AMERICAN EXPERIENCE

COUNTRY CLUBS start in the living rooms, dining rooms, and city club meeting rooms of men and women who wish to establish a private social and athletic domain. They draw a line between public and private space and install a collective (the membership) as the lords and ladies of that private domain. Such was clearly the case with the founding of the Country Club, in Brookline, Massachusetts, perhaps the first and certainly the most important such club in the United States. In early April 1882 James Murray Forbes held a dinner party at his Commonwealth Avenue home. After dinner Forbes, a railroad tycoon, introduced the idea of forming a club in the suburbs of Boston. The gentlemen present that evening agreed to sign a circular explaining the aims of the proposed club; the circular invited Boston's elite to join in the enterprise. Over the next fifty years and beyond this process or one much like it occurred again and again, until most American towns had at least one such club. Solid numbers are hard to find, but by 1930 there were at least four thousand country clubs in the United States.[1]

To understand why Forbes held his dinner party and why the idea spawned there prospered, we need to understand certain aspects of American life in the 1880s and 1890s. The country club idea drew considerable strength from the long and mostly glorious history of the voluntary association in the United States. Well before the Civil War Alexis de Tocqueville noticed the passion with which Americans formed associations. He was particularly interested in political associations; he was also impressed by the fact that Americans of "all stations of life" formed associations "of a thousand different types." He noted that unlike aristocratic societies, a democratic nation needs voluntary associations to overcome the helplessness that democracy and individualism forced on its citizens. Certainly forming country clubs does not have the same moral gravity as forging abolition societies to end slavery, but Tocqueville stressed that once the habit to associate had become general, Americans bonded together to achieve purposes both great and small.[2]

Voluntary associations have indeed been central in American life. Church historians, for example, have added to Tocqueville's insights by showing exactly how important voluntarism or the "voluntary principle" has been in American religious history. Since the early seventeenth century Americans have founded churches on the principle of voluntarism. In time Americans came to see churches as best formed by individuals freely coming together to create them. In the early nineteenth century the New England elite, challenged by a rising commercial elite, rapid migration west, and the influx of new ethnic groups, used various forms of association to maintain their moral and intellectual control in a rapidly changing nation. The result was the vast array of reform and moral uplift groups that did much to shape the history of the pre–Civil War period. They fought drinking, slavery, the oppression of women, and moral decline generally. In the long run they also taught the post–Civil War generation the virtues of association. By 1880, especially in New England, the power of association was being used less and less for reform and more and more in commerce, industry, and government. The tendency to consociate for all sorts of purposes had become a cultural habit. As people sought increased leisure and the desire to pursue games grew, it was not at all odd that they formed voluntary associations to achieve their goals.[3]

Nevertheless, the New Englanders who first employed the voluntary association would have been appalled by the country club and the somewhat frantic pursuit of leisure that characterized the late nineteenth and early twentieth centuries, for the Protestant elite who formed moral reform societies early in the last century clearly saw play and leisure as anathema to the work ethic. Samuel F. B. Morse, the inventor of the telegraph, heard constant injunctions against play and leisure from his parents and grandparents. When he was only eight, his parents wrote him: "Don't let play occupy too much of your time or attention. Remember time is precious and should be well improved." His parents were backed by an equally concerned paternal grandfather who believed that there is "a great danger . . . of carrying Recreations to Excess."[4] Morse was taught what literally a whole generation of Protestant middle-class children were taught. They came to value hard work, the postponement of gratification, and the repression of desire. The good life revolved around family and was sober, conscientious, and orderly. These values add up to what we now call Victorian culture.

It is important to understand that this culture, which I call "Victorian" for convenience' sake, was in its own way revolutionary. Its idea of work was profoundly radical; Victorians took what humanity had long seen as a burden and made it virtually the moral core of life itself. In essence, they constructed an ideology centered in large part on the idea that work is the avenue to virtue. As Morse learned, the Victorians also defined play as one important pothole on that avenue. This ideology was one major engine for the growth of preindustrial capitalism. It provided a worldview for the men and women who inhabited the small shops, counting houses, and capitalist farms of the American nineteenth century. By the middle of the century, especially in the North, the new view of work had combined with geographic and economic expansion to create a new culture that effectively replaced the precapitalist agrarian world of the eighteenth century.[5]

The slow destruction of this new culture and the construction of an even newer one in its stead was the larger context in which the country club idea was born and thrived. Exactly why Victorianism began to decline is a big story, one I cannot tell here, but the country club idea was undeniably a response to its slow demise. In many respects the country club was an attempt to preserve certain aspects of Victorian culture before they were overrun by new values spawned in the burgeoning industrial city.

The typical affluent Victorian of the 1880s felt assailed from both the outside and the inside. The overwhelmingly Protestant elite felt threatened from without by millions of immigrants who were arriving on American shores. Between 1880 and World War I many immigrants came from exotic places such as Russia, Poland, and Austria-Hungary. Perhaps most alarming was the arrival of over two million Jews, mostly from Eastern Europe. These new arrivals shared neither the religion nor the values of the Protestant elite. Thomas Bailey Aldrich, a member of the elite in both Boston and New York, gave voice to deeply rooted nativist fears in his 1885 poem "Unguarded Gates." On the one hand, Aldrich affirmed America's role as the haven of the oppressed; the United States was an "Eden," the "enchanted land" that had liberated millions who wished to work and live as free people. On the other hand, Aldrich feared that the unguarded gates now served as a portal for the massive onrush of "a wild motley throng" bringing "unknown gods and rites," groups who wished "to waste the gifts of freedom."[6] Fears like Aldrich's would grow and spread through the 1920s, when they would lead to immigration restrictions based on a quota system that limited the immigrant flow from Eastern Europe and elsewhere.

Perhaps as alarming as the immigrants was the dramatic rise of the new rich elites, many of whom possessed wealth enough to challenge the older elites, whose social status was rooted in long years of community service, historic family names, and genteel education and manners. In Boston, for example, the Brahmins who had dominated Boston's social and economic life between 1820 and 1860 were challenged by "upstarts" such as Eben Jordan and his department store fortune and Harvey Parker, who grew rich building hotels. Although the older elite could deny such newcomers genteel sta-

tus, the new rich were clearly altering the economic landscape and under-
cutting the long-standing Brahmin control of Boston's economic and political life. By the turn of the century the older elites were withdrawing from
the scramble in the new industrial city. Justice Brandeis remembered that rich
Bostonians often advised their sons that the city was being destroyed "by
heavy taxes and political misrule." He also recalled that the sons of Boston's
beleaguered elite were advised to move to the suburbs and build their lives
around club, home, and family.[7]

In fact, the Victorians faced problems even larger than immigrants and
the rise of new wealth. For much of American history and well into nineteenth century, American culture was decidedly local. Americans lived their
lives and learned what was allowed and disallowed in "island communities."
Informal elites and informal economic relations ruled people's lives; for the
most part, agricultural patterns still dictated the pace of life. On the surface
the social structure seemed remarkably flat, but distinctions that would probably elude a modern observer were clear to the inhabitants. Such things as
a home's location or exact size had precise meanings to the natives. Relatively small variations in wealth, religion, and family history served to sort
individuals into a social order. Even in urban areas, the wealthy of "good"
family enjoyed remarkable isolation. They had little contact with the wealthy
and genteel of other towns, cementing their dominance through exclusive
local institutions and rigid control over the marriage choices of their off-
spring.[8]

Edith Wharton has provided us with a remarkable portrait of this urban
upper-middle-class tribalism. *The Age of Innocence* (1920) is Wharton's retro-
spective look at New York's upper-middle-class society in the years after the
Civil War. It is "a compact little circle" governed by a complex "ruling class."
The novel's hero, Newland Archer, is described in terms that could apply to
all the males in his circle; he "was a quiet and self-controlled young man.
Conformity to the discipline of a small society had become almost his second nature. It was deeply distasteful to him to do anything melodramatic and
conspicuous." The members of this circle seem trapped in their over-furnished
homes, such as the Newport mansion that Archer inherits when he marries

into the Welland clan. It was "one of the houses in which one always knew exactly what is happening at a given hour." Like all who enter such houses, Archer is overcome by the atmosphere; the furnishings, "the tick of disciplined clocks," and "the whole chain of tyrannical trifles binding one hour to the next" nearly suffocate him and make him feel that a less organized existence would be "unreal and precarious."

Of course, Newland Archer does attempt to live a less organized existence. He is attracted to Ellen Olenska, who represents all that is foreign, unconventional, and exciting. The elite sphere that gives him his sense of position and a set of utilitarian values silently but effectively destroys his desire to leave his wife and run off with Ellen. In telling this story, Wharton creates the sense that New York "society" is made up of only some two hundred people who really matter. Even in a city growing at an amazing pace, the Archers, the Wellands, and the others live as if they occupy some tightly knit village. Behavior is regulated by an unarticulated code that silently employs tradition and training to mold people into compliant Victorians. The code, of course, is justly famous for its repression of the sexual, the eccentric, and the overly ambitious. It also put great value on absolute honesty, the family, and the community, and it allowed the past some hegemony over the present. This Victorian code has become something of a joke in the twentieth century, but Wharton understood it better than we ever shall. She knew that the collapse of the tribal values she so clearly dramatized in *The Age of Innocence* was not an unalloyed victory for progress. By the end of the novel, Newland Archer can look back from the perspective of the early twentieth century. He understands that "after all, there was good in the old ways." The changes of the late nineteenth century had destroyed the clans and their tight little island community, and although his tribe had kept him from Ellen, he understands its value in a new age that he does not fully accept.

Newland Archer articulates a sensibility that was an important element in the first stages of the country club movement. The movement was an important attempt to recapture the "old ways." Specifically, it was an effort to counter a world in which, Newland Archer believed, people had become "too busy with reforms and 'movements,' with fads and fetishes and frivolities . . . , to bother much about their neighbors." The country club was also an antidote to a new concept of equality in which a person's past was seen as inconsequential and society became a "huge kaleidoscope where all the social atoms spun around on the same plane."[9]

Island communities like the one occupied by Newland Archer provided the perfect soil for the luxuriant growth of Victorian values. Hard work, self-denial, thrift, and modesty among women all became cultural givens. There was little room for tolerance; the crudely ambitious, the spendthrift, the lazy, the drunken, and the disorderly were dealt with according to a code that almost no one doubted had been ordained by a Protestant God. This was a world in which the word *gentility* had precise meaning and worth, and it was run unself-consciously by a Protestant, Anglo-Saxon elite willing and able to enforce that meaning and worth.

By the late 1870s the island communities were being undermined by enormous and irresistible forces. It is easy to identify these forces as nationalization, industrialization, mechanization, centralization, urbanization, and incorporation, but it is more difficult to describe their precise impact. As Americans brought these forces into being, they experienced "dislocation and bewilderment." As local control gave way, Americans found themselves in a nation without a center. Robert H. Wiebe claims that America "lacked those national centers of authority and information which might have given order to such swift changes. American institutions were still oriented toward community life where family and church, education and press, professions and government, all largely found their meaning by the way they fit one with another inside a town or detached portion of a city. . . . They tried . . . to impose the known upon the unknown, to master an impersonal world through the customs of a personal society."[10]

Wiebe claims they failed in this attempt. Certainly the national political movements of Populism and Progressivism deservedly command our attention as crucial attempts to deal with the dramatic changes of the late nineteenth century. Our sense of the period between 1877 and 1915 is sharply focused on the national scene and on the attempts to find new ways (generally via an expanded federal government) to deal with massive economic and social change. This is one fundamental reason for the neglect of the country club as a historical development. The country club was clearly part of the attempt to respond locally to the nerve-racking pace of change. By drawing a line between public and private space, the country club founders effectively reestablished the vanishing village. They created small, stable, and easily understood corporate enterprises that, although democratic in practice, exercised nearly absolute control over access. While the nation sought national solutions for national problems, the country club arose as a local response that effectively dealt with the dissolution of village America. In the fullness of time, the country club would find that its most potent enemies would be the forces of nationalization, standardization, and the incorporation of American life. Country clubs developed as eccentric local institutions. As such they were left to grow and evolve unhindered (except for the imposition of a federal excise tax during World War I) by governmental interference or corporate competition. The Great Depression and World War II stopped the growth of clubs and set the stage for increased governmental control and corporate competition in the postwar era. Like many other American institutions, the private country club was pressured by the federal government and other national groups to conform to a set of national standardized rules. In addition, after the war the clubs faced increased competition from large corporations that in several ways began to offer a substitute for the member-owned private club.

While Victorian culture was assaulted from the outside by immigrants and the changes associated with capitalism, urbanization, and centralization, it also produced within itself some of the seeds of its own destruction. To put the matter in simple terms, Victorians were taught to work hard, accumulate wealth, and deny themselves the luxury that such wealth might buy. It was the perfect ethic for a preindustrial society in which production was the central problem. Certainly it was the ethic for a society that needed to bring a frontier into useful production and to exploit a technological revolution that yearly spawned new and profitable ways of extracting wealth from nature. Yet this ethic was essentially self-destructive; by 1890 it had produced wealth beyond the dreams of eighteenth- and early nineteenth-century

Americans. Between the Civil War and World War I, Americans experienced unprecedented growth in discretionary time and income. The average work-week for nonagricultural workers in 1850 was seventy hours; by 1910 it had dropped to fifty-five. Wages and profits rose and fell with an increasingly violent boom-and-bust rhythm, but in the long run wages increased and prices went down, often dramatically. For the average American before the Civil War, work had been the crucial foundation of a moral life; work had been the school where Americans learned self-discipline and erected barriers against needless consumption and other unsavory desires. By the end of the century, abundance, the product of all that work and denial, was making most elements of the Protestant work ethic seem superfluous. As one historian has put it, "Of all the acid that ate away at work and self-discipline . . . affluence was among the most corroding."[11]

By the late nineteenth century, Victorian culture seemed to be literally consuming itself. As Victorian culture evolved, growing numbers of its most ardent adherents grew anxious and depressed. They began to doubt that modern life was producing progress, let alone perfection. Drawing on the warnings left behind by their Puritan and republican forebears, many affluent Americans began to see their society as overcivilized. Self-denial, hard work, and self-control had produced a spreading sense of moral and spiritual sterility. Instead of experiencing personal independence and energy, Victorians began to feel trapped in their airless parlors and encumbered by their ample stomachs. More crucial, however, was the feeling that important values such as the primacy of the family, as well as rigid internalized values such as self-control and self-denial, had become intensely repressive and suffocating. Many Americans from the middle class upward began to suspect that somehow the life they thought proper and good was making them sick.[12]

In addition to believing that modern existence was making them ill, these Victorians felt profoundly that cultural authority was collapsing. Again drawing on Puritan and republican sources, many Americans fretted over the vast corruption in local and central government. For most Anglo-Saxon Protestants, however, ultimate authority rested with a benevolent deity who planned the universe for the enjoyment of humankind, his favorite creations. By 1900 this complacent religiosity was no longer possible. Darwin, of course, was crucial in undermining the notion of a divinely ordered universe, but a perhaps more important factor was science's implicit centrality to the worldview of the dominant Protestant creed. In this view evidence of God's existence rests on the idea that the universe is orderly and that his will can be observed working in nature. As scientists revealed more of the universe, they in effect revealed more about its ultimate creator. American Protestants particularly relied on the argument from design. Protestants had based their faith on the idea that science and religion were compatible; by 1900 this easy alliance was no longer possible. For the first time in American experience, important people expressed their agnosticism and, more rarely, atheism.[13]

In sum, the dominant Anglo-Saxon Protestant culture experienced a profound crisis that reached a peak of sorts in the 1890s. The America these Victorians had inherited from the pre–Civil War years dissolved before their very eyes. The cities were overrun by immigrants who spoke strange languages and who often did not share the Victorian values of hard work and strict self-control. Localism disappeared as national corporations, technological advances, and a transportation revolution undercut the power of local elites and constructed national and international elites in their place. As if this were not enough, Victorian Americans began to feel that their own values had somehow turned on them. They felt trapped in their cluttered homes and betrayed by their commitment to work and self-control. Even God seemed less vivid, less able to serve as a basis for a tired, increasingly unreal culture. Protestant Anglo-Saxon upper- and middle-class Americans continued to act much as they always had, but they did so with a sense of exhaustion and a barely repressed feeling that their time was up.

This gloomy mood somewhat paradoxically created a period of frantic activity. Many affluent Americans poured their energies into reform attempts. On several fronts anxious Victorians sought to impose their wills on the industrial cities. They sought moral reform by attacking prostitution, drinking, and the abuse and neglect of children. They attacked political corruption in a number of ways, particularly through efforts to destroy the power of urban political bosses and to clean up corrupt police departments. One historian has characterized this trend by saying that as Victorians became less religious, less confident and less sure of their own beliefs, they became "more concerned than ever to embody their cultural values in institutions."[14] As reformers, for example, they created the settlement houses as a way to teach the new urban dwellers Victorian values. For themselves they founded country clubs to provide private spaces where the values and behaviors associated with gentility could be honored and maintained.

The first of these clubs was formed around Murray Forbes's dinner table in the spring of 1882. The men who put their energy, time, and money into this endeavor did so for a variety of reasons, but the club itself and process whereby it came into being clearly show what their intentions were. The thirty men who began the club came to the effort with some experience. Many of them were members of or at least knew about Winchester's Myopia Club.

Myopia had evolved informally in the 1870s and was formally incorporated in 1879. At first it was a neighborhood boys club with the Prince brothers in the lead. Their father, Frederick O. Prince, had once been mayor of Boston as well as a state senator and representative. His sons—Gordon, Charles, Morton, and Frederick—formed a club on the shores of Wedge Pond, in Winchester, Massachusetts. At first the club was devoted to boating and tennis, but they soon turned to baseball. Their team took the name Myopia since the Prince brothers (really the whole family) suffered from poor vision; local newspaper reports often referred to the team as the "Near-Sighted Nine."

The club seems to have become more formalized when the members turned their interest to riding and fox hunting. They moved from a small cottage on the Prince estate to a handsome clubhouse on nearby Mystic Lake. Lumber tycoon David N. Skilling built the new structure and became one of the leading members. By 1880 the club had begun getting some negative responses; the members had too much fun and drank to excess. To counter this, the membership purchased a pew in the local church. Frederick Prince, moving on from boating, tennis, and baseball, managed to infect a number of his friends with his newfound passion for fox hunting. Among those who caught the disease were J. Murray Forbes and Augustus Hemenway, both founding members of the Brookline club. Indeed, the connections between

Myopia and the Country Club were very close. Frederick Prince claims that as Myopia grew, many of its members became interested in finding a place nearer Boston. It was this interest that led Forbes and Robert C. Hooper to take an option on Clyde Park, a racing track and farm, and to suggest that Myopia move to the new site in Brookline. Prince also claims that at the first organizational meeting there was some interest in retaining Myopia as the name of the new enterprise. The bulk of Myopia blended into the Country Club, but because fox hunting proved impossible in Brookline, those most interested in this activity established themselves as the Myopia Hunt Club, with new headquarters in Hamilton, Massachusetts.[15]

Nevertheless, the Country Club's roots go deeper even than Myopia. Since 1860 elite Bostonians had been seeking a rural and private destination within reasonable coaching distance of their homes in the city. A document from 1860 that still hangs in the Brookline clubhouse proposes exactly such a club. Signed by seventy Bostonians, the document outlines the creation of a club for horse lovers who were apparently appalled by the gambling and bad behavior at public racetracks. These gentlemen sought a private club for horse racing and other related activities at a site fairly close to Boston. This original attempt was probably quashed by the start of the Civil War. The links between the 1860 proposal and the efforts in 1882 are clear, however. More than twenty of the seventy who signed the 1860 document show up on the first Country Club membership list, from 1883.[16]

Fed by the example of Myopia and the long-term desire of Bostonians to have a private destination for their weekend coaching excursions, the proposal to establish a club was a rousing success. The circular calling for members attracted over four hundred Bostonians who agreed to pay an entrance fee of twenty-five dollars and yearly dues of thirty dollars. Led by Forbes, the club rented land known as Clyde Park, in Brookline. The land and buildings had known a number of uses over the years, but in 1882 the property was perfectly suited to the club's purpose. It contained all the elements necessary to satisfy a membership in love with horses. The property included ample stables and a racetrack, as well as a handsome farmhouse. Most of the early improvements were designed to make the property more useful to horse lovers. The stables were refurbished, and a steeplechase course was installed. To serve the needs of those who coached out from Boston for the day, the club added a restaurant, a kitchen, and a taproom. Although riding and fox hunting were crucial reasons for founding the club, it quickly became a destination for those fond of coaching. With the founding of the Brookline club, Bostonians could coach into the countryside, enjoy a meal, have their horses tended, and return to Boston in the evening. Thus the Country Club in its earliest days bore little resemblance to the modern country club, with its commitment to a number of sporting endeavors. In tracing the early growth of the club, the *Brookline Chronicle* often referred to it as "a racing park," which seems more accurate than calling it a country club.

This all suggests that the founding of the club at Brookline is not particularly important in understanding the country club movement. The horsey set dominated the early days at Brookline, but those days were short-lived. By the turn of the century much of the devotion to horses had been diverted into other activities, and the club began its evolution into a multipurpose institution with major commitments of land and money to many sports. The advent of the automobile would quickly extinguish the passion for horses and fundamentally change the leisure habits of affluent Americans. This change is best symbolized by the racetrack, which was initially central but by 1900 had been transformed into the first and eighteenth fairways of the golf course.

Although in its first configuration the Country Club was not truly representative of the clubs that followed over the next two decades, it spawned significant attempts to interpret the motives of Forbes and other founders. Much of this guesswork flows from an animosity to the upper class and predictably finds that the country club reflected upper-class pretensions and a desire among Boston's elites to found exclusive institutions that would protect their economic and social status. Other commentators, most notably Stephen Hardy, have taken a more complicated view. Without neglecting the class-consciousness of Brookline's founders, Hardy notes that they also had other purposes and that the club movement has to be put into context. Clubs and voluntary associations in general can moderate the disturbing impact of rapid change and innovation. Clubs tend to provide approved models for behavior, and these models may be radically new, traditional, or something in between. Furthermore, at the time in question clubs of one sort or another provided protection from an urban scene that was increasingly destroying community. The clubs in essence provided stable communities for anxious Americans who felt that the larger community, if it existed at all, no longer provided a sense of personal identity and belonging. The country club was only one example of such community building; people of many classes and ethnic backgrounds also founded clubs and associations that satisfied the desire to reestablish some sense of community.[17]

The country club was certainly a response to the fragmentation of community, but it was also more. If Forbes and the other founders of the Brookline club had simply wanted to reestablish community, they could have done it in many other ways. The country club movement was devoted to challenging institutions and attitudes clearly present in the city clubs, which had long created cohesion among the upper classes. The founders of Brookline did not set out to create another exclusive bastion such as the Somerset and Union Clubs, to which they already belonged; they wanted to escape such sleepy confines, to respond to more urgent impulses. One member has suggested that "when the Saxon blood . . . , no longer to be controlled, called loudly for the sports of merry England," younger Americans responded by modeling Myopia, and then the Country Club, after the Hurlingham Club, near London. This same member wondered whether the country club movement was not designed to destroy the sedentary habits of Victorian Americans and return them to the affirmation of play and devotion to exercise of the Greeks. Most important, he emphatically claimed that "the Country Club is a potent factor in the elimination of morbid nervousness—that American bugbear—and is equally potent in the work of reconstruction; for all who submit to its healthful, pleasing regime are surely progressing toward sane, normal, active manhood and womanhood."[18]

There is little doubt that the late nineteenth and early twentieth centuries saw Americans of many types begin the search for more active lives, but it would be a mistake to lump together all their attempts to find satisfying activities. We must keep spectating and participating as separate categories. It is one thing to watch a prizefight and quite another to take up the sport yourself. There is also the central theme of violence. One can easily argue that many sports new at the time (e.g., football) were cultural means for dealing with suppressed anger rooted in class and ethnic antagonisms. It is also possible that active, violent diversions served as an antidote to the frustrations caused by the increased discipline and control that industrial capitalism and the realities of urban life were imposing on many Americans. Although they all fall within the search for a satisfying active life, turning to football or boxing should not be confused with turning to golf, cycling, hiking, and other outdoor sports.[19]

Over the last century members of the Country Club have proudly claimed for their institution the honor of being the first country club. Such distinctions do nothing to clarify the real significance and function of the country club as a cultural invention. The story of the Country Club's founding offers only a few tantalizing clues, only the beginnings of an answer to my question. Ultimately the country club was the product of other groups like the one that met in Forbes's dining room. These groups had probably heard of the Country Club, but they had other purposes in mind and often operated in a different environment. Nevertheless, the club that Forbes and his colleagues created at Clyde Park suggested some of the most important impulses behind the country club movement. In it we can detect a certain degree of Anglomania; after 1882 a number of clubs took pride in imitating what they saw as English (and Scottish) upper-class habits and culture. On a more general level the desire to escape the city to a private controlled space in the country, which was basic to the founding of the Country Club, would remain central to the movement. It was, and still is, an anticity movement that sought to provide a rural space for its members to enjoy. This intention to escape the city makes more sense, and seems more significant, in the context of David Paine's remark about "morbid nervousness." As I will show, the country club movement, which took off not long after the Brookline club's founding, commonly promoted itself as medicinal, as the prescription for the malady brought on by the industrial city and modern life.

## ❧ 2 ❧

# GOLF AND THE EARLY CLUBS

A S EARLY AS the mid-1890s commentators on upper-class leisure were beginning to sense the importance of the country club.
They identified the fact that farms near the growing cities were
passing out of the hands of farmers and into the hands of the upper class.
What had once been productive farms were quickly becoming "sanitariums"
for the genteel who sought the soothing touch of nature. These commentators, especially Edward S. Martin, still placed the horse and hunting at the
center of the movement. Martin claimed that it was "a reasonable desire" for
"the city man" to want to go back to hunting. The modern city sapped the
affluent urban man's "vitality" and the "vigor." Once this typical successful
urbanite had established himself, his life became too easy. Overfed and
trapped in overheated homes, the city man was led "to work too hard with
his head and too little with his body." In response to his "fear of the debili-
tating influences of such a life both on his physique and on his character,"
the new urbanite sought the country and club life.[1]

This life was still dominated by the horse and related activities. The clubs provided what horse and coaching lovers needed most: an objective for the day's outing, good care for the animals when they arrived, and a congenial atmosphere plus a good meal. This love of the horse was the product of a rise in discretionary income. As such income increased, it was used to obtain a horse. As one's income increased even more, it was employed to purchase more expensive horsey diversions. Martin listed the typical progression: a horse lover started with "a dog-cart," moved onto "a surrey," and continued moving upward until he finally purchased "a four-in-hand," a four-horse carriage that was the late nineteenth-century equivalent of a modern luxury sedan. After obtaining the ultimate coach, the horse lover with suitable means could move on to fox hunting and polo as other, very expensive ways of feeding the passion for horses. The earliest country clubs were credited with reviving fox hunting in particular. Several observers saw this revival as an attempt to copy the English aristocracy and to connect with early American aristocrats such as George Washington and Lord Fairfax.[2]

This early analysis largely mischaracterizes the situation, for by the mid-1890s golf had become the dominant force behind the creation of new country clubs. In retrospect it is clear that horse-oriented clubs had a limited future: the expenses were high, the land required (especially for fox hunting) was immense, and the number of those truly passionate about horses was small. Golf is a different story. People of both genders and all ages can play the sport, and its costs are small compared to those associated with horses. Golf began to intrude into the American sporting world in the late 1880s and profoundly affected the country club movement. I will deal with its introduction and growth in the United States in the next chapter; in this chapter I present the histories of the clubs that, along with Brookline, truly galvanized the movement. It was the golf country club that sparked the growth in country clubs in general and helped to establish them as American institutions.

The most important of the early golf-centered clubs was St. Andrew's Golf Club, in Yonkers, New York. The club began modestly enough with a neighborhood outing occasioned by John Reid's desire to show some of his friends the game of golf. On a warm February day in 1888, Reid and John B. Upham gave an exhibition of the game to Henry O. Tallmadge, Harry Holbrook, Kingman Putnam, and Alexander P. W. Kinnan. The exhibition took place in Reid's cow pasture near his home in Yonkers-on-the-Hudson. Reid and Upham shared a single set of clubs recently arrived from Scotland, a gift to Reid from his friend Bob Lockhart. The exhibition was a success; when spring came in earnest, the group sought a larger space to experiment with the new game. They preempted the use of a twenty-acre meadow owned by a local German butcher, John C. Shotts. By fall the group was determined to establish itself as a club and find a permanent place to play. On November 14, 1888, helped no doubt by Reid's Burntisland Scotch whiskey and his renditions of several Scottish ballads, the group founded the St. Andrew's Golf Club of Yonkers-on-the-Hudson.

For four years the small band of golf pilgrims played on Shotts's meadow. During this period proposals to find a better site emerged, but Reid was against it, and nothing was done. When the town of Yonkers decided to extend Palisade Avenue directly through the course, however, the club had to find a new home. Not far from the meadow the men discovered an apple orchard that suited their purposes, and thus was born "the Old Apple Tree Gang." The members set six holes in the orchard and established a large apple tree near the first tee as a clubhouse; there they hung their coats and lunch baskets. The larger course drew new members, and according to golf lore, the Apple Tree Gang then grew to thirty-three. At this point it became clear that there was a connection between St. Andrew's and a local city club, the Yonkers Club. Most of the thirty-three belonged to both organizations.

By early 1894, however, St. Andrew's was falling behind as a golf club. Golf had arrived and clubs were proliferating in New York's Westchester County and in New Jersey. This prompted St. Andrew's to find a better site and establish a longer, more interesting course. The members purchased the Odell Farm, near the Sawmill River in Grey Oaks. It was one of the oldest farmhouses in Westchester Country and reportedly haunted. The informal club at this point began to look more like a modern golf club: the group had a real (and historic) clubhouse and hired a pro, a young Scot named Samuel

Tucker, who taught the game and helped the members develop their new course. They finally incorporated on April 14, 1894. The club's purpose as stated in the incorporation papers was "to play the game of golf and provide proper ground for so doing."

The move to Grey Oaks marked an important development in the club's history. From an informal group of friends playing quasi golf in pastures and orchards, the club began to display the signs of tribalism. By *tribalism* I mean the sense that a social entity—in this case a club—has a set of qualities that distinguishes it from all others. As is common, clothing offered one way to mark this distinction. The first moves toward establishing a St. Andrew's uniform came from the early members (who began to disappear through death and attrition and were slowly turned into heroic elders whom the club significantly called "Saints"). Much of this uniform was based on what the early members believed to be golf tradition, especially the red coat. As the outfit evolved, the red coat was made unique to St. Andrew's by giving it special brass buttons and a blue collar with the silver cross of St. Andrew embroidered on the lapels. To the red coat the Saints added blue-checked waistcoats, gray hats, plaid stockings, and gray gaiters. Although the evolving uniform was worn on many occasions, a special blue hat was saved for days when a member was actually on the course. When Reid and the others began playing in 1888, dress had not mattered. Although the later style was still decidedly informal, by 1896 the adoption of a complex, traditional uniform both symbolized and partially constituted the process whereby the members set themselves off from the rest of society and established their group as unique in purpose and style.

Another example of this growing tribalism and increased traditionalism involved the role of women. St. Andrew's was clearly a male-dominated private space. In the twentieth century the membership took a certain pride in the fact that no women had ever played any of the St. Andrew's courses. As the club historian Desmond Tolhurst makes clear, however, women did in fact play in the early days. According to Tolhurst, the club records indicate that Mrs. John Reid and Miss Carrie Law played on March 30, 1889, in what was the first mixed foursome staged in America. It seems likely that women played regularly in the early days and were shut out as the club became more formalized and firm traditions took root.

The clarification of gender roles at the club was only one aspect of the complex process of creating a private space totally controlled by a small self-generating group. At the heart of this process was the land. The club members could hardly have had as much control over Mr. Shotts's meadow as they had over their own property. Once they purchased the land, they began the process of drawing lines, both actual and symbolic. They established rules to keep out the public and laid down traditions for what would and would not happen inside the boundaries.

Equally important, the members began to romanticize their little plot of land, investing it with unique qualities. John Reid was a leader in this movement. In the magazine *Outing* Reid claimed that "primeval forces" had long been at work to create the land on which the club stood. In his view these forces had simply been arranging the land for "the day when true pioneers of golf . . . would be searching for their ideal playground." Reid also claimed that "social revolution" had conspired to bring this land into the hands of serious golfers. He noted that real estate speculation had broken up almost all "the estates" within twenty miles of New York City. The club was blessed to find such a spot "undefaced and undefiled." In a society increasingly undifferentiated, where cities were becoming boring grids of standard streets and buildings, the new country clubs of the 1890s sought to establish places that were special, where traditions and a fondness for a unique place could take root.[3]

In 1891 another group incorporated a club that was as devoted to golf as were the St. Andrew's men. The story of Shinnecock Hills began in Europe. Duncan Cryder and Edward S. Mead became interested in golf while spending the winter in Biarritz. Cryder wrote Samuel L. Parrish, his friend and a fellow summer resident of Long Island's Southampton, asking whether golf might not be introduced into the summer life there. Apparently it was Mead who was most entranced by the game, however; when he returned to the United States, he passed his enthusiasm along to others, especially General Thomas H. Barber. The project began to take shape after consultation with the Royal Montreal Club (founded in 1873) and was pushed along when the professional from Royal Montreal, Willie Davis, came to Southampton loaded down with clubs and balls for the new golfers.

After the men tried the new equipment, their enthusiasm grew. General Barber and George R. Schieffelin took the lead in raising money for the club. Late in the summer of 1891 Schieffelin, Barber, and others invited "all members of Southampton's summer colony" to a meeting at Edward Mead's home. The invitation made it clear that the meeting concerned a proposal for a golf club. The plan was to lease land, with the right to purchase, and to construct a golf course and "a small club house and sheds for horses." The noted architect Stanford White had already submitted a design for the clubhouse. By September forty-four Southamptonites had stepped forward to purchase from one to ten $100 shares in the new venture. Some of these forty-four were female; especially important in the club as long-term members (in their own names) were Mrs. William P. Douglas and Miss H. L. Parish. Unlike St. Andrew's, Shinnecock never developed a tradition of excluding women. In fact, it was the women who organized the first "event" at the club. Samuel Parrish recalled that "the ladies of the colony," who had been actively helping from the beginning, organized a "grand golfing rally" in September 1891.

The women were involved in golf as well as in the social side of the club. The original course laid out by Davis was only twelve holes. The response to golf was very heavy, and this twelve-hole course quickly became congested. As a result the club built a nine-hole course for women players. Samuel Parrish delicately reports that "this distinction between men and women players . . . created a certain amount of dissatisfaction," and the women-only course was abandoned in favor of one eighteen-hole course.

Like St. Andrew's, however, Shinnecock developed a decided tendency toward tribalism. Its members adopted the traditional red coat and the other trappings of what Americans saw as Scottish golf. Most important, the club decided to limit its membership in an interesting way. In September 1891 the trustees responded to the club's growing popularity by voting to admit as members only "those identified with the social life and interests of the immediate vicinity." This suggests that the club did not have to search far for individuals able to foot the expenses of membership. It also indicates that one purpose of the club was to create a local institution under local control with local traditions. Shinnecock Hills Golf Club was for the villagers and by the villagers.

This desire to reestablish a village atmosphere was not limited to golf. In the early 1890s the village of Southampton established the Shinnecock Hills Summer School of Art, naming William Merrit Chase as its instructor. Chase's paintings of the American middle class at leisure had made him famous. Those whom he portrayed now treated art in much the same manner as golf. The Southampton villagers were hungry for diversion and stimulation; they had abandoned the city but sought to bring to their village the genteel entertainments that they had left behind. It is notable that many of the same people who promoted the art school were also important in establishing the golf club. Samuel Parrish and Mrs. William S. Hoyt were deeply involved in both endeavors. Mrs. Hoyt's daughter Beatrix was so attracted to golf that she became the best player of her gender in the United States.

Like their counterparts at St. Andrew's, the members of the Southampton club soon began to characterize their little private plot of golf ground as special. Parrish attempted to convey the "mental condition" of what he called "our small golfing colony" by paraphrasing a statement made by Edward Mead, who believed "that after the creation of the Heavens and the earth, when it was thought that all details had been properly attended to, it suddenly occurred to an all-wise Providence that a golf links had been forgotten, and that then the Shinnecock Hills were created with a special reference to the proper development of the game." Could this have been serious? Did the members actually believe that they had drawn a line around a special plot created by Providence for the playing of golf and that they, the members, had been put in charge of this special place?

The notion that the Shinnecock Club was special rested in a grotesque way on the history of the land and the history of the village as a Puritan settlement. The area had once been the home of the Shinnecock Indians, many of whom still lived in the area as it became the playground for the affluent. Willie Dunn, who laid out and supervised the construction of the course, remembered running across Indian burial mounds, which he incorporated into his design. Dunn employed approximately one hundred and fifty Shinnecock Indians from a nearby reservation as workers during the construction of the course. The *New York Times* thought this situation "unique": "Americans playing a game of genuine Scottish origin and bearing the name of the aboriginal tribes of our own land." The nameless *Times* writer was close to understanding that the summer colony at Southampton was striving to become a distinct tribe possessed of unique lands in a nation increasingly homogenized and centralized.[4]

By 1895 the country club idea was spreading quickly. A number of riding, hunting, and cricket clubs yielded to the growing popularity of golf and built courses. The idea was also spreading geographically. Long Island and the Boston area were centers of club building, and in "the West" (as the Midwest was called at the time) Chicago became the site of a rapidly growing number of clubs. At the root of this development was Charles Blair Macdonald. He was the moving force behind the founding of the Chicago Golf Club and over the years built a number of important golf courses, including the National Golf Links, constructed next to Shinnecock Hills.

Macdonald's reminiscences illustrate the importance of golf to the country club movement. His father had sent young Charles to Scotland's St. Andrews University in the early 1870s to get an education. He returned in love with golf. Over the following years business trips took him to England, where he played on some of the English courses and kept his passion for the game alive. Back in the United States, he was frustrated. He tried for "many weary years" to interest his friends in the Scottish game. Macdonald claims that the 1893 Chicago World's Fair finally shook the town from its lethargy. Golf was only part of a new interest in the outdoors and in the arts, however. More specifically, the fair brought Sir Henry Wood to the Chicago celebration as England's commissioner general. Along with Wood came a sizable group of young Englishmen and Scots. Like Macdonald, these young men were passionate about golf and frustrated by the lack of courses. In response to this pressure and at the request of Hobart Chatfield-Taylor, Macdonald laid out a faux course on the estate of Senator John B. Farwell in

Lake Forest. This course excited some interest, and Macdonald claims that the experiment on Farwell's estate led eventually to the establishment of the Onwentsia Club, incorporated in November 1895.

Macdonald not only excited the players in Lake Forest; he also stimulated the interest of the gentlemen at his town club, the Chicago Club. He "passed around the hat," and approximately thirty of his friends put in ten dollars each toward building a course on the stock farm of "a Musselburgh man, A. Haddon Smith." The course was in Belmont, about twenty-five miles from Chicago and easily accessible by train. In the spring of 1893 Macdonald added another nine holes to the original nine. In July the state of Illinois issued a charter to the Chicago Golf Club. Of the charter's original seven signers, only two were American citizens. The club was similar to St. Andrew's during its Apple Tree period. There were no fancy amenities, not even a clubhouse of any sort. The players stored their clubs and other gear in a neighboring barn. These limitations did not keep the club from prospering, for the membership grew steadily.[5]

In fact, the club proved so popular that Macdonald and the membership began to seek land on which to build a course "comparable with the best inland courses abroad." In 1894 the membership purchased a two-hundred-acre farm near Wheaton, in DuPage County, about twenty-five miles from Chicago. The town and the club were served by the Chicago and Northwestern Railroad. Macdonald established the new course, which became the base from which he developed his reputation as a course designer. The Chicago Golf Club was so closely associated with Macdonald that he was often referred to as the "Laird of Wheaton." At about the time Macdonald established the Chicago Golf Club at its permanent location in Wheaton, the Chicago area saw the introduction of a number of new clubs. Macdonald's original club at Belmont was taken over by an Englishman, Herbert J. Tweedie, and a group of his friends. In 1894 several residents of Lake Forest—among the most affluent and pleasant of Chicago suburbs—established a golf club that eventually became the Onwentsia Club. The establishment of Onwentsia illustrates a change in style in the suburbs. Until the mid-1890s the affluent suburban family spent vacations away from both city and suburb. Many maintained vacation homes in northern Wisconsin or Michigan. The country club changed this habit; the club kept the people in the suburbs, where they spent their vacation time spread out over the entire summer. The nearby clubs allowed the businessman to "sprinkle his vacation all through the summer and at very little cost, much less than would be the case in a trip away." Why were the clubs so attractive? "It was golf that did it and that is the reason golf has come to stay."[6]

The list of these suburban clubs is impressively long; it includes the Chicago Golf Club, Onwentsia, Belmont Country Club, Midlothian Country Club, Exmoor Country Club, Ouilmette Country Club, Glenview Golf and Polo Club, and Skokie Country Club, as well as clubs in Wisconsin, such as the Lake Geneva Club. Each of these clubs was organized along individual lines, but in general they all made large investments in golf courses and were all related to the accelerated move to the suburbs and away from the rapidly growing city. A focus on the Onwentsia Club, among the most prestigious and exclusive of the early Chicago institutions, can thus provide a clear idea of the way the early clubs were organized and financed.

The club was organized under the laws of Illinois in 1895 with a capitalization of $75,000. The membership structure was complex. At the top were the stockholders, who had contributed the original capital. These stockholders allowed club members to use the clubhouse and grounds, demanding no compensation other than the payment of taxes. This arrangement lasted from 1895 until 1910. In 1910 the stockholders changed the club's name to the Lake Forest Club, and all the members became part of a nonstock corporation called the Onwentsia Club. The Lake Forest Club then leased all the property to Onwentsia for fifty years. An important part of this lease was a total ban on games and sports on Sundays. The lease also provided that the Lake Forest Club approve of three-fifths of the fifteen-member board of governors that effectively ran the subordinate club.

As structured in 1910, Onwentsia operated as a complex organization. The governors elected from among themselves a president, vice-president, secretary, treasurer, and chairs of house and grounds committees. Most important, the governors controlled the executive committee, which had broad powers, including control over what was deemed proper in the area of member conduct. Finally, the governors were themselves the committee on admissions. It took only two negative votes out of fifteen to exclude any candidate for membership. Indeed, a potential member had to go through an interesting process even to get to this point. All candidates had to be at least twenty-one years old, and after they had been nominated by one member and seconded by two others, their names were posted in the clubhouse for two weeks. The nominator and the seconders were required to write recommendation letters supporting the candidate's admission before the name could be posted. Finally, the bylaws stipulated that "no proposed member shall be elected unless personally known by some member of the Committee of Admissions."

Membership itself was no simple category. For example, there were resident and nonresident members. Nonresidents were defined as those living more than fifty miles from Lake Forest; they were assessed only half the $200 initiation fee. One could also become a life member by paying $1,000 in addition to the initiation fee. The number of life members was limited to thirty-two. There were also special memberships arranged for consuls stationed in Chicago, army and navy officers, and professors at nearby Lake Forest University, all at reduced rates and privileges.

The club enacted special rules for women and children of members. Widows and unmarried women could be elected to full memberships. Widows of former members were not assessed an initiation fee; unmarried women paid only half the normal fee. Sons and brothers of members between twelve and twenty-one years old could become junior members by paying a ten-dollar "annual subscription." In general these juniors were banned from "the smoking room" and from all sporting events on the club grounds on Saturday afternoons and holidays. When they reached the age of sixteen, however, they could pay an additional twenty-five dollars to be admitted to Saturday and holiday events and to the smoking room. A father could petition to have a son or brother admitted to full membership when he reached eighteen. Young males were thus acculturated to club life and taken into full membership according to a series of precise and clearly articulated steps.

Females over twelve years old connected to a male member could have certain privileges by paying a ten-dollar subscription. This allowed wives, daughters, and sisters to enjoy the clubhouse and to use the sporting facilities, except on Saturday afternoons and holidays. Significantly, there was no set of steps for young females to move into full membership. A full-fledged member who had a family simply had to sort out what he was going to do with each member of his brood. He could purchase positions for his wife, sons, daughters, brothers, and sisters by paying various annual subscriptions. Young males were clearly set on a path to membership, if they choose to pursue it, but women, while allowed a place, were limited and relegated to second-class status.

The bylaws of 1910 had to deal with several other membership issues. The new rules stated that all members of the Lake Forest Club were, without further payment, members of the new Onwentsia. The club also sought to establish its proper size. Excluding all the special-status categories (life members; nonresidents; army, navy, consular, and university personnel; women; and juniors), the membership was set at 425, and the dues for 1910 were established at ninety dollars. One could be expelled by the club for any conduct likely "to endanger the welfare, interest, character, or good name of the Club."

The structural features of the club are not as interesting as the "House Rules" that prescribed proper behavior and provide some insight into life at the club. Onwentsia was open daily from seven in the morning to midnight. Members could and did bring guests to the club. A guest could use the club for a period not longer than fifteen days. No guest could be accorded privileges more than three times in "a season." Under certain circumstances a guest could be tendered a seasonal subscription (the fees were $75 for nonresidents and $100 for residents). Members were held strictly accountable for guests' behavior, especially the acquisition of any debts. Children under twelve were generally not allowed in the clubhouse. They were, however, allowed in a special dining room for children and nurses and into a special section of the main restaurant for breakfast and lunch only. Children were completely banned on Saturdays, holidays, or match days.

Beyond executing its other functions, the club also served as a hotel and rooming house. Rooms in the clubhouse could be rented for the season (May 15 to October 15) or for shorter periods. In addition, the club maintained "cottages" that were open only to members and their families. This suggests that, as mentioned earlier, members could "vacation" at their club instead of buying a vacation home in the North or elsewhere.

There was a decided tendency to keep the reality of commerce out of sight. All purchases at the club were conducted with signed vouchers, the accounts being settled monthly. Indeed, a club rule explicitly regulated virtually all financial transactions: "No cash will be received at the club except in settlement for tickets which have been signed or of monthly accounts." No advertisements, petitions, or "subscription papers" could be posted "except such as relate[d] to Club affairs." Members were also forbidden to "give any fee or gratuity to a servant of the Club." Given the club's ban on Sunday sports, it is not surprising to find that all games of chance were banned at all times and card playing of any sort was forbidden on Sunday. The official colors of the club were navy blue and chrome yellow.[7]

Like most of the 1890s clubs, Onwentsia was tied to changing residential patterns. As affluent families sought relief from increasingly congested cities, they wanted to replace the urban institutions that had provided avenues for social intercourse and recreation. The nature of the country club was shifting subtly. Whereas the founders of Brookline saw their club as a destination in the country, the members of Shinnecock, Onwentsia, and others saw their clubs as additions to new permanent or temporary communities. Both temporary summer colonies and permanent suburbs discovered in the country club a valuable mechanism for providing a social center to their new and largely unstructured communities. The clubs gave a sense of rootedness and history to these new communities. As I have shown, many of the clubs sought to provide their institution with an instant history or specialness, and by so doing, they provided their community with the same uniqueness. This was one reason golf became so central; the game was ancient and had a colorful history. Beyond trading on golf's history, the clubs often sought to associate themselves with the history of the area by taking

Native American names or by including unique local features into their courses. The desire to provide one's club with an instantaneous patina was perhaps best illustrated by the Glen View Golf and Polo Club of Evanston. One of the preeminent clubs along Chicago's North Shore, Glen View (founded in 1897) set out to build a new fireproof clubhouse in 1920. The building's designer included bricks from Chicago's Hoyt Building "covered with the silvery salts of age," limestone bricks from Chicago's Old Trinity Church, and hewn timbers from the U.S. frigate *Constitution*. The dining room in the new clubhouse was modeled "after an old English chapel."[8]

Another attempt to create instant history and prestige was the construction of Tuxedo Park, in the Ramapo Hills, approximately forty miles from New York City. Tuxedo Park was an attempt to create a suburb and a club at the same instant. It was clearly the forerunner of the modern gated community development where all the social and recreational amenities are built in from the beginning. The story of Tuxedo Park began when Pierre Lorillard Jr. undertook a complex transaction with his siblings to assemble a massive tract of land in Rockland and Orange Counties. A contemporary journalist suggested that Lorillard set out to change the seat of fashion from Newport to Tuxedo Park. He brought together a group of wealthy friends, ceded 5,000 acres of land to the Tuxedo Association, and began planning a massive retreat for the upper crust. The association quickly constructed a clubhouse and leased it to the Tuxedo Club; a few of the founders, Lorillard among them, built "cottages," and the project was launched. In the 1890s there was little activity at Tuxedo Park during the summer. Things began to pick up in September as sportsmen arrived to hunt and fish.

The club separated itself from the surrounding area by erecting a massive entrance gate that looked more like a guard tower and by surrounding the property with a fourteen-strand barbed wire fence. Inside the perimeter the club made every attempt to bring nature and community together. A visitor to the park in 1891 claimed that "Tuxedo is proud to boast that science has so effectually been applied to the problems of living as to preserve untainted the unequaled healthfulness of its vitalizing climate." Indeed, massive amounts of money flowed so that members of the club could live (for part of the year) in regal comfort but also close to nature. The trout pond was stocked from hatcheries on the premises. Roads were artfully cut through the forest so one could confront nature from the seat of a carriage.

Judson Nuvman Smith, who visited the club in 1891, was duly impressed by the way Tuxedo Park presented nature to the inhabitants. Bowled over by the "primeval forest," Smith noted, "There is no trace of the hand of men but in the perfect macadam road and its rustic, vine covered railing on the precipitous side." Smith was equally impressed by the clubhouse and the cottages. Structured around a massive central hall, the clubhouse also contained a parlor for women, "leather clad lounging rooms for the men," a dining room, a billiard room, and a ballroom. There was "an aggressively English air about the place." The doorman, named Boots, was very English in manner, and overall the place impressed Smith as evoking "the English country house and the life peculiar to it."

The population of Tuxedo Park was divided into two groups. First, there were the "residents," people who had purchased land and erected a home. Individuals joined this exclusive group by contracting to buy land, at which point they were examined by the Tuxedo Association for admission to the club. If a perspective homeowner was denied admission to the club, his contract to buy property was simply voided. In this way Lorillard and the original group controlled access to Tuxedo Park. Second, there was a class of nonresident members who came to Tuxedo Park for limited periods, apparently established by the club. Nonresident members with families stayed in apartments on the top floors of the clubhouse. Bachelors resided in a separate building. Families with children were also housed in a separate house that Tuxedoites called "the baby kennels." Everyone at Tuxedo Park fell under a set of rigid rules that created an almost impossibly formal atmosphere. For example, first names were never used in public, even by husbands and wives. The rules were created and enforced by the house committee, under the despotic control of George Griswold. Although this may seem like some upper-class utopian experiment, Tuxedo Park was also a capitalist venture. Smith concluded his account by claiming, "The property is now yielding a fair and increasing income." Tuxedo Park was an attempt by "private enterprise" to provide natural beauty, recreation, exclusivity, and "perfect order" to people who could afford a very high price for such things.[9]

It is too easy, however, to dwell on the exclusivity and the vast expense that characterized Tuxedo Park and the other clubs founded before 1895. Although the founders and members of these clubs were clearly seeking exclusive places far from the crumbling cities and their rapidly growing diverse populations, they were also passionately pursuing sport, particularly golf. Hobart Chatfield-Taylor, the first president of Onwentsia, made this clear in a series of articles he wrote for upper-crust magazines around the turn of the century. His memories were of the growth of the country club, but they symbolize the general tenor of upper-class opinion in the decade between 1895 and 1905. Chatfield-Taylor told a relatively simple story. Chicago's upper class had until the early 1890s been enamored of racing and polo, diversions they had pursued at Washington Park. The club began to change as racing declined, however, and by 1895 "golf fever had become an epidemic." Washington Park laid out a nine-hole course, but this was unsuitable. Too near the heart of Chicago and surrounded by "tenements," the players sought a better stage for their newfound game. The prevailing attitude was that "smoking chimneys and elevated railways are not the proper background for polo and golf." This feeling helped lead to the rush to create golf country clubs in the suburbs; because they needed vast amounts of wild and open land, the polo players and fox hunters either gave up their sports or separated from their original clubs (the case at Onwentsia) and established themselves on larger, more isolated sites.

The rush to create golf clubs was fueled as well by a more important shift in attitudes toward health and sport. Chatfield-Taylor recalled that in the early 1880s "there was but one occupation—business; but one God—Mammon." Men were divided into two classes, "the workers and the loafers." Sports in general were for "the weak-minded," and the upper classes viewed sport as a diversion from the prime obligation to work hard and lay up riches. This changed radically in Chicago toward the end of the century. Between 1885 and 1895 "a new creed of health and happiness" evolved, and golf clubs were a potent expression of that creed. Chatfield-Taylor concluded: "An era of honest sport has commenced, and through its influence Chicago society is becoming healthier and better. Money-grubbing and gossip are no longer the all-dominant pursuits."[10]

Eight years later Chatfield-Taylor added some depth and detail to this portrait of the clubs. For one thing, he offered a clearer image of sport in the 1870s and early 1880s. Sport in this era was marked by racetracks, "where fast young men gambled their patrimony away. . . . Sport was for the 'Sports' and it meant gambling and drinking." There were a few clubs where young sons of the rich idled away their time at tennis or sailing, but they were too often involved with professional racing events, where the "sports" watched hired jockeys compete on the horses of the rich. Chatfield-Taylor suggests that society began to see the problems with racing in this format; there was drinking and gambling, and the society patron stood by passively watching his or her investment. It was "the Ancient and Honorable game of Golf that changed all this." It had such an impact because it is "a game for old and young, the hale and halt." This "exasperating pastime" worked untold good because "it is the only game which has ever dragged the sluggish business man from his desk."

The year 1894 was a turning point: "Golf was in the air—the microbe had begun its deadly work." Chatfield-Taylor, a Chicago partisan, claimed that the golf club bug had rapidly spread from the Windy City to the whole of the Middle and Far West. All major cities sprouted clubs, and what had been localized to Chicago, Boston, and New York City spread to Pittsburgh, Milwaukee, Cincinnati, Detroit, Denver, and San Francisco. The result was nothing short of the salvation of American businessmen, who were "no longer sallow dyspeptics who toil from 8 A.M. till 6 P.M. Golf . . . made their blood flow and the color come to the cheeks." They no longer despised a sportsman.[11]

Chatfield-Taylor was not the only upper-class commentator who sought to explain the rise of the country club. In 1901 Gustav Kobbé offered an explanation for the proliferation of country clubs that confirmed and expanded on Chatfield-Taylor's observations. Kobbé places the growth of the country club in the context of suburbanization. He admits that he lives in a suburb but claims that life in his suburb "more nearly resembled premature burial." The little unnamed community occasionally aroused itself and unlocked "the casino or town club and gave a dance." It did so, according to Kobbé, "to prove to its own satisfaction that it was not yet ready to be invited to its own funeral."

It was the country clubs, "which now fairly swarm all over the United States," that transformed Kobbé's dreary suburbs. It was the rise of sport that changed the suburban communities from places to sleep to living places. An important contributing factor was the "general adoption of the Saturday half-holiday," but more central was the introduction of "that sensible, democratic, and reasonably economical sport, golf." Like Chatfield-Taylor, Kobbé concludes that golf turned the affluent businessman away from work and toward play. He suggests that "the Nation [was] beginning to find as much fascination in driving a golfball as in driving a bargain."

Kobbé makes a distinction between suburban and summer colony clubs that escaped Chatfield-Taylor. Summer clubs were not truly rooted in the local population, he concludes. They were part of the growing number of summer and winter colonies that overlaid local areas. Clubs of this type (Kobbé mentions Tuxedo Park and Shinnecock Hills) would open for the season only and then close and return the area to the locals. The "real, all-the-year-round country club," however, was clearly rooted in permanent suburban communities. Such a club existed not as a plaything of the very rich but "because the American who does business in a city, or lives there, has been seized with an uncontrollable . . . desire to be outdoors and it promises to be the safety-valve of an overworked Nation . . . . it has attained the dignity of National Importance."

Kobbé correctly sensed that by 1901 the country club had evolved from a limited upper-class invention rooted in horsey sports to a more generally useful suburban institution based on the popularity of golf. He cites as the perfect example of this new kind of club the Brooklawn Country Club in Bridgeport, Connecticut. It offered golf and archery in the summer and bowling and skating in the winter: "sensible and inexpensive sport." "Social enjoyment" all year around characterized the club, but this enjoyment came not from "the elaborate social function" but from everyday informal social contact.

Since its organization in 1895, Brooklawn had developed what Kobbé believed to have been a typical profile and schedule for the suburban club. The clubhouse was a remodeled "farm dwelling" only a ten-minute trolley ride from the center of the city. Kobbé claims that a lawyer could leave his work, get to the club for nine holes and lunch, and still be back in his office "for a very fair afternoon's work." This is a sharp contrast to Tuxedo Park and Shinnecock, where the leisured used their club unencumbered by work obligations.

Women were in complete charge of Brooklawn's social schedule. The all-male board of governors appointed twelve women, each of whom took charge of the social calendar for a month. The woman in charge of a month's activities gathered other women around her, and together they planned a series of events. At the beginning of each month the members would receive a schedule of "the entertainments for that month. In the summer the events [would] include afternoon teas, putting contests and archery matches." In the winter there was a more varied schedule. The members could attend bowling parties, ice carnivals, dances, minstrel shows, "salmagundi parties," and "candy pulls." Bowling was very big at Brooklawn. Apparently everyone, regardless of age and gender, was expected to compete; the finals, however, pitted the best men and women against others of their own genders. Perhaps the most popular events were the informal one-dollar dinners prepared by "the steward," followed by a dance or card party. Although this schedule illustrates that the club was active all year, Kobbé is adamant about the central role of golf. He asserts that golf was the mainstay of the Brooklawn Club, as it was of nearly all the other country clubs: "Most . . . were in fact founded solely because of golf, and that game is the only sport to which they are devoted." Kobbé concludes by noting that seven years earlier a magazine article on country clubs "barely mentioned golf." By 1901 the cornerstone of the clubs had changed from the horse to golf.[12]

By the mid-1890s, and even more clearly by the turn of the century, golf and the country club had bonded tightly. Other diversions and sports found

places at the clubs but were most often seen as additions to the main attraction and the largest investment—golf. This bond was pulled tight when a
group of clubs came together to form what grew into the United States Golf
Association (USGA). The general outlines of the meeting that formed the
USGA are well known. Henry O. Tallmadge, secretary of St. Andrew's, invited representatives from a group of leading clubs to discuss organizing the
game of golf in the United States. Both St. Andrew's and the Newport Golf
Club had staged so-called national championships, but both matches had
ended in controversy. The source of the controversy was Charles B. Macdonald; since he lost in both cases, Macdonald found reason to criticize and
ultimately negate the results of the two tournaments. In response Tallmadge
invited representatives from Brookline, Shinnecock, St. Andrew's, Newport,
and the Chicago Golf Club to meet in New York City. It seems clear that
there had already been formal discussions about creating an interclub association to run tournaments and establish rules. All the clubs sent two representatives except Newport, which sent only the fabulously rich Theodore
A. Havemeyer.

The group elected Havemeyer as their first president, largely because
they thought his wealth and prominence would give the new organization
a much needed boost. An executive committee composed of a representative from each club was formed. Macdonald then introduced a motion that
set out the purposes of the organization. The new organization, he suggested,
should take as its prime purpose the promotion and protection of the game
of golf. The organization should also establish and enforce a uniform set of
rules, act as the final judge for disputes, create a consistent system for establishing handicaps, and choose the sites for both amateur and open championships.[13]

It is crucial to remember that this was a meeting of the *clubs*, not individuals. The document creating the organization was actually signed by the
club presidents, not the representatives at the New York City meeting. The
pledge to fund the organization was made by clubs, which each contributed
fifty dollars for expenses and trophies. This structure had profound implications. The clubs had created a complex, self-perpetuating autocracy that ruled

over all aspects of golf. This became important in several key aspects of the game, the most important being membership; article 4 of their constitution created the mechanism whereby other clubs could become members of the USGA. The mechanism created two classes of clubs, "associated" and "allied." Full, or associated, membership was granted to any club whose course, buildings, and bylaws were "such as to make it representative": "Such clubs may be admitted on a four-fifths vote of the Executive Committee of the Association." What made a club "representative"? It is impossible to say with certainty, but Macdonald gives us a hint. He thought this division of the clubs into two groups was "a wise provision" because golf was in its infancy, "and the community had to be educated." He clearly wanted the leading (oldest and most prestigious) clubs to run the show, giving sharply reduced voting rights to clubs with courses "laid out in any old place" or "hotel courses." Macdonald's views on this matter were clear: "I firmly believe the ruling of any sport by an intelligent autocratic body is infinitely preferable to mob-rule, which always lowers the morale of games." This division of the membership was hotly debated in 1905 and finally changed in 1927.[14]

During its first decade the USGA was bedeviled by the issue of amateurism. The founders were obsessed by a desire to keep their game free of commercialism, to keep it, as Macdonald often said, "clean." Periodically they tightened the definition of an amateur to exclude anyone tainted by professionalism in even the smallest way. The country club as an institution played an important role in these exertions. The USGA used its control of the national championships to frustrate faux amateurs. Section 10 of the constitution, as amended in 1899, allowed only members of the association to compete for the amateur championship, thus making the clubs admitted to the association the sole source of approved players. Furthermore, entry into all USGA championships was contingent on approval by the secretary of an association club. In this way golf country clubs took on an important role as gatekeepers to prestigious tournaments. To compete at the highest level, a player had to belong to a club.

This struggle to define amateur status also reveals some interesting elements of the evolving country club ethic. The creation of an amateur status was in part a process of exclusion. The USGA elite and the elite clubs sought to eliminate "unsavory" competitors from their championships. The definition of amateur status accepted in 1897 suggests what clubs sought to exclude not only from competition but also from the institutions in general. Anyone who had played for "a money prize" of any sort was banned, as was anyone who had been paid for giving lessons or exhibitions. In fact, just about anyone who had received money for anything related to golf was considered a professional. Caddying after the age of fifteen, laying out or administrating a golf course, and making or selling golf clubs made one a professional. The most interesting element of the amateur definition, however, was the clause that defined anyone "who plays the game or frequents golf courses for the purpose of exploiting his business" as ineligible for the amateur championship. It seems that the struggle to define amateur status was very much a battle against commercialism. Using its member clubs, the USGA created a barrier against anyone who sought to commercialize golf; in the process it limited the field of competitors for the much-prized amateur championship to an unduly narrow elite. For those who could not qualify as an amateur, the USGA also provided an "open" championship, which in the twentieth century evolved into a much more important event than the amateur championship.[15]

All this debate about amateurism tended to obscure a more important point about the founding and early evolution of USGA. Country clubs and their leadership used the association to take control of golf in the United States. This tended to give golf an upper-class ethos and to suggest to the public a tight association between golf and the country club. The USGA was immensely effective in promoting the game, with its aura of gentility and emphasis on manners and tradition. The USGA, golf, and the clubs seemed in the end to be part of an attempt to save traditional values while at the same time promoting a sport and emphasizing healthful and redemptive leisure.

The USGA and the clubs that made up its membership were clearly in the business of inventing tradition. In fact, the entire process of establishing golf and country clubs was profoundly influenced by the desire to establish traditions as landmarks in an era of rapid social and economic change.

It seems clear that at clubs such as Brooklawn middle-class families were actively creating important if prosaic traditions. The country club and golf offered an annual schedule around which the family could structure its life. Monthly suppers, Sunday dinner at the club, the spring dance for high school seniors, Men's Day, Ladies' Day, the fall member-guest golf outing, the club championship, coming-out parties, the Christmas party, and countless other events became ritual landmarks in the lives of affluent country club families. Golf was in many ways the ideal sport for those interested in the revival of tradition. With its long history, and with Anglo-Saxon traditions already in place, golf was ready-made for Americans hungry for tradition. The following chapter focuses on the story of golf's arrival and early evolution in the United States.[16]

## ❧ 3 ❧

# GOLF TAKES ROOT

**B**Y 1900 the number of country clubs had reached 1,040. Leading the states were New York, with 165 clubs, and Massachusetts, with 157, but the movement was widespread: California had 43; Illinois, 57; and Pennsylvania, 75. Even thinly populated states such as Maine (33 clubs) and Vermont (20) were responding to the demand for clubs and courses. By the turn of the century several types of clubs had appeared, as I discussed in the previous chapter. Lavish suburban clubs served a stay-at-home population—Onwentsia provides a good example. Less lavish clubs such as Brooklawn served the middle- and upper-middle-class of towns such as Bridgeport, Connecticut. Shinnecock was the model "colony" club serving the needs of a temporary population escaping the city's summer heat or winter cold. By 1898 *Outing* magazine claimed that the upper-crust sailor could navigate the Atlantic seaboard and never be out of easy sailing distance from a golf club. The magazine traced the yatchman-golfer from the

Algonquin Club in New Brunswick to the Atlantic City Country Club with a total of twenty-seven stops along the way.[1]

The popularity of golf was the major reason for this growth in the number of clubs. The older horse-oriented and cricket clubs discovered that adding golf increased their membership and expanded the value members received. The Staten Island Cricket and Baseball Club installed a course and reported a decided shift among its members from cricket and baseball to golf. In 1896 the Agawam Hunt Club in Providence, Rhode Island, put in a course and soon thereafter reported that golf had "become the principal sport at the club." Brookline was also part of this movement; it added a modest course at first but over the years purchased more land to create a first-rate course. Even the Myopia remnant who had split off and established a riding club in Hamilton, Massachusetts, put in a very fine course and joined the USGA.[2]

Golf came to America in the 1890s. The game had been played in various places in America as early as the 1770s, but these courses and clubs quickly faded away. Golf was a vital part of the rapid increase in the time and money spent on sport and leisure as the nineteenth century drew to a close. In the late 1880s, however, American ignorance of the game was almost total. An 1889 newspaper story, for example, claimed that the game was played "generally at a dead run," especially by the caddie. The writer admitted knowing little about golf but maintained that the victor is the player "who makes the largest number of holes within a given number of minutes, say twenty or thirty."[3] By the first years of the new century, however, golf had established itself as a part of American culture. It had developed an image, a language, and a rationale. In the press at all levels, but particularly in magazines for the middle and upper classes, commentators puzzled over the arrival of this new diversion. At first this puzzling assumed that golf was a fad much like the passion for cycling, but this quickly proved untrue, for too much time, land, and money were poured into the game. In addition, the USGA, with its highly visible and prestigious leadership, signaled that golf was more than a fad. Why did the game take root and grow? What did Americans see in it that they liked?

Any investigation of this question must take into account the biggest hurdle golf faced in America. The game was very widely understood to be the possession of dudes, swells, and the effete. Discussions of golf from the 1890s include many examples of this attitude. One of the early histories of golf refers to the period from 1890 to 1915 as "the Dude Era." In 1926 the upper-class socialist reformer Robert Hunter recalled: "Less than thirty years ago the game was looked upon as something effeminate—an unmanly sport suited to the pink-coated fops and dandies who played it. And what moral courage was required in those days to walk the town streets or board a train dressed in knickers and carrying a bag of clubs." There can be little doubt that this attitude was rooted in class sentiments. The first players were affluent and socially prominent, and when they donned red coats and began pushing a small ball around converted pastures, the lower classes could not resist turning to satire.[4]

There was, however, much more to this image of golf as less than manly. For one thing, the sport *is* less than manly. Golf was popular among women, and many of the early clubs were open to women. Moreover, golf is militantly nonviolent, and strength alone is of no use. This last aspect ran counter to the image of sports as strenuous and violent and as intensely competitive exertion. In this way golf was a stark contrast to boxing, football, and even baseball.

The fact remains that thousands of Americans ignored the ridicule directed at golfers, taking up the game and building clubs at which to play. They did so for many reasons. One of the most commonly cited was the game's ancient roots in Holland, Scotland, and England. Almost every attempt to explain the rapid adoption of golf in America cited its deep traditions in Scotland. As early as 1895 Henry E. Howland, writing in *Scribner's*, presented the game as a "royal and ancient" pastime whose origins were "lost in obscurity." He presented a long list of English royalty and aristocrats who had played the game. The list included James I, James II, the marquis of Montrose, and Mary, Queen of Scots, who played "after the death of Darnley, perhaps as solace in her widowhood." This anecdote concerning Queen Mary became one of the standard stories in the presentation of golf as it made its way from Great Britain to the United States. Equally common was the story that as the duke of York, James II combined with an Edinburgh shoemaker to win a high-stakes match. In fact, the stakes were so high that the shoemaker used his share to construct a new home. Such stories indicate that golf was rationalized as an aristocratic *and* democratic game. It could be embraced by potential aristocrats and commoners alike.[5]

Early commentators also associated golf with the image of Scotland as the land of churchgoing, hard-working Presbyterians who had also, ironically, invented the finest alcoholic beverage known to humankind. One writer noted, "It is not for nothing that the game of golf comes from Scotland." The player begins at the first hole with a sense of mastery and control; he arrives at the eighteenth "with a sense of defeat," knowing he had "no real opponent but himself." Such a game could only have been the product of "the Scottish Calvinist mind." In much the same spirit Howland pointed out that golf "illustrates the analytical and philosophical character of the Scotch mind." This association of golf with Scotland was made all the tighter by the fact that virtually all the professionals who staffed the early clubs were Scots. One writer, Price Collier, in a view somewhat tinged with myth, characterized the early pros as "natural gentlemen" and "kindly, sweet-tempered, pure-minded and charitable old Scotchmen [sic] who goes to church, says his prayers, and refuses to play golf on Sunday."[6]

This stress on the game's connection to Scotland was part of a larger development in the dominant culture. In many ways, middle- and upper-class Americans were attracted to the past in general. In this they were part of a larger movement that historian T. J. Jackson Lears has called antimodernism, an important part of turn-of-the-century cultural ferment. Lears argues that the American elite came to see contemporary America as both a failure and oddly unreal. In contrast, images of premodern societies fascinated Americans deeply. So-called simpler times offered Americans attractive images and activities in which life seemed more meaningful and authentic. The rapid expansion of industrial capitalism, the increasingly violent relations between capital and labor, and the multitudes of non-Anglo-Saxon immigrants all combined to make Americans, especially established Anglo-Saxon Americans, very nervous. In this context an ancient game from Scotland must have seemed an appropriate antidote to a confusing world.[7]

Golf, however, grew in popularity for many other reasons as well. More important perhaps than its historical roots was the claim that golf could save the health of Americans. In the 1890s Americans in general became very concerned about their health. *Outing,* for example, suggested that the typical pattern for "men born since the war" was to "graduate directly from college into sombre-hued clothes and business—not to mention dyspepsia." For these men, an interest in games was "a mark of frivolity."[8]

Golf's image advanced through testimonials from men who extolled the game's health-inducing qualities. The early golf magazines often published stories that related the experiences of businessmen whom golf had saved from illness. In 1897 *Golfing* told of a Chicago businessman who thought that golf was for women and children. His business career had cost the erstwhile college athlete first his robust figure and then his overall health. A doctor prescribed golf, and it worked wonders. The businessman claimed that golf had "added years to [his] life" and that the game kept him "in mild but perfect training." He concluded that even during some recent financial problems, by playing golf he had "kept up without feeling blue or depressed."[9]

One of the most passionate testimonials on behalf of golf came from Andrew Carnegie. Born in Scotland and possessed of deep romantic feelings for the country, Carnegie was an easy convert to the game. He began playing late in life, but this could not dampen his enthusiasm for golf and its charms. Carnegie praised golf as a diversion that required absolute devotion and an ability to put aside "business cares." He described golfers as "worshipers of God of the open air": "Every breath seems to drive away weakness and disease, securing for us longer terms of happy days . . . even bringing something of heaven here to us." Carnegie also praised the social nature of the game because it tends "to make men dearer friends than ever."[10]

A number of writers on golf noted that American development had come to a decided turning point in the early 1890s. Without mentioning Frederick Jackson Turner, they adopted his views on the impact of the frontier. These writers suggested that Americans had found their challenge in subduing the wilderness, but with the closing of the frontier and the growth of cities, natural human instincts had been suppressed. More than one writer argued that modern man needed "the sense of space and freedom" found on golf courses far from "the exhausted air of some great city."[11]

Much of this commentary assumed that the typical American was an urban businessman. This may help to account for the tradition of associating golf with the tired and anxious executive. Golf was often promoted as little more than an antidote for an obsessive concern with profits. One writer, for example, praised golf as the answer to "a boring one-dimensional existence"; especially since the arrival of the "Saturday half-holiday" he said, "the Nation is beginning to find as much fascination in driving a golf-ball as in driving a bargain." This sort of commentary occasionally took a racist tone, for not surprisingly, the typical businessman turned out to have "Anglo-Saxon blood" that poorly tolerated the realities of urban life. Several writers subtly connected golf to "the mental peculiarities of the Anglo-Saxon race."[12]

Still, this sort of racism and exclusiveness was rare in discussions of golf. It was much more common to see golf presented in relation to a general change in attitudes toward work and play. One writer, describing golf's arrival in the Midwest, voiced this attitude clearly: "A revolution has been wrought, and now, a love of healthful exercise throbs in the heart of all, from office boy to lawyer, doctor or merchant prince. A leisure class I am proud to say does not exist in the Middle West . . . our money-makers have been converted from work fanatics to rational men who realize the extremes, either of work or play, are equally to be avoided."[13]

Thus golf was a significant part of the growth of a new, more congenial attitude toward sports and leisure. Its penetration of the American consciousness went though several clear stages. Like all new games, golf was at first wildly misunderstood. It was taken into American culture much like any immigrant would have been. Mr. Dooley, the widely read columnist, claimed that when the game first arrived, men thought it was played "on a rainy afternoon in the front parlor" and that the results were "submitted to the *La-*

*dies Home Journal."* He also thought golf was the most cheerful new thing to come from Scotland since "the theory of infant damnation."[14]

As the essence of the game became clearer to Americans, many writers began to interpret the game in the light of classic American values: democracy and equality. It is ironic that golf passed this test easily, or at least seemed to do so. Many Americans in the 1890s and immediately after 1900 heard the game of golf praised for its democratic, individualistic, and egalitarian character. For example, it was standard to note that in Great Britain golf was most often played on public courses by all classes of people. Henry Howland claimed that "the game is a leveler of rank and station. King and commoner, noble and peasant, played on equal terms in days gone by." Almost all the early commentators noted that the game could be enjoyed by all ages and both genders. It was common to read that golf "was open to middle-aged and elderly as well as the vigorous young men." The *New York Times* concluded that golf's popularity was largely based on "the fact that the game can be played with physical benefit by middle-aged and even older men, whose time for active indoor exercise has passed." Also in the *Times*, the Reverend Dr. Rainsford, one of New York's most prominent clergymen, extolled the virtues of golf and claimed that it "is a thoroughly democratic game."[15]

It would be wise to take all this talk of democracy and equality with some suspicion. Golf was clearly explained and promoted on exceedingly complex grounds. While extolling its democratic features, many writers also noted that golf is highly individualistic. Some noted that the game can be played alone or in foursomes with only limited team spirit. In trying to get to the essence of the game, many struggled with and often celebrated the way the game reveals and at times improves the individual character. Price Collier noted, for example, that "you do not play against the powers of an opponent; you play against an inanimate, will-less, unprejudiced gutta-percha ball. The good and the evil are in yourself alone." Charles B. Macdonald wrote that "no game brings out more unerringly the true character of the man or teaches him a better lesson in self-control." He also noted that men, women and children can all "be interested [in golf as] expressing, maintaining and developing their individuality." In *The Living Age* a writer noted an often-repeated theme: in golf, unlike other sports, "you are absolute master of your ball all the time; what is done, well or ill, is done by you." The writer went on to note that in a world where such control is rarely possible, the attraction of golf can be "very powerful."[16]

Writers such as Macdonald took pains to argue that golf teaches hard, true lessons. He criticized those who argued that all games should be equitable and fair. Macdonald thought that golf inculcates exactly the opposite lesson and that sport and life should teach one to accept the inequity and randomness of life's rewards:

> Does any human being receive what he conceives as equity in his life? He has got to take the bitter with the sweet, and as he forges through all the intricacies and inequalities which life presents, he proves his mettle. In golf the cardinal rules are arbitrary and not founded on eternal justice. Equity has nothing to do with the game itself. If founded on eternal justice the game would be deadly dull. . . . The essence of the game is inequality, as it is in humanity. . . . Take your medicine where you find it and don't cry.[17]

Given all this confusing rhetoric about golf, a typical upper-middle-class white American could have been confused about golf, but he probably was not. The nature and significance of golf were clear by the turn of the century. It was an ancient game with British roots, and this differentiated golf from recent homegrown games such as baseball and basketball. The nature of the game allowed almost everyone to participate equally. As people became aware of golf's unique handicap system, they also understood golf to be one of the few games in which everyone can compete on an equal footing. Crucially, it was apparent that golf allows the genders to play together, in sharp contrast to most other sports, where the genders were kept apart or women were completely excluded. Finally, a typical American would have comprehended that such factors as size, speed, weight, and strength are largely irrelevant in golf. It was not uncommon to read or hear of golf described along the lines of Twain's remark about it, that is, as a good walk spoiled. It also did no harm to claim, as many writers did, that golf is a pleasing antidote to urban anxieties and that it teaches its devotees sound lessons about life and character—in short, that the game instills virtue.

On a more practical level, golf took hold because it was relatively cheap. Indeed, magazine writers routinely extolled the game's cheapness and simplicity. Unfortunately, estimates of the costs of taking up golf around 1900 are unreliable, since they often confuse costs in England with those in the United States. Whatever the exact costs were, however, upper-class commentators tended to see golf as inexpensive because it was much cheaper than traditional upper-class sports.[18] Although the expense of golf still excluded many Americans, it was much less than the costs of traditional club activities such as yachting, horse racing, and fox hunting. In addition, it is crucial to remember that the number of Americans who could afford twenty-five to fifty dollars a year for golf was growing rapidly. Golf was quickly becoming the sport that opened the clubs to the white middle class.

In this regard, the activities of the USGA are particularly interesting. As I have shown, the prestigious clubs maintained tight control over the organization, relegating newer, less wealthy clubs to a subordinate status. Nonetheless, the USGA, and especially its first president, Theodore Havemeyer, pursued policies that could best be called moderately democratic; he also sought to keep the cost of golf down. Although Havemeyer was wealthy from interests in the sugar trust, he also understood that golf needed to be promoted as suitable for everyone, not just the country club set. In January 1897, not long before his death, Havemeyer complained about the lavish clubs Americans were building. He was among the first to understand that country clubs comprised two inherently separate entities—the clubhouse, with its social life, and the golf course. Havemeyer criticized those clubs that spent large sums for clubhouses and installed cheap, poorly designed courses. He argued that "the genuine golfer cares far more for a first-class sporting course than he does for elaborate club fixings."[19]

Havemeyer served as president during the early years of the USGA. During this period the organization created a magazine as a vehicle for spreading its views and for generally promoting the game. *Golfing*, as the magazine was titled, took up Havemeyer's position on the issue of the game's cost. In a series of unsigned editorials, *Golfing* argued that although the wealthy, leisured class had introduced golf, its reputation as expensive would slow the game's general spread. The magazine repeatedly praised Havemeyer for his criticism of the high cost of clubhouses and related elements and argued that the focus should be on the golf course. The magazine claimed that golf "can be a comparatively inexpensive game in this country as it is in Great Britain or Canada." The idea that the game is expensive and suitable only for the wealthy "is detrimental to its progress."[20]

The USGA, again through its magazine, supported the creation of public courses. In a series of editorials *Golfing* argued: "Those who want to keep the game as the exclusive property of the wealthy who belong to clubs are not carrying out the ancient and honored traditions. In the old country, it is possible for everyone to play and no one has ever objected to this." *Golfing* also argued for maximum access to the few public courses in existence. It fought bans on Sunday play on the grounds that golf is "not a disorderly game." The magazine applauded court decisions in a number of states that exempted golf from laws prohibiting baseball and football on Sundays. In taking this stand the USGA aligned itself against powerful forces, most notably the conservative Christian establishment, which sought to keep Sundays completely free of all games and recreation.[21]

Further evidence of Havemeyer's generally democratic approach came during the USGA Open Championship in 1896. The USGA had arranged to hold both the amateur and the open tournaments at Shinnecock Hills. The amateur portion went off without a hitch; H. G. Whigham won the title and decided to compete against the professionals in the open championship. Before the tournament began, Havemeyer knew there would be trouble. The controversy revolved around the participation of John Shippen and Oscar Bunn.

Shippen and Bunn were products of golf's arrival in the Shinnecock area. Shippen's father was an African American minister of Jamaican origin who held the posts of teacher and minister at the Shinnecock reservation. Bunn was almost certainly a Native American. Both Shippen and Bunn (about whom little is known) caddied at the club and learned to play, helped along by lessons from the pro, Willie Dunn. Shippen became so proficient that Dunn allowed him to give lessons and to become an assistant at the club.

When the USGA decided to stage the open championship at Shinnecock, some members encouraged Shippen and Bunn to test their game against the professionals.

On the day before the championship began, the other professionals met and threatened a boycott if Shippen and Bunn were allowed to compete. The job of responding to this threat fell to Havemeyer. What happened next has been the subject of much speculation. In the most likely account, Havemeyer simply informed the potential boycotters that the open would be played with or without them. We shall never know exactly what Havemeyer said or why he said it, but the plain fact is that Shippen and Bunn played and the boycott collapsed. It is fair to add that this happened in 1896, not 1996; from the USGA's standpoint, the truly important tournament was the amateur event. Havemeyer and the USGA leadership tended to look on professionals as akin to hired help and no doubt viewed their demands as inappropriate uppityness.

Shippen nearly won. During the morning round he played with Charles B. Macdonald and shared the lead with a seventy-eight. Macdonald was five strokes behind at eighty-three; he withdrew from the afternoon round and served merely as Shippen's scorer. An eleven at the thirteenth hole in the afternoon ended any chance that Shippen might win. Shippen finished seven strokes behind the winner, James Foulis of Chicago, but he proved beyond any doubt that he belonged in the field. He played in the open occasionally after 1896, appearing last in 1913.[22]

The story of Havemeyer, Shippen, and Bunn at Shinnecock should give us pause. This modest victory for openness in a world tightly associated with exclusion and racism should not obscure the fact that golf and the country club were very much defined by the racism of the era. Yet Havemeyer's actions deserve more than a footnote. By allowing Shippen and Bunn to participate, he was being true to the game's traditions as he understood them at the time. The United States inherited a set of values regarding golf that emphasized the game's openness. The Scottish tradition as Americans came to know it celebrated the fact that royalty played with commoners, that merchants played with carpenters. This tradition has never been completely overwhelmed by

American racism and class antagonisms or by the exclusive nature of the clubs where the game has been played. Golf's emphasis on openness has long battled the desire of many to exclude all but the socially prominent.

Havemeyer's actions at Shinnecock, however, were not part of the public discourse on golf. The USGA and its officials never publicly challenged deeply ingrained American attitudes. The golf clubs that constituted the USGA were created by generally conservative Americans who were understandably products of their time. Yet this cannot be the end of an investigation into the impact of golf, into how people conceptualized the game. The golf-oriented country club was created so that people could pursue a particular game. As these clubs emerged, the world of print presented a persistent stream of discussion, guesses, odd views, jokes, and serious commentary that sought to provide golf with a meaning and to explain its attraction.

Perhaps the most substantial attempt to explain golf's attraction appeared in 1908. Arnold Haultain, a Canadian writer, published *The Mystery of Golf*, which remains one of the most substantial attempts to philosophize about golf—or any game, for that matter. The first edition was limited, but it met with some success, and a larger edition was published in 1910.[23] Haultain became for a brief period the guru of golf. He published several shorter versions of his ideas in magazines such as the *Atlantic Monthly*.[24] Haultain's book differs from almost all other golf books in that there is not one word of instruction in it. His goal was to explain the game's attractions and plumb its meaning for those who play it. For those who believe that games are ephemeral, Haultain's musings will probably seem silly; he takes golf very seriously. Those who believe, however, that people choose their games based on the distinct issues a given sport evokes may well find Haultain to have taken up an interesting issue.

Haultain structures his book around the question of the game's significance. He creates an imaginary golf club member who has joined for the social life but who has never played. This member, the author relates, has always seen golf as silly and without purpose. He has therefore been much puzzled by the other club members' fervid devotion to the game. Finally the unnamed member begins to play and sticks with it. Haultain tells us that "then indeed did the scales fall from his eyes. He discovered that there was more in golf than meets the eye—much more."[25] The rest of the book is an attempt to describe that "much more."

In his little book Haultain occasionally adopts common views concerning golf. For example, he contends that golf reflects the national character of Scotland and its religious proclivities. He uses words such as *slow, sure, quiet, deliberate,* and *canny* to describe both the Scottish temper and the skills needed in golf. Both the Scot and golf are individualistic; in the game "there is no defensive play, no attacking an enemy's position, no subordination of one-self to the team, no captain to be obeyed, no relative positions of players." This, Haultain suggests, contrasts sharply with cricket, the English national game. Cricket is "communistic, political. The nation that evolved cricket evolved the British Constitution." Golf is Scottish and different; it "is self-reliant, silent, sturdy. It leans less on its fellows. It loves to overcome obstacles alone."[26]

Nevertheless, these ramblings about golf and the differences among the British are merely a prelude to the book's main point. Haultain begins to construct his larger view by noting that the world around him was in the throes of "a sporting mania"; to account for golf, we have to understand this mania. To do this Haultain adopts a Darwinian position. He suggests that all sport is simply "amicable combat" and that prowess in sport is "proof and symbol" of prowess in the larger combat of individual versus individual and individual versus nature. This larger combat (evolution) has been the vehicle for human-kind's rise to dominance and for the triumph of "special races." Haultain argues that humans "instinctively" comprehend that skill in sports means more than physical skill; it means intellectual and moral superiority as well. Sporting success or failure reveals the true nature of an individual as he or she engages in the struggle with others and with nature. Thus, in the end, sport becomes "a symbol and analogue" of the larger evolutionary conflict in which is revealed humanity's "true and secret character . . . [a] real and inner self."[27]

Haultain admits that this theory does not fully explain the fascination of golf. To explain this fascination and to extol the game, he presents several arguments that are occasionally interesting but often devolve into mysticism and leave a reader more bewildered than enlightened. For example, Haultain contends that golf, more than other games, combines physiological, psychological, social, and moral skills. He argues that golf is unique in calling for a delicate balance of strength, intellect, and character. For the most part he continues in a simple way to extend his evolutionary, Darwinist viewpoint: "In golf we can see a symbol of the history and fate of human kind: careening over the face of this open earth, governed by rigid rule, surrounded by hazards, bound to subdue nature or ere we can survive, punished for the minutest divergence from the narrow course."[28]

Haultain's attempt to find the attraction of golf in a crude analogy between sport and evolutionary struggle is an abject failure. Anyone with a rudimentary understanding of the gentle game understands that it has little in common with "the joy of combat." The people who play with an abiding passion are more likely to reject the joy of combat than to embrace it. Haultain reached for the language of the day, drawn largely from Darwin's popularizers, to provide golf (and sport generally) with a philosophical underpinning.

Nevertheless, in the course of his ramblings Haultain stumbles on several insights that ring true and help to separate golf's popularity from that of other sports. Most important, he emphasizes the golfer's direct contact with nature. For the most part he discusses the golfer's contact with nature in the context of a struggle that has tested humankind and brought forth the best in the human character. To his credit, however, Haultain also understands that this contact with nature has other aspects and benefits. The golfer never tires of the stage on which the game is played. He or she has some understanding that golf is played over beautiful spaces where "every sun-lit day composes a symphony beautiful to behold." The golf course (clearly not a seaside course) is a place of modest, familiar, but increasingly meaningful beauties: "There are nooks, and courses, and knolls, and sloping lawns on which the elfish shadows dance. Smells too, curious smells from noonday pines, and evening mists, from turf, and fallen leaves. . . . What is it these things say? Whither do they beckon? What do they reveal? I seem to be listening to some cosmic obligato the while I play; a great and unheard melody swelling from the great heart of Nature.—Every golfer knows something of this . . . . these be holy things whereof I speak not."[29]

In addition to offering lyric praise for the golf course, Haultain also praises the clubhouses and the general atmosphere of the game. He finds much to like in the local pleasures of the typical golf clubs, such as the "spacious verandahs and arm-chairs, shower-baths; teas and toast; whiskey and soda; genial companionship; and the ever delectable pipe." To these things he adds the comradeship, the sense of community, and the growing circle of friends a club provides. Haultain suggests that both the course and the club develop in players and members an affection that borders on reverence.[30]

Haultain seems to understand that golf's attraction somehow involves our fascination with nature. He senses that the beauty of the course, enjoyed with satisfactory companions, is one reason for golf's popularity. Yet this does not fully explain the manic attraction to the game that many players feel. Haultain again turns to nature as a basic element of golf's growth. He points out that of all games, golf is the only one played over natural terrain and that the fundamental foe is not your opponent but nature. All other games are played on artificial fields with rigid, artificial boundaries. In golf, unlike almost all other popular games, you proceed through nature unimpeded by a human foe or even alone if you wish. In this Haultain sees something like a reenactment of human fate. Having asked about the purpose of it all, he answers his own question with an analogy that many golfers would find preposterous; the point of golf and life, he concludes, is "to reach an exiguous grave with as few mistakes as may be—some with high and brilliant flight, others with slow and lowly control."[31]

This flight of philosophic excess is suggestive. Golf is peculiar, as Haultain claims, because the foe is nature and the game essentially revolves around movement through nature, where your fate (score) is determined by nothing but your own skill and character. This was neither the first nor the last attempt to see in the nature of a game some analogy to life, but it certainly was a unique one. It suggests that unlike other sports, golf bears a close resemblance to economic life as defined by capitalism and the Protestant ethic.

To understand this fit, we have to understand that golf is essentially a "spending" game. You stand on the first tee equal to everyone else in at least one way: you have an infinite number of strokes to expend. Your pockets are jammed with an infinite amount of money. The goal is to keep expenses to a minimum; the outcome of the game (at least in medal, or stroke, play) is the total you have spent. The task that produces this spending is a simple contest against nature, or if you like, space. Time theoretically plays no role in the game; the only matter of importance is the expense. Thus a good golfer is a thrifty golfer; a bad golfer is a spendthrift profligate. It is therefore no accident that golf has evolved a language that expresses in countless ways the realities of waste, saving, and spending. One praises a golfer by calling him or her economical. It would be easy to expand this analogy between golf and capitalism. If you have played the game, you will understand, for example, the ways in which risk and reward are factors in golf just as they are in capitalism.

Haultain's musings also suggest a connection between golf and the ageless diversions of fishing and hunting. All these activities take place in nature, generally unencumbered by the rigid lines and borders that characterize modern sports such as baseball, basketball, and football. In golf, fishing, and hunting the "score" begins at zero, the result is in effect an accumulation, and the player is very much on his or her own, unable to turn for aid to teammates. The player in these activities is governed by an unspoken code that he or she is responsible for policing. Finally, the fishing or hunting guide bears a striking resemblance to the golfer's caddie.

The point of this chapter has been to seek out the reasons behind golf's rapid growth between 1890 and World War I. In American popular culture and among students of upper- and middle-class attitudes, golf has been often characterized as aristocratic. For example, in his study of American suburbs Kenneth T. Jackson concludes that golf has been the "aristocratic pastime *par excellence*," as well as part of a larger trend in which "sport became almost an end in itself" and "compulsive play became an accepted alternative to compulsive work."[32] The survey of what people actually said about golf tends to cast doubt on this view. Golf was adopted by the upper and middle classes because it fit, or could be made to fit, with widely shared

American values. When golf arrived from England and Scotland, it came with a reputation as the game of kings and commoners. Americans quickly understood that the game was cheaper, more accessible, and more egalitarian than were traditional upper-class diversions such as yachting and fox hunting. Americans took to the game because they seemed to believe that it could be an antidote to the stresses of business and city life and because it arrived with an association to an ancient (and largely democratic) tradition that emphasized the game's usefulness to all. Golf may also have benefited from its unique qualities. It differs from the other games that were attracting adherents. It is nonviolent, playable by men and women of all ages, and can could be enjoyed by all members of the family.

I have spent far too many hours debating the virtues and vices of golf. People tend to have strong feelings about the game. The antigolf forces point to its social exclusiveness and lack of strenuous physical demands on the player. Progolf people argue that the game is difficult to play well and point to the amazing number of professional athletes who turn to golf at every available opportunity. Debate on these grounds clearly misses the point. The most crucial point is that golf can in no way be associated with combat. Virtually all the major sports to which Americans are addicted are surrogate forms of combat in which one struggles directly with an opponent or, in a team game, seeks to gain territory or some other advantage over a clearly defined opponent. In these combat sports, the action is often quick, putting a premium on reflex actions, say, to block a punch in boxing or volley a ball in tennis. Golf is played slowly, even gravely; the actual play takes up a tiny portion of a four- or five-hour round. The majority of the time is spent in planning, considering, worrying, and socializing with your playing partners. Because golf is unlike the combat sports, it is the one sport in which people of vastly different sizes, ages, and genders can easily compete. Golf requires none of the basic traits required of combat sports: physical fearlessness, physical strength, quick reflexes, or a willingness to dominate others physically. As Haultain states, golf brings "frail and mortal men" into conflict, not with other humans, but with "sempiternal Nature." It is the one game you can play, truly and fully, alone.

## ❧ 4 ❧

# GOLF, THE COUNTRY CLUB, AND THE AMERICAN FAMILY

> American manners, as they stand, register therefore the
> apotheosis of the family—a truth for which they have
> by no means received due credit; and it is in the light
> of Country Clubs that all this becomes vivid. These or-
> ganizations accept the family as the social unit—accept
> its extension, its *whole* extension, through social space,
> and accept it as many times over as the question comes
> up: which what one means by their sublime and success-
> ful consistency. No, if I may still insist, nothing any-
> where accepts anything as the American Country Club
> accepts these whole extensions.
>
> —Henry James, *The American Scene* (1907)

IN SEPTEMBER 1900 E. S. Martin provided the readers of *Harper's Weekly* with a short but penetrating analysis of the country club's rise to prominence. He understood that the clubs resulted from several factors. A general increase in discretionary income, the "centralization of the population," the love of horses and related pursuits, the wish to escape the city for the country, an increasing number of urban train and trolley lines into the country, and especially the rise of golf—all these led the number of clubs to grow rapidly. Martin cites golf as the central factor that ballooned the country club membership rolls. As the membership grew, dues shrank, and joining a club became a possibility for more and more Americans. Martin concludes: "Golf keeps up the membership and makes the clubs strong."

All this is true and illuminates the basic and obvious reasons for the success of the country club idea. Martin, however, goes further; he casually labels the clubs a "valuable adjunct of democratic social life." This is a surprising claim, but Martin has his reasons. He sees the country club as a device that allows the average family to extend its typically urban home into the countryside. The clubs are "democratic" in that they allow those in the new urban middle class to possess, after a fashion, a country estate. Martin argues that "country clubs seem to have attained by co-operation many, if not most, of the advantages which people of wealth derive from country estates. The payment of a moderate annual fee gives them the usufruct of a well-kept country-place, with sports and society furnished ready to hand. To the poor whose poverty is not of exasperating exigency all this is a great boon."[1]

Although Martin's analysis is insightful, it raises as many questions as it settles. For one thing, even given his qualification, can he possibly mean that the poor enjoyed the benefits of country clubs? In the context of the early twenty-first century this claim sounds preposterous. Martin is, however, accurately reflecting a common tendency in turn-of-the-century discourse. He and many other commentators viewed *society* as a term defined by a number of unspoken qualifications. Without thinking about it much, Martin limits society to white, solidly employed homeowners. His analysis applies only to a given portion of the total population; it most likely excludes affluent Jews and other non-Anglo-Saxons. Thus we can reasonably assume that by "the poor" he means the lower reaches of the white, Anglo-Saxon, property-owning group. His concern is not with the classes below these people but with the quest of solidly affluent middle- and upper-middle-class whites to acquire access to country living, long a prerogative of the aristocracy.

Martin's analysis of the clubs only lightly brushes against the issue of gender. He briefly notes that golf's influence on the clubs was in part a product of its popularity and usefulness to both genders and to the family in general. If we read him as we should, however, it is obvious that within the limits of his definition of society, the country club idea had immense implications for the relationship between the genders and for the family as a whole. If the stage for the family drama is the home, then any extension of the home will by necessity project that drama onto a new stage. Therefore, if we understand the years around the turn of the century as a time of contest and change in gender relations, then the country club becomes a site at which this contest should be evident.

The Victorian family and its home have been the subject of much investigation and debate. The white, bourgeois family of the late nineteenth century was constructed around three crucial images. The first image was that of the adult male, or patriarch, as the competitor and achiever who sallied forth into the world seeking material resources. Loosely employed Darwinian rhetoric underscored the biological roots of aggressive male behavior. Such rhetoric also helped to define the Victorian adult female, the second important image. She was crucially different from her mate; the home, children, and moral and cultural concerns formed the boundaries of her life and purpose. Children were her special project; she could more closely attend to them because the bourgeois family had been getting smaller during the nineteenth century. Each child was to be trained by the mother to develop easily and thoughtlessly into his or her biological destiny. Males were taught to struggle and compete; females were taught to be modest, nurturing, and homebound.

The third image was of the home. For the affluent Victorian family, the home was a complex place: for the male, who needed respite from the competitive wars, it was a haven; for the woman, it was the canvas on which she expressed her taste and control; and for children, it was a haven and school, a calm place where they learned life's lessons before moving into the larger world. The home had lost its purpose as an element in productive economic life and was largely cut off from the public realm. It increasingly served as a focus for the desire to escape the chaos of capitalist society and the bewildering transformation of American life. As T. J. Jackson Lears suggests, "In the bourgeois imagination, the home became an oasis of tenderness and affection in a desert of ruthless competition."[2]

The images of male, female, and the home were compelling cultural realities in the late nineteenth century, yet they were also losing much of their cultural force. More and more women were attending college and pursuing opportunities that often led them to put off marriage for a few years or forever. Victorian women had been taught by their mothers and by medical experts that exercise is generally ill advised. The emphasis on female modesty and decorum had either eliminated female exercise or limited it to a few boring alternatives. As the new century approached, however, college programs that encouraged participation in sports and changing medical opinion led women to begin to play, and as they did, they slowly shed restrictive clothes and the sacred notion that women would not, could not, or should not compete.

Victorian culture at its most restrictive had sought to maintain clearly defined boundaries. Civilization itself seemed to be at stake. The borders between male and female, human and animal, black and white, and public and private were monitored by cultural arbiters who saw them as very nearly sacred. The good life, the moral life, depended on the militant maintenance of these boundaries. By the middle of the 1890s, however, this monitoring had become an insufferable burden; people paid homage to the old values (they influenced much of what happened at country clubs), but affluent Victorians were eager to explore the option that the old boundaries could be quietly breached and the world would not end.[3]

A portion of this exploration took place at the country clubs that sprang up during the 1890s and the years before World War I. In some measure the old values held sway. Acquiescing to the notions of separate male and female spheres, some of the early clubs excluded women entirely or limited female participation to the barest minimum. In doing so, these Victorians were no doubt following the pattern set by urban male-only social clubs. Much more common at country clubs was the separation of male and female activities. This division is symbolized by the invention of the term "golf widow." The birth of this term in the 1890s suggests that golf and the country club drove a wedge between men and women and shattered the idea of a social life engineered by women. When a Newport "society woman" was asked what the term meant, she replied: "Simply drive over to the golf club and see our dutiful husbands steaming with perspiration in chasing a bouncing ball over half the expanse of the island. Then look at us, sitting on our verandahs, waiting for them to come home to fill a dinner engagement and you will understand what a golf widow means." She went on to complain that this also happened on vacations "down South," where the men played golf and left the women "to amuse [them]selves." From the golf widow's point of view, the game had produced a "new species of men" who no longer cared about their dress, men who, the woman complained, "growl when we expect them to appear in evening dress at night."[4]

In many ways clubhouses reflected the desired separation of men and women. While the men sought to rule the fairways, the women ruled on the verandas and in the "social" rooms. Clubhouses evolved with clearly gendered areas. By 1905 the Country Club, at Brookline, had enlarged and improved the site's farmhouse, making it a full-scale clubhouse. It had two main entrances, one for "the ladies" and one for "the gentlemen." By this time the clubhouse had taken on most of the features of a luxurious home. There was a reading room, a smoking room, a general reception room, and a dining room capable of holding 270 people. David Paine suggested that a "progressive *fin de siecle* movement" had forced the club to recognize the presence of women and children at the club. This led to installing special accommodations for women as the structure was enlarged. There was, for example, a "ladies reception-room" to the right of the women's entrance. The room was papered to suggest a Japanese flower garden and was furnished with "dainty green willow furniture." The room had a decided Japanese tone; the mantel was decorated with Japanese pottery, and the overall intention was "to impart to the room an elusive, fascinating Oriental atmosphere." There was also a "ladies boudoir" upstairs and adjacent to the women's locker room. Thus, like many other clubs, Brookline had re-created the expansive upper-class home with special areas for men and women and common spaces, such as the dining room, where the genders could mix. In time many clubs would organize themselves around three concepts: a men's wing, a women's wing, and a common area.[5]

All this becomes more meaningful when we understand that the affluent Victorian home underwent an important transformation between 1890 and the war. As servants became less affordable, houses tended to become less formal and to lose their central role as a site for entertaining. Candace Volz has claimed that, especially after the turn of the century, as the homes of the affluent employed increasingly "fewer servants. . . [and] a less formal lifestyle became the norm . . . , many of the rooms in the Victorian home that were related to formal entertaining and servants became obsolete." Typical homes no longer contained reception rooms, conservatories, sitting rooms, billiard rooms, or rooms to house servants and to create work space for a large household staff. Most of these changes can be linked to the slow evolution of a more informal way of life. The appearance of the breakfast nook during this period clearly suggests that Americans were developing less formal eating habits that required fewer servants.

As rooms began to disappear from the typical upper-and upper-middle-class home, other features began to appear. Homes began to open up, and owners sought more access to the outdoors. Sleeping porches, for example, became common; they were one way for families to regain some connection with the outdoors. The front porch began to move around the house. At first it traveled to the side, where it was reinvented as the sun porch, which could be screened in good weather and glassed in during winter. The porch kept moving and ended its journey at the rear of the house, where it was reinvented as the loggia or, more familiarly, the patio.[6]

Another crucial feature was the garage. Among the automobile's many transformations of American life and homes was a reduction of the home's role as a cultural site. Victorian families had been trapped together in their homes. To many this seemed to be a virtue; the family was the mechanism whereby the young learned values and sexual identity. The home was the site where adults controlled children and instilled in them the behavioral code we tend to call Victorian. The rebellion against this system began before the advent of the automobile, but the automobile proved to be a crucial and perhaps determinative instrument in reducing the importance of the home in the construction and transmission of values and rules of behavior.[7]

The role of the country club in all this seems obvious. As the home became less important and people spent less time there, American families found substitutes. The evolving American consumer culture grew increasingly adept at inventing these sites that in part replaced the home. The birth and growth of the movie theater constitutes one example of such a substitution; the department store (shopping as recreation) offers another. The country club, too, became an important destination outside the home, a place where functions that once took place in the home could be carried out. Nevertheless, country clubs differed in important ways from places such as movie theaters and department stores. The clubs were private and member owned; they were odd elements in the evolving consumer culture, if they were part of it at all. Still, joining a club was at bottom a consumer decision. Many families decided to spend some of their time and money for entertainment, recreation, and socializing outside the home. This decision transferred a small measure of the drama and tension of family life to the club.

The most central problem transferred to the club was the tension between men and women. To understand this tension, we need to grasp the evolution of the "new woman" in the late nineteenth century. The new woman had a decidedly public persona. She emerged from the middle- and upper-class homes of the Victorian era and became much more visible and influential in the public realm. Jane Addams, the Chicago reformer, stands as one of the best symbols of this new public woman. She represents countless affluent women who, rejecting the rigid boundaries of Victorian gender rules, began to carve out new ways of being female and new sites for activity outside the family home. Large numbers of these new women attended college, became involved in reforms, remained single longer than their predecessors, and had fewer children when they did marry; most important for my purposes, they often challenged the notion that robust physical activity is not central to the life of a healthy woman. Also important was the new woman's affection for clubs in general. Women in the 1880s and 1890s flowed easily into a wide array of voluntary associations, such as temperance groups and general purpose (usually intellectual uplift) women's clubs.[8]

An emphasis on the dramatic increase in women's public and political activity, however, can obscure a subtler change in the attitude toward the female body and its maintenance. The new woman learned a new attitude toward her body at colleges such as Wellesley. An *Outing* article summarized the college's attitude toward physical activity: "There is an attempt made to insure an intelligent interest in physical culture and outdoor life." Wellesley women learned the joys of exercise and play in several ways. In the gym they did routine exercises and played basketball under the learned eye of Miss Hill. Outdoors they rowed on Lake Waban and played golf on the course donated by Dr. Channing, who also gave the college an assortment of golf clubs. Golf was by 1898 "a very popular sport," one that offered recreation without intense competition. Concerning golf, a Wellesley woman said: "We play simply for the pleasure of being outdoors . . . . Everyone plays golf, which means that a universally popular game has found no particular champion of Wellesley and awakes but little spirit of contest." Tennis, however, was a different matter. Spirited contests occurred on the college's six courts. In 1897 the college championship was hotly contested, and the winner was raised to her friends' shoulders for a victory march up College Hill.[9]

Throughout the 1890s and beyond, colleges such as Wellesley were producing a generation of women dedicated to sport and "the outdoor life." These women, largely from affluent backgrounds, moved easily into country club life with a desire to continue their pursuits of golf, tennis, and other sports. This generation of females routed the golf widow and sought to make the country clubs their own. The clubs were perfectly suited to their purposes: they were private and voluntary associations, and the athletic and organizational skills learned at college transferred smoothly to country club life.

The country club thus became an agent in undermining the Victorian notions of separate spheres for men and women. It was part of a complicated process that men and women around the turn of the century struggled to understand. Magazines of all sorts, and particularly magazines for the upper classes, devoted considerable space to the task of understanding the new woman and her sporting urges. In the process these magazines also reflected the subtle shift of the boundaries between men and women at the club. In general this shift varied greatly in its radicalism; some women wished only to increase their physical activity modestly and openly stated that women at the club should take second place to the men. Other women pushed harder; they founded their own clubs or demanded rough equality with men. Finally, some even broached the radical notion that women could compete with men on equal terms.

Mrs. Reginald De Koven, writing in *Cosmopolitan* in 1896, neatly summarizes the timid approach to women's golf at the club. She frankly admits female frailty as an inevitable bar to excellence in golf and other sports. Women, she claims, are weaker than men, and women are also encumbered by the iron rules of proper dress. Both these factors, which she fully accepts, place women forever "very far behind the men." De Koven also suggests that women in general cannot see as well as men, and this will also limit a woman's ability to play golf. Only in one area, putting, does De Koven believe that women might "get the better of their masculine opponents."

Given this somewhat dismal outlook, one might ask, Why play the game? De Koven provides two answers. First, golf allows "the possibility of companionship with husband, brother, or friend," and this stands as an" alluring reward for the practice of the game." She expressly rejects the term "golf widow" as "a term of misfortune" but also advises women who would play with the men to be "modest and self-effacing." Second, De Koven urges women to play for the same reason men were advised to take up the game— it is both good for your health and egalitarian: "A game which will bring weak and idle women off their couches, and by its fascination carry them over miles of hills and meadows, among the sunbeams and breezes, should be considered in the light of a great blessing to humanity. Its rewards are for women as well as men, for all ages and conditions, irrespective of rank or of wealth; a real game for America—democratic and free."[10]

De Koven represented the mildest sort of position that women could take concerning their roles at the club and in the game of golf. Lillian Brooks took a decidedly more radical stand in 1900. Brooks welcomes open comparisons between men and women, claiming that they reveal the emancipation of women to have been "almost entirely intellectual, not physical." Brooks argues that female frailty is the product of an environment that blocks the physical training of women. Her two main enemies are "fashion" and "conventionality"; she is particularly hostile to the "tyranny of clothes." In a larger sense Brooks is a militant Darwinist in that she attributes the differences between genders almost entirely to environment. She claims that men have been taught to compete and enjoy struggle while women have been kept from the battle. Women, she suggests, would have evolved in the same ways as men if they had been exposed to the same environmental challenges.

Brooks expressly objects to the idea of all-women clubs. She much prefers the traditional club, where genders must mix and, even on a gentle level, compete with each other. She sees these clubs as beneficial, claiming: "Country clubs are now looking after our golf and are doing more to further our interests than we could hope to do by ourselves." Of course, Brooks admits that there are a few "old gentlemen" who become agitated by "the sight of a petticoat on the golf links," but they are usually tolerated because their wives have spoiled them and their daughters have neglected their education.[11]

Brooks's charge that women need competition to pursue their physical emancipation fully was quickly answered by the USGA and the New York Metropolitan Golf Association. By 1900 Americans in most large towns could regularly read reports of women's tournaments in their local newspaper. Beginning with the USGA Ladies Championship in 1895, American women quickly developed a keen interest in the progress of the game. There was much discussion regarding how good American women could become and when they might equal their English counterparts, who had been playing longer. The early American standards were not high, but the scores began to go down, and a clear elite of players developed, particularly among the younger women. At the top of this group in the 1890s was Beatrix Hoyt, who won the USGA championship three years running between 1896 and 1898. Hoyt had been nurtured at Shinnecock Hills, where the first women's USGA champion, Mrs. Charles Brown, had learned her golf. In November 1895 Brown defeated ten other entrants in an eighteen-hole medal-play tournament; her winning score was 69-63-132. There was obviously a lot of work to do, and Beatrix Hoyt began to do it. She won the next three years while only a teenager; her scores in qualifying rounds and in match play tended to be in the low nineties. In each year Hoyt won, the number of entrants increased, crowds at the final matches grew, and newspaper coverage expanded.

It would be easy to make too much of this developing world of women's golf competition. Nonetheless, in retrospect it was in its small way momentous. The women were upper class and young and tended to drop out of competition after a few years, but they also made the newspapers. The idea of increasingly intense competition among women was accepted and institutionalized with barely a whimper of protest. Women golfers protested restrictive clothing simply by finding apparel in which they could take a full swing. The idea that a true woman should take a half-swing (raising the club only to her waist) died a quick and silent death. Competitive golf among women also added much to the popularity of the country club. The privacy of the clubs was probably necessary for women who sought to play but still felt the pressure of the Victorian code, which told them to stay home and stay calm.

One of the fullest looks into the world of women turning to golf came in *The Book of Sport* in 1901. Clearly designed for an upper-class readership, the book contains essays on various sports and includes a piece by Ruth Underhill, the 1899 USGA women's champion, entitled "Golf: The Women." Underhill was impressed by the rapid changes in the world of women's golf. She claims that in 1890 women were relegated to short, special courses. They were taught that a full swing is "not particularly graceful when a player is clad in female dress." In little more than five years American women were eagerly discussing the best forms of competition (match versus medal and team versus individual) and what measures were needed to help American women catch up with the English. Underhill makes it clear that the country club was the major factor in the growth and improvement of women's golf in America. As did the men, women represented their clubs at championships, and trophies were held not by the individual but by the winner's club.

Underhill's essay contains several tantalizing hints that provide some insight into the new world of women's golf at the clubs. First, many of the better players were young. Hoyt was sixteen when she won her first championship, and Margaret Curtis, from the Essex County Club, had established a reputation as a fine player at the tender age of thirteen. It seems fair to suggest that golf was making its biggest inroads among young and unmarried women. Underhill names ten women as "All-America" players; of the ten, eight are comparatively young and unmarried. Like many commentators of the time, Underhill compares the women with the men. She concludes by establishing a modest goal for the ladies: "There is no reason why women should not play as clean and perfect golf, on a more limited scale, as men do."

When discussing the genders' competition for space on the course, Underhill deals with the issue tactfully and with deference to men. At the same time, she reveals that by 1900 the country club was already contested ground:

> It is greatly to be hoped that the evermore pressing question of women's privileges on the men's links will be decided by those with whom the decision rests, the men, in a spirit of favor for women. The latter ought not to be turned off the course *en masse* on certain days, as many of the men would like to have done; but, instead a certain grade of play on the women's part might be made a basis for their admission. While, of course, it cannot be asked that the men shall subject themselves to being bothered on their holidays by women beginners, it would none the less be ungracious and generally hurtful of the game if women of keen interest and enough proficiency in it to entitle them to enter in class B should be shut out, as many purpose. The men, by sharing the courses with us from the first, a courtesy which would never have been dreamed of in the foreign homes of golf, have shown that it is not as women that they object to us on the links, but merely as the cause of delay and interruption. We may, therefore, hope as the courses become more crowded . . . that to such women as are fairly entitled to compete with many of the men there will be accorded the privileges they deserve.[12]

One way of dealing with Underhill's concerns was to establish women-only clubs. We will never know exactly how many such clubs existed, but we do know a little about the most famous one—the Morris County Golf Club. Formed in 1894, the club was the product of affluent women in and around the exclusive village of Morristown, New Jersey. Some Morristown residents, both men and women, had seen golf being played at Brookline, Shinnecock, and Newport. They returned to Morristown and sought a site at which to create their own course and club. In the beginning women clearly took the lead; they leased a sixty-acre site and laid out a rudimentary seven-hole course. The *New York Times* noted that the women had also secured the services of "a genius Scotchman," James Campbell, as professional.

The club was clearly not strictly for women only. There were three levels of membership: "regular," limited to the thirty-two women who had financed the club's beginnings; "limited," limited to two hundred women; and "associate," limited to two hundred men. The original thirty-two women were clearly crucial in starting the club. Nevertheless, from the beginning the group's executive committee had an all-male advisory committee attached to it. Success apparently destroyed this original club structure. Golf proved to be popular, and with over four hundred members in the club, the demand for a larger and better course to accommodate this growing interest eventually caused the women to lose their dominant position. The women may have started the club, but when it began to expand and grow, the men took over. This change took place with some measure of resistance from the female founders. The club, incorporated in 1895, issued stock and sold bonds to raise money to buy the leased land along with some additional acreage. With incorporation the men took control of the club, bestowing on the original female officers honorary titles and allowing them to control the house committee and the social life within the club. Miss Nina Howland, who was apparently at the center of the controversy, was allowed to keep the title of "honorary president."[13] She never played at the club again.

The club at Morristown was hardly a radical experiment; indeed, it was hardly an experiment at all. After its first year it became a typical upper-class suburban club. As they did at most of these clubs, the genders fought a subtle battle for control and space. This battle was an extension of the one fought in the Victorian homes across America. To put it bluntly, the transformation of America into an urban capitalist rat race had made both genders "nervous": *neurasthenia* was the name they gave to this nervousness. The cloistered and cluttered Victorian home exacerbated the malady; elite families with tensions transferred their contests to the country club. It became an extension or an annex of the home. Both genders were seeking escape from the intolerable predictability and moral straitjacket of Victorian domesticity. Men found escape and release on the golf course and the club's bar. Women sought much the same thing; they could maintain an element of their domestic role by dominating the social life of the club.

If there was a true winner in this process (and I doubt there was), it was young females. The club became a private and supportive site where they could experiment with new personalities and explore new ways of doing things, such as finding a mate and a purpose in life, that had once been done in the strict confines of the home.[14]

A surprising number of the early short stories about golf and country clubs focus on the endlessly fascinating subject of courtship. In these stories young and sometimes not so young women court and are courted by men. As the stories unfold on the golf course and in the clubhouse, the woman learns to separate men of good character from the bad. One of the best of these early stories is "The Duffer," by Frank A. Spearman, which appeared in *Munsey's Magazine* in 1898.[15] The action takes place at a fictional Chicago-area club called Glen Ellyn. The central character, Blanche Bryson, is being courted by three men: Garrett Brynham, a transplanted Englishman and a good golfer; Jim Macalester, a young businessman and a duffer; and General Florence, a wealthy older man and lifelong hacker.

In the course of the story the author does two things. First, he describes the country club as largely a world of the young. In his longest description of club life, Spearman presents a world where the young dominate:

> Supper parties chatted and laughed around the porch tables, and young men in smart ties and peaked caps hung around the big porch columns pulling gravely on briar pipes. . . . Young women well up in diplomacy, and girls but peeping from their shells, strolled arm in arm across the lawn. . . . To watch the young people disappearing around shadowy corners awakened envy; their voices, echoing, brought a regret; so vast a happiness—and passing unshared. . . . It was Saturday night on the golf links at Glen Ellyn.

As the story unfolds, Blanche comes to know her three suitors. In an atmosphere described more than once as a "fairyland," Blanche learns that Brynham is a complete fraud; he is not even a real Englishman. She quickly rejects General Florence as too old. Jim Macalester emerges as the winner of Blanche's heart even though his golf is so pathetic that when playing a round with him, Blanche is rendered helpless from laughter. Blanche's parents are nowhere to be seen during this courtship process; the young woman sorts out her love life unencumbered by parental influence. Victorian rules are maintained only marginally by the presence of Mrs. Van Der Hyde, who plays the role of club chaperone. She remains generally clueless until the very end, when she awards the union of Blanche and Jim some minimal adult approval.

Young women could find more than a mate at the country club. They could also uncover that they had a passion for sport and that the club setting would actually nurture that passion. In the typical Victorian household young women were watched closely for signs of masculine traits, which were ruthlessly repressed when they appeared. The country club was not helpful in this process. As an extension of the home, it provided a new kind of private space in which women could, within limits, explore new ways of being female. They began to compete with one another in tournaments, both national and local. The winners served as models for a rising generation that sought to erode the rigid rules imposed on women and their desire to play and compete.

The country club's role in this erosion is vividly illustrated by the early career of Glenna Collett. She was one of the most popular women sports figures of the 1920s and 1930s. The average American followed her career in the newspapers that recorded her progress as a tournament player. Collett was also an important element in the American assault on European and British dominance in golf. At the 1929 British Women's Amateur Championship she played what some have called the "match of the century" against Great Britain's Joyce Wethered. She often competed against men in benefit matches, an experience she vividly recalls in her autobiography, *Ladies in the Rough* (1928).

The foundation of Collett's career was laid at a country club. Born in 1903,

Collett moved with her family to Providence, Rhode Island, when she was six. At an early age she yearned to play baseball, as her brothers did; her mother objected, but she could not completely suppress the girl's desire to play and compete. The influence of Collett's father and the environment at the Metacomet Country Club led mother and daughter to agree that tennis was more suitable than baseball. Golf, however, soon replaced tennis as a passion in Collett's life.

On an ordinary day in 1917 Collett accompanied her father to the club and stood on the veranda to watch him tee off. He hit an excellent shot down the fairway. She was "tremendously impressed" and ran out on the course, asking to play along. Operating under the poorly understood influence of "beginner's luck," her first shots were long and straight. These shots "stirred the enthusiasm of [her] father and several spectators." One "sun-browned veteran" called out "the coming champion!" Her father and other members of the club eagerly bestowed "lavish praise and warm encouragement" on this talented fourteen year old.

More than a decade later Collett recalled that day: "My head was bursting with the soaring dreams that only the very young and ambitious live and know. . . . My destiny was settled. I would become a golfer." She quickly discovered a small number of models to follow; she avidly consumed all she could about Alexa Stirling, Elaine Rosenthal, Marion Hollins, and other leading female amateurs. She came to understand that she had taken up golf at a time when women had "won two rights": to vote and to play sports. Collett also implies that women had been liberated from the tyranny of Victorian dress regulations as well. Women's desire to play had forced restrictive clothing into the closet and had produced what she calls "modern dress." In addition, she claims that she saw the word *tomboy* change from the term of reproach it had been in her youth. She argues that a tomboy is nothing but a flapper, who is markedly different "from the old-fashioned conception of a little girl who must, like Goldilocks, sit in a corner and sew a fine seam."[16]

It would be preposterous to suggest that the country club was the sole agent in producing this change. It would be equally absurd to forget the role the country club played. Not every young affluent female achieved what

Glenna Collett did, but her experience with her father at the club was indicative of a common experience. The country club provided all young, affluent people a space devoted to play and shielded from public scrutiny. Such spaces let them learn to love games such as tennis and golf in an atmosphere that can best be called tribal. The clubs were in part constructed to promote these games, and as the young took them up, something like an initiation took place. If you had talent, the feeling of belonging, of joining a community, could be unusually strong. Gender stereotypes did not die, of course; they were only challenged by this new reality.

Although Glenna Collett grew up in a welcoming atmosphere at her parents' club, such was not the case everywhere. In 1916 the *New York Times* noted that the issue of women on the golf courses was a hot topic in the metropolitan area. A survey of local clubs found several where women were all but completely banned. The *Times* labeled the Garden City Golf Club "the most monastic of golf clubs." Other clubs imposed restrictions on women, forcing them to play only during limited time periods and requiring them to let men play through. The Piping Rock Club, for example, banned women before 11:30 A.M. and after 3 P.M. on weekdays and banished them from the course completely during the weekends. Many clubs, however, such as Baltrusrol, had no rules inhibiting play by women. The *Times* no doubt correctly concluded that no one was winning the gender contest at country clubs. What the *Times* did not do was to compare the situation in 1916 with the amount of female participation two decades earlier. In this context, women had made great progress.[17]

That progress was part of a much larger process of which the country club was only a small part. Affluent white Americans went through a remarkable transformation between 1895 and 1915. A major element of this transformation was the decline of the home as the moral, economic, and social center of the family. Along with the department store, the movie theater, and the college, the country club allowed for the extension of the family in time and space. In what amounted to a slow-motion escape from the stifling control of the Victorian home, both men and women were compelled to create new values and confront new realities.

What is considered to be the first golf photo in the United States depicts (left to right) Harry Holbrook, Warren and Frederic Holbrook, Alexander P. W. Kinnan, John B. Upham, and John Reid on St. Andrew's Yonkers course in 1888.

A ceremony of some sort at the first tee of the Midlothian Country Club, circa 1898. The clubhouse, considered among the grandest in the Chicago area, was designed by the architectural firm of Frost and Granger. (#201257)

The first tee at the Midlothian Country Club, 1897. The box to the left is probably full of wet sand, from which this man is forming a tee for his female companion. (#201259)

The Chicago Golf Club at the turn of the nineteenth century. The club, located in Wheaton, Illinois, was the creation of Charles Blair MacDonald, who raised $28,000 to buy the 200-acre farm on which it was built. (#200496)

The Onwentsia Club in Lake Forest, Illinois, became the center of suburban North Shore upper-class social life. This photograph was taken in 1899. (#201630)

The clubhouse at Shinnecock Hills Golf Club in Southampton, New York, circa 1892. Designed by Stanford White, who was perhaps the most fashionable architect of the day, the structure illustrates the central role of verandas and porches in the creation of clubhouses. (#202255)

A group of women on the course at the Shinnecock Hills Golf Club in the late 1890s. (#202253)

This converted farmhouse, which still serves as the clubhouse at the Country Club in Brookline, Massachusetts, is little changed from the structure purchased by members in the early 1880s.

For many years sheep were used to keep the lawns trimmed at the Country Club in Brookline, Massachusetts. (#200567)

A triumphant Francis Ouimet (center) and his heroic caddy, Eddie Lowery (with the towel over his shoulders), at the U.S. Open in 1913.

The clubhouse at Olympia Fields, south of Chicago, was completed in 1923 and is perhaps the best example of the monumentalism that influenced country clubs in the 1920s. The building, designed by the Chicago architect George C. Nimmons, was truly immense, providing an aristocratic country house for more than a thousand members. (#201579)

## ❧ 5 ❧

# FROM SIMPLE TO COMPLEX

COUNTRY CLUBS could have remained an upper-class fad. Golf could have become merely another elite sport, such as fox hunting, polo, or yachting. But that did not happen. By World War I the country club had become a significant feature on the social land-scape, and golf had become a major sport. Exactly how this happened is a complex story. As outlined in the previous chapter, the decline of the home and the desire of the whole family to extend itself in time and space played an important role in the growth of country clubs, but several other factors propelled the movement as well. For one thing, country clubs in general became more complex and attractive to larger numbers of Americans. The first clubs were simple affairs, with crude courses and clubhouses consisting of hastily remodeled farmhouses or barns. By 1920 all this had changed; golf courses were becoming more complex in design and construction, and club-houses had in many cases become virtual palaces.

This growing complexity becomes apparent in the development of the Country Club, in Brookline, from its beginnings to 1920. Founded as a coaching destination and a site for other horse-related sports, Brookline slowly became a complex organization. The introduction of golf dramatically changed the club; the horse and rider gradually gave way to the caddie and golfer. Soon, however, other activities took their place at the club. To encourage wintertime patronage, the club arranged for curling and skating. At the turn of the century a group of members at their own expense opened squash courts in the old locker building behind the main clubhouse. At about the same time the club held several automobile races, symbolizing the decline of the horse at the club. In 1901 the executive committee announced that polo matches would be discontinued. The remaining polo players transferred their enthusiasm to the clubs at Winchester (Myopia) and Dedham. Golf steadily grew stronger; the club was the site of the USGA Women's National Amateur Championship in 1902. The public was allowed on the course for this event, but not in the clubhouse. As many as two thousand spectators watched the final matches.

The growing complexity of the Country Club was illustrated by growth in membership, dues, and the club's physical plant. In 1902 the club voted to limit membership to eight hundred. The waiting list was well over one hundred. Like many other clubs, Brookline often found itself caught between a desire to expand its membership to raise revenue and the desires of the existing members to resist such increases. Adding new facilities and sponsoring events tended to call for more members and increased fees. The original annual dues of $30 had risen to $50 by 1888. In 1901 the executive committee heard a request to raise the annual levy to $100. Several reasons for the increase were put forward, but the executive committee probably suggested the most fundamental: "The buildings were old when we got them in 1882. They are nineteen years older and have been repaired and patched until now replacing a rotted post or board involves the very safety of the whole structure." This increase in the annual fee was defeated twice; not until 1902 were dues lifted to $85. At the same time, however, the club agreed to increase its bonded indebtedness from $123,000 to $275,000. These borrowed funds were used to make the much-needed capital improvements and to cover a $25,000 deficit in 1901. In 1902 the club began an ambitious program of improvement and expansion of its buildings, adding a new ballroom and dining area to the first floor of the old clubhouse. It also decided to install electricity in the new quarters. In 1903 the club increased its membership to 850 to raise revenue; as one club historian put it, the additional money was helpful, "but the resultant crowding of the golf course caused many headaches."[1]

All this must have bewildered the original members. In the beginning the club was to be a country lark, a simple, relatively inexpensive place for those weary of town to enjoy their horses. The problems multiplied. In 1903 the older section of the clubhouse was condemned. There was no choice but to raze and rebuild. Again the membership was increased (more revenue); in addition, money from newly created life memberships went to fund the construction, and the club increased the mortgage on the property. At about the same time the club purchased twenty acres of adjoining land to permit improvement and expansion of the golf course. Finally, in 1912 the membership approved the long-resisted increase in dues to $100. In 1912 the growth in the club was illustrated by an appraisal of just its buildings, which included the clubhouse, lockers, a squash court, three stables, some sheds, the Myopia stable, a blacksmith shop, a tool house, the grandstand, a judge's stand, a superintendent's home, and the employee's cottage. The total value was $262,000. This number would have been dwarfed by the value of the golf course and other acreage.[2]

Most of the early clubs went through something like Brookline's experience. Courses had to be expanded and improved and tennis courts installed, and perhaps most important, clubhouses took on new functions and grew like luxuriant plants. More important than this growth of the early clubs was the adoption of the country club movement by the American middle class. Discussing the middle class during this period (1890–1920) introduces exceedingly complex issues. There is no truly acceptable definition of this group, for there are many variables. Is a skilled worker making $5,000 a year in the same class as a teacher, government bureaucrat, or businessperson making the same amount? Sectional differences were also important; the middle class in New York City was different from the middle class in a small town in Kansas. Nevertheless, although important differences existed, many contemporary commentators knew there was a definable group out there, and this group was shaped not so much by income or occupation as by its members' own perceptions of their positions in the rapidly changing American class structure and by their attitudes toward consumption, saving, and money in general. There was, after all, an upper class, which by virtue of wealth and position had grown increasingly free from older social norms concerning work, play, and consumption. There was also a lower class, which was composed more and more of immigrant stock; this class, too, exhibited new attitudes toward work and play. While the upper crust created country clubs and supported sumptuous new resorts, the lower classes literally invented the American saloon. The lower orders also created a vibrant street life and with their nickels and dimes supported places such as Coney Island. As the great American consumer culture wore away at the Protestant ethic, the middle class of the late nineteenth century was the last rock washed loose.[3]

Simply put, old-fashioned middle-class Americans slowly became modern. They put aside attitudes toward saving, work, and leisure that emphasized the denial of desire and the rejection of play. Especially in smaller towns, middle-class Americans adopted the country club as their own. In doing so, they reflected the rationales that the upper classes used as they established their own clubs. The middle-class clubs were different, however; they were simpler, less ostentatious, and tended to be seen by their creators as more closely tied to the larger community.

It is interesting to note that between 1909 and 1912 two magazine articles appeared with identical titles: "Country Clubs for Everyone." The first of these essays, which appeared in *Country Life*, was essentially a survey of country club growth. Its author, C. O. Morris, contends that country clubs, which were once the sole possession of the upper classes, are now available to "everyone." He puts this claim into a community context, presenting the club as an asset to the whole community. Most of the clubs Morris discusses were in smaller towns; if they were near larger cities, they were "less elabo-rate." In listing the factors behind a club's success, Morris presents some fa-miliar notions. The beginning stage is the hardest. Once the club is operat-ing successfully, "everyone will want to join," and "golf will prove to be the most attractive single feature." There are, however, some new realities. Morris points out that clubs tend to raise the real estate values in the nearby area. More important, Morris discusses the club as if it were a community asset: "The desirability of such organizations in any community is beyond ques-tion. The verdict is unanimous. With sufficient impetus to start it going, a club will be like a snowball rolling down hill. After a few years it will come to be regarded as just as permanent a feature of the town as its library, churches, or town square."[4]

Morris acknowledges that the general wealth of an area will influence the way a club is founded, developed, and operated. He assumes that larger cit-ies contain enough wealthy people to overcome any financial problem eas-ily. His focus, however, is on towns such as Kenosha, Wisconsin, where people have founded a club "with practically no money, but with vigorous *esprit de corps*." The Kenosha Country Club was simply a group of people who had rented two large fields near town. Each year the club ran a small deficit that was paid "by popular subscription." The club existed for social purposes only. Each summer night the club served a simple dinner at a low price. Al-though the club hired a cook and a small staff, the waiters and waitresses were club members who received a free dinner for their service. The secretary of the club noted that this serving system had produced "no feeling of social inequality."[5]

The Montrose Country Club, in Montrose, Pennsylvania, provides an-other example of "a simple but successful club." Begun by fifty people who pledged three dollars per year for three years, the club rented land and in-stalled a six-hole golf course and one tennis court. In 1909 the membership stood at two hundred, and the club was growing; it had acquired more land and built a modest clubhouse. Morris describes club after club like the one in Montrose. They are all similar. Dues and fees are low. The members make do with simple clubhouses and the plainest of food and drink. Financial arrangements vary widely, but clearly the key to success is a growing membership willing to pay slowly increasing fees and to buy club bonds when the group needs funds for expansion and improvement.[6]

The second essay entitled "Country Clubs for Everyone" appeared in *Outing* in October 1912. The author, Edward L. Fox, subtitled his work "Ways of Securing Playhouses for All Who Have a Little Money and a Little Time." This piece is unique because it presents the true story of an individual who decided he "needed" a country club. The man is John Blake, from Pierre, South Dakota, who had an idea that was "little short of treason." He wanted a "vacation," but in Pierre work was virtually a religion, and people like Blake kept their noses to the job six days a week, fifty-two weeks a year. "Most of his kind were sorry that fifty-two Sundays cut in." Anyone who wished for a vacation was labeled "an idler," a "trifler," or worse. In short, John Blake was a hard-working, middle-class American with a deep commitment to the Protestant ethic of hard work and denial.

The more he thought about a vacation, however, the more he liked the idea. He assembled ten of his friends and told them his idea. Blake explained to them that they worked too much, too hard, and foolishly." He exhorted his friends to mend their ways: "We are not getting the best results that we should . . . . we should give ourselves a rest." His friends had thought the same thing but had been afraid to speak up. They wanted to hear Blake's idea, which turned out to be much more than simply taking a vacation. He wanted to create a country club in the Black Hills where they could, as he said, rest their minds and rebuild their bodies. It was quickly agreed that each family would buy one share of stock to fund the venture. In the end fifty families purchased bonds for sixty-six dollars, and this money was used to build a clubhouse that would sleep seventy people.

The resulting organization was apparently democratic. The *Outing* essay reports that from the outset there were no class distinctions. The lodge brought everyone to a common level: "The wealthy proprietor of Pierre's largest drygoods store sat down to dinner with one of his clerks. (Sounds like a Socialist farm, but it's true.)"

What John Blake had set in motion in Pierre spread to other parts of South

Dakota. Another group in Pierre founded the Pierre Country Club much nearer the city than Blake's Black Hills Lodge. Other Dakota towns followed suit. Fox notes that these clubs reflected the same democratic tendencies seen in the early Pierre ventures. He claims that the nature of the country club was changing; for him the country club "ceased to mean something aristocratic. No longer does it suggest a gated place of pillared verandahs and smooth lawns where only the wealthy may go."[7]

Indeed, by the time America entered World War I, many middle-class Americans had fully adopted the country club idea and made it their own. Compared to the upper-class clubs, the middle-class clubs were simpler and more open, but above all they were cheaper. Both the *Outing* and *Country Life* essays are uncharacteristically frank about prices. Middle-class Americans may have been altering their attitudes toward leisure and play, but they, like the rich, wanted a bargain. Morris concludes his story of the country club's proliferation with the blunt claim that Americans have increasingly adopted the club idea because they have seen "that the dues will be kept very low. . . . For only because of that reason . . . has the country club received its present and ever-growing vogue."[8] By bonding together, middle-class Americans could and did create versions of the upper-class clubs; through the magic of collective action, they purchased for themselves inexpensive access to the leisure and recreation of the rich.

The flow of middle-class Americans into golf and country clubs was propelled by more than lower prices, however. A number of factors made such clubs attractive to Americans. Golf historians have made much of Francis Ouimet's victory in the 1913 U.S. Open. At the age of twenty Ouimet defeated two veteran Englishmen, Harry Vardon and Ted Ray, in an eighteen-hole playoff. His victory was front-page news, and at the very least, it stirred American nationalism. Nothing could have been better suited to lift America's golf inferiority complex than Ouimet's victory. More important, however, were the domestic implications. Young men from the middle classes could identify with and envy Ouimet. Al Laney, who later became a notable golf writer, was a teenager in 1913 and remembered that Ouimet's victory had been unusually compelling for him because the young golfer was not yet able to vote and, moreover, was from the wrong side of the tracks. Ouimet was the son of a workingman and lived across the street from the exclusive club where he had caddied since he was old enough to tote a bag. He had become a pretty good golfer, too, by imitation, although (like Laney) he had to work summer jobs all through his school years.[9]

Clearly Ouimet's upset of the English legends helped to undercut the image of golf as being only for the elite, the old, and the unheroic. Ouimet proved that golf could put you in the national spotlight and that golfers, like baseball players and prizefighters, could be national heroes, celebrated on the front pages of big city newspapers.

Ouimet's story also raises the issue of the caddie as part of the growth of golf and the country club. Caddying has no parallel in any other sport. Young men (and a few young women) could accomplish a great deal by toting the bags of the wealthy. They could make a few dollars, learn the game of golf "by imitation," and get a firsthand look at the gentility of upper-class life. No other job offered such a valuable blend of benefits. Caddying would become the conduit through which many of the early greats of the game would pass—Sarazen, Hagen, Hogan, Nelson, and many others. This reality clearly indicates that the exclusivity of the country club is a myth. The snobbish country clubbers faced a dilemma, for they sought both to wall themselves off from the undesirable classes and to have people carry their clubs for small wages. The latter desire led the memberships to let the caddies into the clubs, where they became a part of a complex institution. Arrangements had to be made (hence the caddie shack), the caddies had to be supervised (hence the caddie master), and upper-class duffers had to learn how to look foolish in clear sight of their social inferiors.

These arrangements make for an interesting story. In large part country clubs sought to hide the caddies from view. Members adopted an attitude of condescending forbearance toward these young and not so young "servants" in their midst. I will discuss this in more detail in the next chapter when I consider country club design. There was, however, another side of the story illustrated by the Ouimet legend. In the best tradition of upper-class paternalism, country clubs, or at least some club members, took on the responsibility of training and shaping the young men who carried the bags. Ouimet, for example, often cited the influence of a Brookline member, Theodore Hastings, who had invited him to play eighteen holes on the supposedly private links at Brookline. With one eye on the ball and the other vigilantly on the watch for the caddie master, Ouimet played for the first time the course on which he would later defeat Vardon and Ray. When Ouimet had achieved that victory, the club recognized its responsibility to golf and to all the young men who sought to rise in the world through golf. The club granted Francis Ouimet full use of the course without dues for one year; it renewed this gift annually until Ouimet was made an honorary member of the club for life.[10]

The year 1913, when Ouimet had his great victory, saw another broad-gauged development that would influence the evolution of country club life. In the 1880s golf courses were laid out and developed in a simple way. Following Scottish and English precedents, most country club courses were shaped by nature. Men such as Charles B. Macdonald believed that the proper golf course was a seaside course. In 1897 he wrote that there were no "first-class golf clubs" in America. Such a course for him had to meet a strict set of qualifications. It had to have eighteen holes; it had to have rich, sandy soil; and it could develop only over time, with nature taking the lead but guided gently by the human hand. Even though Macdonald was from Chicago, he felt that Long Island and other such seaside sites would be the home of true golf courses. Simpler and less affluent men built courses with less regard to British models than Macdonald had. They found an open piece of land for sale or rent and in a matter of hours laid out nine or eighteen tees and greens. With the addition of a few bunkers, the process was complete.[11]

By the time of America's entry into the war, all this had changed. Golf course construction (the most important and often the most expensive element in founding a country club) was transformed by several factors. Perhaps most important, Americans wished to have courses in all sorts of environments, not just seaside ones. No one ever seriously thought that golf would be played only within sight of the ocean. The result was the American woodland golf course. Americans quickly learned to carve golf courses from heavily wooded land and, in the process, to call on the best science and technology had to offer. Macdonald, for one, never made his peace with the woodland course. He wrote: "No course can be ideal which is laid out through trees. Trees foreshorten the perspective and the wind has not full play."[12]

The construction of American golf courses grew increasingly complex and expensive. Americans took to this process with perhaps more alacrity than the English or Scots might have exhibited. The American identity was deeply linked to the land and especially to the process of taming wild land, of hacking a route through the wilderness, seeking the promised land. Perhaps no club illustrates this development more vividly than Pine Valley, in Clementon, New Jersey. The club was the product of George A. Crump, who owned Philadelphia's Colonnades Hotel. Sometime between 1910 and 1912 Crump became obsessed with a piece of heavily wooded, sandy land ten miles east of Philadelphia. Eventually he sold his hotel interests, moved to the site in Clementon, and supervised the construction of the course. At first Crump lived in a tent as he oversaw the removal of more than 22,000 trees from the site. Using the latest in technology, such as steam-powered dredges and other equipment, Crump literally imposed his will on a piece of intractable land. Crump died of an infected tooth with only fourteen holes completed; he had spent more than a quarter of a million dollars on his obsession. Others took up the task and finished the course in 1918. The club that emerged from Crump's effort was and still is famous for its modest amenities. A writer noted in 1927 that the interior of the clubhouse "has absolutely none of the atmosphere characteristic of the ordinary suburban golf or country club." The act of so violently reconfiguring the land was quite enough; there was no need to build a luxury clubhouse or otherwise to gild the perfect lily.[13]

Even Charles Macdonald was not immune to the temptation to expend vast sums of money and effort to build a notable golf course. In 1913 Macdonald was approached by a group of New Yorkers, including Cornelius Vanderbilt, who asked him to build a course on 115 acres of marshland and swamp. At first he refused, but when told he was to have vast resources and could experiment as he wished, Macdonald accepted the challenge. He recalled his feelings when he undertook to build the Lido course: "To me it seemed a dream. The more I thought it over the more it fascinated me. It really made me feel like a creator." So much for letting nature construct the golf courses.

Macdonald's first step was to hire Seth Raynor as the construction engineer. Next Macdonald arranged for the English magazine *Country Life* to hold a design contest to solicit plans of par four ("two-shot") golf holes. The Lido course eventually used parts of sixteen of the entries. The Lido Corporation, which directed the construction of the club, eventually spent approximately $800,000 on the course. This figure included the price of the land. The total cost of building the club was $1,430,000. To create a golf course out of what was essentially a swamp, Raynor and Macdonald had to reconfigure the 115 acres entirely. The oceanfront had to be protected by groins, and a huge bulkhead had to be built along a channel that ran through the property. After this had been accomplished, the entire site was filled with two million cubic yards of sand sucked from the channel by power dredges. The sand was covered with fifteen-by-thirty-inch blocks of meadow bog to create a foundation for the fairways. The meadow bog was topped with muck removed from a nearby bog, and this was top-dressed with lime, topsoil, and manure and then seeded. To oversee the seeding of fairways and greens, Macdonald hired Peter W. Lees, who became responsible for the early development of the course. As these events indicate, by 1915 the construction of golf courses had clearly entered a new era. Clubs increasingly proved willing to expend vast sums to have an interesting course, and they were willing to place them on sites that literally needed to be destroyed and rebuilt.[14]

Two prewar developments both contributed to and reflected the growing complexity and expense of golf course construction. The first was the arrival of professional golf course architects. In fact, George Crump and Charles Macdonald were transitional figures, passionate golfers who wandered from other professions into course design and construction. The early history of the golf course architect is best understood by tracing the career of the man who many think was the greatest of all time, Donald Ross.

Ross was born in Scotland, and after his school years he became a carpenter in the Highlands town of Dornoch. He was also a golfer and a member of the golf club at Dornoch, which to this day occupies a legendary position as home to very nearly the perfect course. The members of the club decided they needed a professional. As a carpenter, Ross fit the job description, since the professional's main task was to build clubs. After apprenticeship years at St. Andrews and Carnoustie, he took up his duties at Dornoch. During this period he also served as greenkeeper, learning much about the care of turf.

After a few years Ross was approached by Robert Wilson, a professor at Harvard. Wilson invited Ross to come to America, where golf was in its infancy and many lucrative opportunities were available. As his mother pointed out, Ross had the best job in Dornoch, but he nevertheless accepted Wilson's offer and sailed for New York. The trip to New York and eventually to Boston left Ross flat broke. Wilson came to his rescue and put him to work at the Oakley Country Club, where he remodeled the existing nine holes and added a new one. In one year Ross was able to save $2,000, which he sent to his mother.

Ross then began to spend part of each year at Pinehurst, North Carolina, where he was gradually transformed from a golf professional into an architect. Pinehurst in 1900 was a struggling resort, the audacious dream of the Tufts family of Massachusetts. After assembling a fortune selling marble soda foundations, the family's patriarch, James Walker Tufts, purchased a vast tract of North Carolina sand barrens. He wanted to create a retreat for people of modest means seeking, as was Tufts himself, a respite from the New England winter. Soon the visitors were knocking a golf ball around the village cow pastures, and a rude course was installed to satisfy them. James Tufts knew that he needed an overseer of golf in Pinehurst. In 1900 he invited Donald Ross to his home in Medford, and they struck a deal. Ross would spend the winters in North Carolina and keep his position at Oakley (he later spent a short time at the Essex County Club). By 1910 Ross had moved permanently to Pinehurst and made it the center of his course-design business.

There may never have been a more fortuitous meeting between a man and a parcel of land. Between 1901 and 1907 Ross created three courses at the resort, giving them numbers instead of names. These courses were like a source of infection; people came from the North, saw what Ross was creating, and returned to their homes with the desire to have similar courses. The demand for his design and construction services became so great that Ross gave up all his other golf-related activities. By the time the war had begun, Ross had designed or remodeled an amazing number of courses, mostly in the eastern half of the United States. Some of his notable creations were the courses at the Beverly Country Club (1907), the Brae Burn Country Club (1912), the Balsams Resort (1915), and the Chevy Chase Club (1910) and the North Course at the Detroit Golf Club (1916). After the war his business truly took off; when he died in 1948, Ross had designed or remodeled nearly four hundred golf courses.[15]

Ross's career neatly illustrates the growing complexity and specialization in country club life. In 1890 a club would hire one man, usually a Scot, and he filled three roles: professional, club maker, and course designer and greenkeeper. By 1920 this system had evaporated; clubs needed three separate individuals for what was once done by one. A club's prestige and its prospects rested to a great extent on the prestige of the designer and the professional. A skilled greenkeeper who could keep the course playable through drought and flood was invaluable. This division of labor cost money and drove up fees. This may not make much sense to those unfamiliar with golf, but remember tribalism's significance to the early formation of the clubs; the possession of a unique design by Donald Ross or any other notable designer was crucial for establishing a feeling that a club was special. For those obsessed with golf (not a small group), a great course is like a famous artwork; they will travel vast distances and pay vast sums to play on a special course. A famous professional can have a similar effect; people expend great efforts to take a lesson from such a person. To call them gurus would not be an exaggeration. The near deification of the late Harvey Pennick, of the Austin Country Club, is a recent case in point.

As golf courses became increasingly complex, the people responsible for them clearly began to see them as artworks. As designers and country club founders were confronted with developing less than ideal sites or rebuilding an abandoned or mistreated course, they turned to science and technology for solutions to difficult problems. For example, insofar as golf was the driving factor in club creation, the extension of the country club idea into the Southeast and areas such as Southern California was inhibited by the inability to grow suitable grass there. Ross was unable to install grass greens at Pinehurst until the mid-1930s. For many years clubs and courses in hot, arid regions had to make do with sand greens. Such greens produced a low quality of play, and they usually had to be swept with a small carpet after each group putted out. Attempts to construct greens from cottonseed hulls, clay, sawdust, and other waste materials proved equally unsuccessful. To many golfers, it became clear that golf called for special types of grass. One of the first people to work on developing new grasses for golf was Frederick Winslow Taylor, the pioneer in time-motion research and scientific management. As in work, so in golf. Taylor, a devoted golfer, spent the last years of his life in the quest for a grass that would produce a standard, uniform putting green.

Although Taylor's quest was interesting, it paled in comparison with another obsession that blended with the desire to produce better golf course grasses. Driven by increased suburbanization, Americans had begun the search for the perfect lawn. Both searches naturally focused on the U.S. Department of Agriculture (USDA). The department had modestly dabbled in turf grass research prior to 1912. It had constructed a demonstration of lawn-growing techniques at the Philadelphia Exhibition in 1876 and had sporadically issued reports on proper lawn growing. By 1910, however, two groups were increasingly looking to the USDA for guidance: lawn growers and golfers.

The golfers had an able and well-placed advocate in the department's Bureau of Plant Industry. Charles V. Piper, a devoted golfer, apparently conducted research on golf grass as early as 1912, doing so in response to a growing number of requests from clubs and course designers seeking help with turf problems. Piper was able to obtain some of the funds necessary for his research from golf and country clubs. In 1915 the USGA's executive committee suggested to the USDA that the two groups establish a formal relationship (Piper was also a member of the USGA executive committee). At that point the USGA claimed that clubs were spending over $10 million a year on turf and that most of this sum was wasted because they simply did not know what they were doing. By 1916 the two groups were conducting joint experiments at the USDA experimental farm in Arlington, Virginia. In 1920 the USGA undertook the task of spreading the results of the turf research to member clubs when it began to publish the *Bulletin of the Green Section* under the supervision of E. J. Marshall.[16]

This discussion of Donald Ross as designer and the increasingly complex search for better grasses suggests that the rapid rise of the country club was part of a larger movement in American life. Between the Civil War and the onset of the Great Depression, cities, states, and the federal government were animated by a desire to preserve natural scenery for public viewing or to construct natural settings that could provide a crucial antidote to the artificial urban landscape. On the one hand, in 1864 the federal government set aside a wild tract of land in California that came to be known as Yosemite. On the other hand, in the 1880s and 1890s Frederick Law Olmsted took a piece of abused urban land in Boston and crafted a natural setting for Bostonians to enjoy. In the process Olmsted designed and built a marsh, or what today we would call a wetland. Of course, the most well known example of creating a natural setting for scenery-starved urbanites was Olmstead's Central Park, in New York City.

The thousands of country clubs built before 1930 were basically a private version of the public park movement. The general intention was essentially the same: both the park and the golf course were designed and manipulated natural settings offering people an easy route along a "course" through nature. In both cases the intention was not to preserve nature untouched (wilderness) but rather to impose design and human needs on a piece of land. Of course, country clubs had one important advantage: they could limit access to the land. As park designers discovered by the early twentieth century, opening the land to the public inevitably leads to the transformation and often the deterioration of the landscape itself. As I have shown, at country clubs the land often evoked reverence as the club took root and grew.

It would be nearly impossible to overstate the depth and importance of the movement to provide designed natural settings for Americans to enjoy. In the twentieth century the job of creating and maintaining these sites fell to state and federal agencies. Around the turn of that century, however, there were very significant private attempts to purchase and redesign apparently worthless land for similar ends. Perhaps the most famous example of this was the construction of Biltmore, near Asheville, North Carolina. George Vanderbilt had acquired thousands of acres of very poor woodlands. In 1888 he hired Olmsted to transform this land into a managed natural setting that would complement the enormous house Vanderbilt was constructing. Olmsted's goal for the "Biltmore Forest" was clear. He wished to show that humans could impose a plan on a piece of otherwise worthless land and transform it into an economically valuable and aesthetically pleasing venture. The design that Olmsted created for Vanderbilt was clearly similar to the design Donald Ross or any of the golf course architects would have submitted to the membership of a private club planning to build a course. In both cases the goal was to impose human needs on nature, to change the land into something useful and perhaps medicinal to people increasingly cut off from the refreshing embrace of nature.

Firms such as Olmsted and Vaux and the company formed by Donald Ross rarely if ever competed for work, but in one important instance the connection between them became clear. In 1894 James Walker Tufts employed Olmsted and Vaux to design the village that would be the heart of his Pinehurst resort. The resulting plan was remarkable; it featured broad curving roadways with sixteen-foot spaces between the road and the lot lines. The plan called for massive plantings along the roads and elsewhere in the village. Working from the Olmsted plan, the builders and landscapers soon made a small part of the desolate sand barrens Edenic. Nevertheless, it did not work well enough to draw a profitable number of customers from the North. For this Tufts hired Donald Ross, who continued the task the people at Olmsted's firm had begun. Ross transformed useless sandy land into green golf courses that eventually became important additions to the original village.[17]

The period between 1900 and the American entry into World War I was a positive one for the country clubs. Although the affairs of the typical club became more complex and expensive, they also became more attractive. It seemed that everything was moving in the clubs' favor. President Taft, against the advice of Teddy Roosevelt, came out as a spokesman for golf. To his credit, he urged the creation of more public courses in 1913. In a letter printed in the *New York Times*, Taft argued for the installation of courses in public park space. He claimed that "golf is not a mere play thing of faddists, as some suppose, nor is it a rich man's game. . . . It is the game of all classes." The public course was a significant factor in the growth of country clubs. Thomas Bendelow, the foremost designer and promoter of public golf courses, stated in 1916 that the public courses were excellent for teaching Americans to love the game. Once hooked by golf and successful "in their business affairs," they would move on to private clubs.[18]

Even the ball helped the clubs grow. Late in the nineteenth century everyone played with gutta-percha balls. It took some real muscle to hit these balls a great distance, so that they tended to inhibit participation by women and children. Coburn Haskell, an avid golfer from Cleveland, changed all this. While at a Goodyear Rubber Company plant at Akron, he discovered waste rubber strips, which he wound around a core and at first covered with gutta-percha. These balls came on the market in 1898, but they needed much improvement. The discovery of balata for the cover and the practice of dimpling or scoring the cover improved performance. The Haskell, or rubber-core, ball greatly enhanced the game, making brute strength less important than grace and skill.

All this pales alongside two culture-wide developments that decisively influenced the growth and expansion of country clubs. First, the clubs benefited from the decline in Sabbatarian laws that inhibited Sunday play and recreation. From the earliest days the country club and prohibitions against Sunday play were on a collision course. Because golfers played on private property and their sport, unlike baseball, did not draw large or unruly crowds, ancient laws prohibiting Sunday recreation were rarely enforced against country clubbers. Also, Sabbatarian restrictions were local laws, and the enforcement of such laws against individuals who were almost always members of the elite seemed unpromising and unwise to local police.

By the turn of the century those battling Sunday play of any sort were clearly in retreat. A court case in Yonkers, New York, neatly illustrates the situation. In May 1901 Benjamin Adams was arrested at the Saegkill Golf Club for playing golf in violation of a local ordinance. The case was tried before Judge Kellogg and a jury of Adams's peers. In fact, they were too much his peers. One of the jurors, J. Bell, was also a member of Saegkill and might have helped his fellow golfer. Unfortunately Bell appeared for duty wearing his golf clothes; the judge smelled a rat and dismissed him from the jury. Adams's lawyer, Joseph F. Daly, built his defense on two tactics. First, he ridiculed the laws as seeking to make infants of grown men and women. Newspaper accounts quote Daly as saying that the Sunday laws and their supporters sought to put adults "in the boots of the small boy." Daly then told the story of the small boy who asked his mother what heaven was like. When his mother replied that in heaven everyday is Sunday, the boy replied: "I guess I'd rather go to the other place then." The judge was not amused.

Daly's defense rested on a second, more substantial point. The local statute forbade Sunday recreation only on public ground. The judge repeatedly left out the words "public sports" when he read the law to the jury. The defense violently objected, and the judge finally admitted that he had misread the law. The jury was out for forty-five minutes and returned an innocent verdict. It also recommended the repeal of the law against Sunday play.[19] The Yonkers case reveals several aspects of the conflict between the largely Christian forces seeking to ban Sunday recreation and those fighting the laws. Clearly the laws were the subject of much ridicule. They were portrayed as a remnant of an earlier and more oppressive time. Also, the relationship between such laws and country club life was problematic. Did the community have the right to intervene on private property? By 1915 many Americans would have answered no. The country clubs benefited from this development; as Sunday gradually became a leisurely day for many Americans, it became a day to spend at the club.

The historian Benjamin Rader has correctly connected the slow decline of Sabbatarian laws to the rise of the consumer culture. Although the consumer culture did not completely destroy traditional values and rituals such as Sunday church attendance, Rader notes that "it spawned an alternative set of powerful dreams and expectations." The "immediate pleasures" that increased leisure and play could bring slowly eroded the values of work, duty, and self-denial. Rader claims that, partly in response to this change in attitude and aspiration, "many states repealed or neglected to enforce their Sabbatarian laws." Nevertheless, he notes that this transition was far from smooth; people experienced agonizing doubts and attempted to find ways to enjoy the consumer culture while remaining true to the older values. Attendance at church and Sunday morning golf waged a long and sometimes bitter battle that many still fight. By 1920, however, the country club had become a significant challenge to the notion that Sunday should be a day of rest and worship in church.[20]

Suburbanization was the second cultural development that spurred the growth and expansion of country clubs. Suburbanization has been a long and complex process in the United States. The country club became part of this process, as I have shown, when upper-class city dwellers added the country club to their rural or semirural enclaves. By doing so, they were replacing the urban institutions that had provided a social life and recreation for them. There were subtle differences, however, among these early suburban clubs. In one version the clubs served a seasonal population of individuals and families who owned a second home in the country. Such clubs as Onwentsia, Tuxedo Park, and Newport had clearly defined "seasons" and equally clear "off-seasons." Another more important version served a group permanently in residence; the club was an extension of their permanent homes, and it was an attraction drawing more residents into the suburb.

After 1900 this second version became a major force behind the growth of country clubs. Slowly the relationship between the suburban community and the country club began to change. Whereas the rich had added the club to an existing community, the post-1900 environment featured the availability of a country club as an inducement to buy into a suburban development.

In a 1911 series of articles on suburbs, the *New York Times* concluded that "something besides a plot of ground, some trees and abundance of fresh air is recognized today as a prime necessity for the proper development and growth of a suburban community." The *Times* reported that developers were convinced that they had to install "social and open air amusements" *before* starting to develop their communities. The same developers concluded that "a well sustained club" was often a crucial factor in the success of a project. Long Island illustrated this point; clearly undergoing a real estate boom, the island's popularity with potential suburbanites had been much influenced by the establishment of a number of clubs. Glenwood Country Club, Nassau Country Club, the Garden City Golf Club, and the Oakland Golf Club had all stimulated suburban growth.

The *Times* also suggested that these clubs differed somewhat from earlier clubs. For one thing, the new clubs were open all year to serve permanent residents: golf, tennis, and swimming dominated the summer season, whereas winter sports, dances, and cards characterized club life in the winter. These new clubs were presented as less exclusive. In 1914 the *Times* claimed that the new suburban clubs did not foster "an effete, aristocratic club life." Instead they offered more open admission; the emphasis was on "healthy sporting and social amusements, not social exclusivity." In a conclusion of sorts the *Times* claimed: "The suburban district virtually abounds in clubs offering friendly, healthy and enjoyable associations in every case, and wherever one may be pleased to locate within reasonable distance from the business limits of New York he may be tolerably certain of finding a well organized club free from ultra exclusiveness and to which he will doubtless be welcomed as a member."[21]

Beneath the connection between suburbanization and the expansion of the country club idea lay certain major population shifts and the nature of the American attitude toward the post-1900 city. Between 1900 and 1920 perhaps the most important trend in the American population was the steady movement of people from rural to urban areas. During this period the urban population grew nearly 80 percent. Most dramatic was the growth of metropolitan areas, cities with more than 200,000 inhabitants and significant suburbs. Between 1910 and 1920 these areas grew slightly more than 25 percent. In 1920 the United States contained thirty-two metropolitan areas with a combined population of 30,188,543 people.[22] It is reasonable to infer that one of the major dramas of this period was the adjustment of rural and small-town people to the big city. As these transplants responded to their new situations, they were confronted with many choices, but none was more important than the choice between city and suburb. What mind-set and values directed this choice?

A 1927 essay by the humorist Ellis Parker Butler provides a clear view into the values of a transplanted rural dweller who came to the city (New York) but choose to live in the suburbs. Butler came to New York from Iowa just after the turn of the century, and in 1906 he moved out of the city. By 1927 he had accumulated twenty-one years of suburban experience. Butler clearly acknowledges that the city dweller thinks "that the suburbanite must have something seriously the matter with him." Central to this impression is the sense that the suburbanite is "petty and ineffectual" and afraid of real life, which can be confronted only in the city. Believing that all this is unfair and distorts the true nature of the suburbs and their inhabitants, Butler sets out to correct the record.

Butler argues that suburbs have quietly improved since the turn of the century. Although they were once isolated, uncomfortable, and lacking the services only a city could provide, this has changed. Modern suburbs are like "the prettier residential sections of a small city. They offer all that people need within easy reach; schools, churches, theaters and clubs of all kinds are common in the new suburbs." The defense of suburbs, however, tends to focus more on the nature of cities and their decline. According to Butler, "a big city is a nucleus that has outgrown itself, and cannot stop growing because it does not know how." It is also no place for children. He was a city-dweller until his children arrived at "the doorknob-reaching age." Out of general disenchantment, he and his wife began looking for a house outside the city. The Butlers moved often during their time in New York City; they came to understand that many urbanites moved often, driven by "an innate feeling that life is not being lived in the best way. The apartment dweller senses that something is wrong but does not know just what it is, so he moves to another apartment. Then he moves again. And again." In the end, "apartment life is at best a makeshift substitute for real life." Real life, a happy life, would always be defined by the memories of village life (in Butler's case, Muscatine, Iowa) that many carried to the city with them.

Indeed, Butler's positive defense of suburban living rests on his sense of the similarity between suburbs and villages. When he moved his family to Flushing, he described it as "a village suburb," calling it "the most beautiful place we had ever seen; it looked like a home town." As if in a nineteenth-century village, one had a sense that one could control the conditions of life. The Butlers quickly became part of a number of associations that sought to improve everything from the sewers to the cultural life. Friends and a sense of belonging developed quickly; Butler concludes, "I might have remained on Manhattan forever without being more than a frightened individual at whose check the bank teller looks with a suspicious eye."

What has all this to do with the country club? The answer is that the country club was one of the associations that knit together the newly suburbanized individuals. Butler, who joined a club, extols golf as an important social ingredient in Flushing and all the suburbs. With mild exaggeration he claims: "All the golf courses are in the suburbs. The suburban men and women in these United States who meet regularly on the golf courses week after week must run into the millions." Golf and the country club serve also to banish idleness, one of the great fears of people leaving the city for the suburbs. The country club was a small but not an insignificant factor in the process whereby rural people, forced to the city, shaped a suburban world that reflected their desire to retain important elements of the village life they had left behind.[23]

Thus major forces such as suburbanization and gradual secularization not only shaped the new contours of American life but also carried golf and the country club along for the ride. By 1916 the country club as a voluntary association and golf, the main reason for the association, had escaped the persistent charge that both were upper-class fads. The cultural commitment to the country club by white upper- and middle-class Americans was deeply rooted when the war began.

World War I was a severe challenge to the country club movement in at least two ways. As America entered the war, the country adopted strict controls on basic materials such as fuel. In 1917 the Federal Fuel Administration requested that country clubs close during the winter. Since their operation was deemed nonessential, the use of fuel to warm country clubs ran counter to the calls for sacrifice. Several New York area clubs began cutting wood on their property and selling it as fuel. The Dunwoodie Club, near New York City, began raising food crops on part of its course and selling the produce on the local market. It turned over the proceeds to the war effort. The war effort also inhibited the construction of new clubs and new courses, as well as stopping the rapid growth in both public and private golf courses.[24]

Both during and after the war, however, the country clubs' biggest threat came from taxes. As America was drawn into the war, President Wilson and members of his administration slowly came to understand the financial challenge that lay ahead. In addition to paying for its part, the nation faced British and French requests for huge loans. In the spring of 1917 Congress passed several measures to raise money for the war effort. These measures put considerable emphasis on borrowing, and by war's end the nation had borrowed approximately $23 billion. Progressives and radicals in Congress believed that the corporation and the well-off should pay a heavy share in the form of higher income, inheritance, and excess profits taxes. This view that drastically higher taxes should be part of the effort to pay for the war triumphed when Congress passed the War Revenue Act of 1917. In addition to mandating much higher tax rates, the measure called for a wide assortment of levies on luxuries of all sorts. Americans focused on the stunning increases in the income tax and the controversial excess profits tax; few, however, paid much attention to section 701, which imposed a hodgepodge of secondary taxes. Included was a 10 percent tax on "any amount paid as dues or membership fees (including initiation fees), to a social, athletic, or sporting club or organization, where such dues or fees are in excess of $12 per year."

After this relatively clear point, things became intensely confused. Tax code writers were forced to confront a number of issues, including how to treat life memberships, the differences (if any) between membership fees and dues, and the taxability of the purchase of club bonds or stock. In a series of bewildering rulings beginning in November 1917, the Revenue Service attempted to clarify matters but managed only to create a nightmare for clubs as they sought to obey the law. After the war the tax on admissions and dues remained in place, and the clubs grew increasingly infuriated. In 1925, acting through the Association of American Clubs, the country clubs sought the elimination of all taxes on them. In their appeal their spokesperson, S. Franklin Pearce (from Westchester Hills Golf Club, White Plains, New York), claimed that the law and related rulings were "so vague and confusing that numerous clubs [were] taking the matter to the highest courts individually and collectively at considerable cost. In addition, large sums which were illegally collected [were] refunded to the clubs." Pearce also argued against the imposition of any tax on clubs, which he characterized as nonprofit, socially beneficial organizations. Taxing such organizations during the war might be appropriate, Pearce admitted, but such levies are unjust during peacetime. Both Pearce and Wynant D. Vanderpool, president of the USGA, put great stress on the nonprofit aspects of clubs. Vanderpool claimed that the clubs were nonprofit social, athletic, literary, and educational organizations that were "a beneficial influence to the country."[25]

None of these appeals substantially changed the situation. Indeed, the 1920s saw repeated attempts to eliminate or modify the tax on club dues and stock held by members. The only clear triumph for the clubs came in early 1927, when the U.S. Court of Claims ruled that stocks, bonds, and notes issued to members as a condition of membership were not taxable. The Internal Revenue Department agreed not to appeal the decision and to set up a procedure whereby club members could file for a refund (a procedure, by the way, that sounds depressingly familiar to modern taxpayers). The tax on dues and other fees remained in place, in one form or another, until 1965, when it disappeared from the federal tax code without comment or controversy.[26]

The significance of this adventure in tax history is hard to determine.

There was no detectable class bias in the long history of the tax on dues and fees. The real conflict came over the IRS's inability to define the nature of the tax clearly. This was more important than it may seem. The country club was lumped together with other "amusements," and in some sense it clearly belongs in that category. In other ways, however, it does not belong there; clear differences exists between a person buying an equity interest in an organization that provides him or her sport and leisure and a person buying a ticket to a ball game or a movie. The long history of conflict over the tax illustrates that the country club as a commodity does not fit neatly into any slot. This becomes clear when we remember the persistent claim by clubs and their spokespeople that country clubs are nonprofit enterprises. It is worth noting that other nonprofit groups, such as fraternal organizations, were exempt from taxation under the original law in 1917 and remained so.

In the end, however, the war and the resultant tax bite did little to slow the growth of country clubs. As I have indicated in this chapter, there were too many forces in American life to slow the proliferation of the club idea. When the war ended, secularization, suburbanization, and increased prosperity returned to create the conditions for a rapid increase in the number of clubs. Indeed, all the factors that called forth the country club had their day in the 1920s. Discretionary time and income increased for many Americans, and well-to-do whites increasingly abandoned the Protestant ethic and adopted new values that justified increased leisure and pleasure. As the 1920s began, the country club was already fully developed as an idea and institution. Between 1919 and 1930 the country club experienced something like a golden age that, like the decade, ended with confusion, collapse, and despair.

## ❧ 6 ❧

# THE GOLDEN AGE

IN 1977 THE historian Benjamin Rader produced one of the best explanations for the rapid rise of sport in American life. According to Rader, between 1880 and 1930 sports experienced a "takeoff" stage in which organized sporting activity became an important part of American culture. Focusing on the social functions of sport, Rader argues that "a quest for subcommunities in the nineteenth century furnishes an important key to understanding the rise of American sport." As small, coherent villages and towns declined and metropolitan areas began to dominate, Americans sought to create new forms of community. Employing the voluntary association as a tool, Americans created small, often exclusive communities that mitigated the burgeoning influence of rapid urbanization. As America became more centralized and as individuals found themselves unwilling members of national corporate communities, they found coherence and meaning in small socially and ethnically homogeneous communities. Rader contends that there were two types of these subcommunities: "status" and "ethnic" communities.

In most cases, however, the sporting club was a "multifaceted social agency." It could practice social exclusion, training the young in the manners and mores of a social class or maintaining ethnic tradition. At the most complex level, the new sporting clubs could take on some of the functions of church, state, and community. Of course, as Rader notes, they could also become an important force promoting American sports.

In applying his ideas to country clubs, Rader emphasizes their social function. He notes that golf clearly became "the most potent agency" for the growth of country clubs after the founding of St. Andrew's Golf Club, in Yonkers. While accepting this fact, he relies on the testimony of George Birmingham, a visiting Irishman, to establish the essentially social nature of the American country club. Birmingham noted that English clubs were "devoted to particular objects, golf clubs, yacht clubs and so forth." According to Birmingham, the American clubs of the time were very different; they were the social center for the surrounding area, and they encouraged sport "for the sake of general sociability." Focusing on the Tuxedo Club, Birmingham claimed that it existed "primarily as a social center": "It not only fosters, it regulates and governs the social life of the place."[1]

Rader is clearly right on a number of issues, but he falls victim to a confusion of names on the issue of the golf club and the country club. Is the country club a golf club? Is a golf club a country club? The answer to both questions is almost always yes. There have been a few interesting exceptions, but for the most part golf and country clubs evolved together between 1880 and 1930. Thus one institution took on two very different tasks; on the one hand, it sought to create a subcommunity based on ethnic or status factors, while on the other hand, it sought to provide access to an ancient game with a tradition that was in its own way democratic and egalitarian. Furthermore, Rader fails to notice that the country club was a full extension of the home and family and, as such, an attempt by some Americans to attain a possibly aristocratic status to which their income and class did not entitle them. They also sought a status that ran counter to strong antiaristocratic attitudes deeply rooted in American culture.

In the 1920s the dual nature of the country club grew increasingly pronounced. Golf as a sport expanded rapidly and became more democratic, albeit slowly. At the same time the country club in its nongolf guise grew more and more luxurious; goaded by ambitious architects, clubs built increasingly pretentious and complex clubhouses. Many in the affluent classes believed without question the notion that postwar America had entered a period of endless prosperity. Under the spell of this delusion, groups spent vast sums on the construction of incredibly elaborate country clubs that were designed to serve their members as grandiose second homes. Golf thus became inextricably linked with the growth of pretentious country clubs. When the 1929 stock market crash came, and the expensive country club quickly became a symbol feeding the national sense that the 1920s had been a decade of excess and overspending, golf was caught up in the national stocktaking. Although the game survived, its image as the pursuit of the upper crust, the spendthrift, and the unmanly hardened into a widely shared belief.

In addition, during the 1920s the country club evolved in ways that made any image of it stereotypical. Social history, sociology, and gossip have a certain tendency in common. Their characterizations (of the country club, for example) tend to flatten differences and discount the variety of human intentions and purposes. To focus exclusively on issues of social class and status blinds one to the complex reality that was the American country club in this era. In its most blatant form, this stereotyping sees the country club idea as solely the pet project of the white, Anglo-Saxon male, who used it to maintain his position in the social hierarchy. Without denying this reality, it is crucial to understand that other groups—women and Jews, for example—found in the club a valuable element relevant to them. During the 1920s the country club idea spread to all corners of the nation; Americans organized and built many kinds of clubs that allowed them to achieve many kinds of purposes. Of all these purposes, none was more important than the promotion of golf, a game that for many became a way of life.

There were many signs that golf was changing in the decade after World War I. As America entered an era in which sport in general became more important, golf began to shed for good its upper-class image, and growing numbers of Americans made it a part of their lives. Public courses became increasingly common; Americans of small means could play an eighteen-hole round for twenty-five cents, and many were hooked. In 1927 the Playground and Recreation Association announced that golf had a "greater number of active participants than any other game in America." In 1929 Americans spent over $17 million on clubs and balls, easily outstripping the amount spent on baseball, football, and tennis equipment combined. The rapid expansion of golf did not go unnoticed by observers of the American sport landscape. In 1926 Robert Hunter, in his book *The Links*, noted the passion and creativity being poured into the construction of public courses. He also noted that "private companies" were entering the field; some of these companies built courses to enhance their real estate developments, while others sought profit solely from greens fees. Hunter claims: "Golf has been taken to the heart of Demos. Pink coats are no more, but knickers are universal and the time seems not far distant when every man, woman and child will have a set of clubs." For Hunter, this was a case of golf being true to its Scottish democratic roots. When an American of great wealth yearns to play a round with an ex-caddie, they are simply being true to the game's ancient tendency to bring the rich and powerful together on the links with the poor and lowly.[2]

In the February 24, 1923, issue of *Saturday Evening Post* the magazine's middle-class subscribers learned about the game's egalitarianism in an article by Bozeman Bulger entitled "The Growing Golf Germ." Bulger suggests that golf "has taken class distinction by the nape of the neck and shaken it to pieces." A playwright of sorts, he points out that it was once easy to suggest that a character had aristocratic pretensions: "Put a bag of golf sticks over his shoulder and call him Van Courtland Parks." But by 1923 the situation had changed. Bulger claims that the clamor for more public courses will further democratize the game. He notes that people from "all walks of life" mingle on the public courses of his time, and he illustrates this with a story about the golf partnership of a dentist and a hotel porter.

Nevertheless, the push to expand access to the game was motivated by more than a commitment to democratic and egalitarian tradition. Towns sought to establish public courses because they were a way to enhance a town's reputation (the booster spirit) and to provide recreation for the young.

The story of a public course in Janesville, Wisconsin, offers a case in point. The local newspaper was a prime mover in getting the course built; the paper argued that the course would help draw tourists and that the young of Janesville would have access to cheap and wholesome recreation. The course was financed by private individuals and was operated and developed by an independent group, the Janesville Municipal Golf Association. Although a public facility, the course clearly bore the marks of private control and resembled a private country club in many respects. The cheapest way for Janesville citizens to participate was to purchase "golf in advance"—a ten-dollar book let you play fifty rounds. This procedure was little more than a modification of the standard dues system at a private club.[3]

More subtle but equally important in democratizing golf was the appearance of the modern golf professional. Certainly the figure of Bobby Jones dominated the decade, and he was the product of the country club world and the rigorous code of amateurism. Nonetheless, he was a most accessible young man and popular beyond anything Francis Ouimet or Jerome Travers might have imagined. Jones may well be the most extraordinary of the heroes produced in the world of sport during the 1920s. He played serious tournament golf for only fourteen years and then quit at the age of twenty-eight. He studied engineering at Georgia Tech, literature at Harvard, and law at Emory. He was arguably the most literate and gracious athlete in American history. As a role model and popularizer of golf, his influence was immense. After his retirement he and a group of associates established Augusta National in the early 1930s. It has become in the minds of many the most well known and controversial golf club in America.

Although Jones no doubt helped spread the game to the masses, his influence was probably secondary to the role of the caddie. Every country club where golf was a major attraction drew a large number of young boys, and some young girls, to the grounds to carry clubs, rake traps, and replace the divots hacked out by the members. It was a rare club that did not include as a structural element a group of caddies, often a hundred or more. The social tension caused by the close contact of upper-class golfers and lower-class caddies was revealed by a growing tradition of humor surrounding the relationship. This humor often focused on the fact that golf sometimes led the supposedly social superior to look foolish, venal, or dishonest in clear view of the caddie, the social inferior. The best of A. B. Frost's golf drawings show an innocent caddie aghast at the behavior of his affluent employer.

In 1900 Price Collier conveyed some sense of the odd and contradictory role caddies play in the game of golf. The duties of the caddie seem simple enough: tee the ball, follow its flight, find it, and remove the flag before the golfer putts. Collier notes that at one time the caddie was usually a friend working to aid his companion as they sought victory together. Gradually the friend became a "paid assistant," one that "must be obedient as a servant, but . . . also interested as a friend." Collier admits that the caddie is in some sense un-American. In the land of radical individualism, "the American caddy finds it difficult to bury his own personality in the success of another." In fact, the caddie versus the player remains to this day a subtheme in golf literature. From the point of view of the player, the caddie is often a poorly trained and ungrateful libertine. From the caddie's position, the employer is a cheating cheapskate with a golf game that deserves only contempt.[4]

The caddie posed a problem that American golfers failed to solve until the late 1950s. Technology eventually provided the method for eliminating the caddie. The electric or gas-powered golf cart has since the mid-1950s slowly pushed caddying from the game. The loss has been immeasurable. The golf cart is an abomination; it requires paths that ruin the look of the course, and it reduces the exercise required to near zero. Perhaps more important, the cart has eliminated the social mixing between caddies and players that was a crucial element of both the game and the clubs as social realities. To their credit, many private golf clubs work hard to maintain a caddie program, which they rationalize as an effort to be true to the spirit of the game. Such programs have to battle the electric cart and government regulations that seek to "protect" the caddie from "oppression."[5]

The caddie has been an important part of golf as an economic reality and as an element in the life of the country club. In 1921 Grantland Rice argued that caddying was a real threat to baseball. Quoting Connie Mack, Rice claimed that young boys were giving up baseball for caddying. Unlike playing baseball, toting golf bags paid "real money" and introduced the caddie to a game with a future. A caddie could move into a number of jobs as he grew up; the most interesting, of course, was golf professional. Rice noted that there were many role models for this jump from caddie to professional: Gene Sarazen, Walter Hagen, and Jack McDermott were well-known pros who had begun as caddies. Rice estimated that there were 150,000 caddies in the United States and claimed that some of the larger clubs had as many as 350.[6]

The position of caddie has no exact parallel in other organized sports. All sports have coaches and assistants to the players, but in no case is the coach such an active participant in the action. The player and the caddie essentially form a partnership, and the rules in many respects treat them as essentially one person. More important, caddying has served as an introduction to the game for millions of young people, mostly boys. As was mentioned previously, Francis Ouimet was celebrated perhaps as much for his caddying background as for his victory in the U.S. Open. Ouimet's victory led also to the celebration of *his* caddie, ten-year-old Eddie Lowery. Bernard Darwin recalled that before the playoff, young Lowery was offered a large sum to give his job to someone else, "but he stuck firmly to his post and was not to be seduced." Darwin claimed that Lowery "was a most heroic child, and as cool as his master."[7]

Images such as this may have drawn hundreds of thousands of youngsters to America's country clubs. The money and the convenience were probably equally important. Caddying was the perfect summer job, since the most lucrative time coincided with vacation from school. Caddies could often work when they wished; moreover, they work outside, and the job brought them into contact with the upper crust and the game of golf.

All these factors were dramatized by the early life of Gene Sarazen. Born in 1902, Sarazen was an unlikely sort to find his vocation and passion at a country club. The son of an Italian immigrant, Sarazen's earliest memories were of work. His father wanted Sarazen to be a carpenter, and at age four the boy began to work with him, learning the trade. Sarazen was not content with this arrangement, however, and portrays himself as "a rebel" even before he

entered school. For several years he enjoyed a successful career selling the
*Saturday Evening Post.* In the summer he yearned to work outside, and for a while
he became a fruit picker, the job "all the kids were looking for."

At the age of eight Sarazen was introduced to golf and caddying. Many
young boys in his neighborhood in Harrison, New York, caddied at the
Larchmont Country Club, where a neighbor, Fred Biscelli, was the club pro,
caddie master, and greenkeeper. This connection to the Biscellis served
Sarazen well. He learned the way to carry a bag, as well as golf etiquette and
the uses of the various clubs. Soon he was on the course earning what for
him was big money. On that first day he earned twenty-five cents (the fee
for eighteen holes) and a twenty-cent tip: "That forty-five cents was the most
money I had ever earned in a single day. When I handed it to my father at
the dinner table, it made a great impression on him."

As he became an accomplished caddie, Sarazen was attracted to the game
itself. One day, using a member's club and ball, he took his first swing on a
real course. Using what was called a "jigger" in those days, he hit a nearly
perfect shot. He dates the start of his infatuation with the game to that event:
"I had the golf bug very, very bad after that jigger shot." To pursue their
passion, Gene and some of the other caddies created a makeshift course in a
vacant lot near their homes. There they would play until late at night, guided
only by the faint glow from streetlights; significantly, they called their
"course" the Lower Harrison Country Club.

After several years at Larchmont, Sarazen moved to the Apawamis Country Club because it was larger and offered a chance to make more money.
At Apawamis Sarazen competed with a much larger group of boys, one of
whom was Ed Sullivan, who later became a noted columnist and television
host. At his new course Gene learned to supplement his income by selling
lost balls found in the woods and water hazards. More crucial, however, he
was allowed to play the course. This was the direct result of Ouimet's victory. The members responded to the ex-caddie's victory by establishing a
caddie tournament, hoping that among their caddies "there might be another
Ouimet who in future years might make the world safe for American golf."
In his first appearance, Gene shot 105 and finished last.

Sarazen, however, made decided progress as a caddie. One member, an excellent player named Harold Downing, made him his regular caddie and began to take him to tournaments. After one trip Sarazen returned with a twenty-dollar bill to contribute to the family fund. By his own account he was well on his way to being a professional caddie when the war started. The start of the war coincided with a disastrous economic move by his father that wiped out the family's savings and threw them into debt. Sarazen was forced to go to work with his father and give up golf and caddying. Ironically, he was saved from a life as a carpenter when he became gravely ill with pneumonia. At one point he was given last rites. After a near miraculous recovery made possible by an experimental operation to drain fluid from his chest, his doctor told him not to return to his job in a war plant but to find work in the fresh air. He was to rest completely and get plenty of sun for six months. Using the authority of the doctor to blunt his father's protests, Sarazen knew that the solution to his dilemma was golf. For him, the success of Ouimet and Walter Hagen "had washed away . . . earlier doubts that a poor man's son could not climb in a rich man's game."

So Sarazen had six months to *play* golf, but the problem was where. He could not afford a country club, so he turned to a public course, Beardsley Park, in Bridgeport, Connecticut. The professional at the course, Al Ciuci, generously allowed Gene to hang around the course, playing for free as long as he did not interfere with the paying customers. Sarazen was proud of Ciuci's reaction when the pro heard of Sarazen's caddying career and his devotion to the game: "He had me feel as if I were a veteran on an equal footing with him in the golfing fraternity." Over the violent objections of his father, who harbored a deep bias against golf, Sarazen learned the game that would serve him so well. In a matter of months Ciuci was bragging about Sarazen as the best golfer in the area. Ciuci also began the crusade to obtain a club job for him. The object of this crusade was George Sparling, the Scottish head pro at nearby Brooklawn Country Club. Infected with the common notion that only Scots make decent professionals, Sparling at first refused even to interview Sarazen and then, after acquiescing, rejected him until two members pressured the pro to reconsider. Gene was in as an assistant pro, making eight dollars a week. The two members, twin brothers, befriended Gene and protected him from Sparling's obvious bias against Italians. As time passed, however, Sparling and Sarazen became friends, and Sarazen was released from much of the drudgery in the pro shop. He began to play big money matches with the members, and this experience honed his ability to play under pressure. Soon he was playing in local events and occasionally winning fifty or a hundred dollars. Sarazen's future was set; he began to spend the winters in the South, playing tournaments and working on his game. He found summer jobs at northern clubs and soon made a name for himself as a tournament player. In 1922 Sarazen won the U.S. Open and went on to become a prominent figure in the world of golf, remaining so well into the 1930s.[8]

The story of Gene Sarazen and other pros of the 1920s and 1930s has much to do with a dramatic change taking place in the world of golf and the country club. By the middle of the 1920s figures such as Sarazen, Hagen, and Jones had altered the public's image of the red-coated upper-crust golfers of the 1890s and the prewar years. They had also pushed aside the tweed-coated, pipe-smoking Scottish professionals who ran the early courses. Moreover, the professionals had clearly pushed the amateurs from center stage. Even Bobby Jones, the great amateur, could not save the old days, when professionals dressed in their cars and ate in the club kitchens. The golf professional, dashing in his knickers and silk shirts, took over the golf world and democratized it to a significant extent. Americans could certainly relate to Sarazen, the son of an immigrant and only five feet, five inches tall. They also loved Walter Hagen, the son of a blacksmith, who added excitement to the game. Hagen played the game as a series of wild mistakes and improbable recoveries. Alistair Cooke, who saw Hagen during one of his "invasions" of Britain, recalled that Hagen "looked like the 'lounge lizard' all nice girls are warned against." Cooke understood that Hagen was stealing golf from the aristocracy. Hagen hit balls from the Savoy's roof into the Thames, arrived at the course in a chauffeured limousine, and called the prince of Wales "David," and it was clear that Cooke delighted in the "pained cries from the Old Guard whom the Lord sent Hagen to mock." And it was Hagen who first said, "Take time to smell the flowers"—a cliché today, but as Cooke noted, it would have made "the perfect epitaph" for Walter Hagen's gravestone.[9]

The rise of these dashing men was more complex than it seemed at the level of mere images. To some extent it was based on the existence of public courses, where poor boys such as Sarazen could play and practice. It was also influenced by the founding and growth of the Professional Golfer's Association (PGA). Founded in 1916 by Rodman Wanamaker, heir to a department store fortune, the PGA gave professionals an advocacy group and for the first time a tournament for professionals only. Wanamaker put up a purse of $2,500 in 1916; the first winner was Jim Barnes. From these modest beginnings the PGA has steadily grown into one of the most successful professional sports organizations. By the middle 1920s a fledgling tour with significant prize money had developed, especially in the South during the winter months. All these developments tended to "Americanize" the game. In the late nineteenth century and earlier in the twentieth, the average American had tended to think of golf as somehow connected to Scotland and the English upper crust. The rise of caddies to national renown, the creation of a national professional organization, the establishment of public courses, and regular victories by Americans in English tournaments slowly made the game more appealing to the average American. All this takes on more meaning when we remember that in 1925, at an obscure country club in Fort Worth, Texas, two young caddies took up the game knowing it was American and that it offered them a career in sport. They were Byron Nelson and Ben Hogan, who came to dominate professional golf in the 1940s and early 1950s.

This democratization, however, applied only to whites. The PGA did not officially have a "Caucasian only" policy until the 1940s, but since its founding it had been dedicated to keeping the professional ranks free of African Americans. Thus, the situation in golf was much like that in baseball. Young blacks could learn the game and earn money as caddies, but if they wished to continue in the game, they were pushed to the margins. The few African Americans who carved out a place for themselves did so at a tiny number of black clubs and public courses. John Shippen, who rose to prominence at

Shinnecock Hills, was able to make a place for himself in golf at the black-owned Shady Rest Golf and Country Club, in New Jersey.

Dewey Brown was another African American who faced obstacles quite unlike those of his white counterparts. Born in 1898 in North Carolina, Brown began caddying when his family moved to New Jersey. He began to learn the golf business and obtained a job at the Morris County Golf Club, where he learned to make clubs under the direction of pro Tom Hucknell. Slowly his game developed, and he became as well known for his play and teaching as he was for his skill as a clubmaker. Brown made a living in several ways. He owned a restaurant and catering concern but was always involved in golf. He worked on and off for many years at Shawnee-on-the-Delaware. Many prominent people, including President Harding, purchased sets of his hand-made clubs. In 1928 the PGA, apparently unaware of his race, admitted him to the organization, but it revoked his membership without explanation in 1934. Disappointed, Brown made his living as a restaurant and resort manager. In 1947, however, he purchased his own resort golf course, the Cedar River House and Golf Club, in Indian Lake, New York. In the early 1960s the PGA readmitted Brown to full membership.[10]

As the image of golf changed, so did the demand for country clubs. More and more Americans took up the game and, if they could afford it, bought a membership in a private club. More and more players could try the game at one of the growing number of public courses, and if they caught the golf bug, they could seek a place at a private club. Public courses were very popular during the 1920s, no doubt because, unlike many other facilities, they were self-sustaining and often produced a profit that could support other public athletic facilities. The experience of Grand Rapids, Michigan, was typical. In 1929 the city had four public courses; the first had been built only in 1924. Although it had been self-sustaining from the beginning, in 1929 it produced a profit of over $2,100. In some cases cities made every attempt to duplicate country club life at their public courses. Indianapolis was a hotbed for public golf. As early as 1920 it boasted two eighteen-hole courses and one nine-hole course, and it was taking over a private club that had leased land from the city. *Golf Magazine* reported that the city was constructing a new clubhouse that would serve two of the courses. The new structure was modeled on private clubs "with every feature, even to the dance hall that a country clubhouse affords." One group in the city wished to raise fees and make the courses "more exclusive," but it was checked by the city's park board, which fought higher fees and aimed ultimately at providing free golf to all.[11]

Counting the number of courses and sorting out the public from the private is exceedingly difficult. In *Americans at Play* (1932) George Steiner provides the most useful numbers. Steiner's general conclusion is that "the spectacular growth of golf [between the war and the depression] is unparalleled in the history of American outdoor sports." He claims that between 1916 and 1923 the number of courses jumped from 752 to 1,903. By 1930 the number had further increased to 5,856. Of these courses, 543 were public or municipal while approximately 700 were daily-fee or commercial. Thus the total number of private country clubs in 1930 stood at approximately 4,613, almost four times the number of public courses. Steiner also suggests that geographically clubs and courses had spread quite rapidly in the 1920s. In 1916 there were four states with no courses and sixteen states with fewer than 10. In 1930 there was only one state with fewer than 10, and eighteen had between 10 and 400. The total worth of "golf plants" Steiner puts at approximately $830 million. The total dues paid at private clubs was $450 million. Using reasonable assumptions, since many private clubs did not report membership numbers, Steiner concludes that at the time there were 880,000 club members and 200,00 family members, for a total of 1,080,000. Steiner estimates that at least 900,000 were playing public courses and sets the number of American golfers at 2 million.

One fact emerges from these numbers: the private club was still the dominant venue for golfers in the 1920s. Although the country club had begun as an experiment among urban elites, by the mid-1920s it had spread to all parts of the country. New York and Illinois led the nation in total number of courses, but by other measures they were back in the pack. If we look at the number of courses per 100,000 in urban population, Kansas had the highest density of clubs, at 31:100,000; Iowa was second, with 21:100,000; and New York trailed badly, with only 5:100,000.[12]

It is impossible to capture the essence of all this club building. Clubs ranged from simple affairs to the almost impossibly grandiose. The affluent of small towns installed nine holes, built a simple clubhouse, and took pride in their country club. One such club was the Oak Hill Country Club, in Red Oak, Iowa, a town of 6,000. The history of this venture shows that even simple clubs were based on complex financial maneuvers. The club was incorporated as the Red Oak Country Club in January 1920, when the membership purchased eighty acres of land two miles east of town. Unfortunately this purchase was made when farmland prices were very high; in two years the original $30,000 investment had shrunk to $15,000. To save the club, a local group founded the Club Land Company, a holding company that took over the club property. Each original member surrendered his or her share of stock in the Red Oak Country Club for a share in the new Oak Hill Country Club, a nonstock enterprise. The Oak Hill membership then leased the club back from the holding company at a rate that gave the financiers an 8 percent return. The club created a constitution and bylaws that stabilized the future of the club. Each member was assessed a $100 membership fee that became a building fund since there was no clubhouse. Male members paid $25 per year and $10 into a sinking fund; females paid $10 for dues and $5 dollars into the fund. The sinking fund was used to buy the stock of the Club Land Company. Eventually the membership would own the holding company and thus the country club, with all its improvements. This arrangement suggests that local affluent elites were important in the early stages of rural country club growth.

*American Golfer* magazine sent Earl Chapin May to Iowa to report on the Oak Hill Country Club. On his arrival he was told that Oak Hill was typical, that "strictly rural country clubs" were "sprouting . . . like mushrooms." The club was clearly a golf club with a strong emphasis on family. Women played a major role in the club through the Ladies Auxiliary, which arranged the few non-golf-related social events there. Children were allowed limited use of the golf course; they were banned every weekday after five P.M. and all day Sunday. Children could not be at the club without a parent or guardian at any time. Chapin noted that the club had constructed a playground and that it was always full of happy children watched over by parents. He also claimed that the club was democratic, basing his assertion on the fact that members, male and female, carried their own clubs. There were only three caddies at Oak Hill, and they had a hard time finding work. Chapin was of the opinion that golf lured members into the club but that, like all rural clubs, Oak Hill was a "community social center of the best order."[13]

Not that far from Oak Hill but separated by a vast gulf of expense and pretense was the club at Olympia Fields, approximately twenty-seven miles south of Chicago. The planning for this club had begun in 1914; the first course opened in 1916, and the fourth, in 1923. The million-dollar clubhouse was finished in 1925, completing what was arguably the largest country club in America. The club was the idea of Charles Beach and a group of Chicago business and social leaders; there were 500 charter members. Amos Alonzo Stagg, the athletic director at the University of Chicago, was club president from 1916 to 1919 and shepherded the enterprise through the war years. Before the war the initiation fee was $60 and the annual dues were $25, but these figures rose throughout the 1920s. In 1927 the value of a membership was approximately $1,100. In the late 1920s there were 1,000 regular members and 300 members of other classes.

The original impetus for this massive project was golf. Beach and his colleagues, who were "not men of large means," wanted from the beginning to build a four-course golf club, with the courses radiating out from a huge clubhouse. The club was established on a 700-acre site, and the first stage of development was financed by a $500,000 bond sale to the members. In 1927 the club was a tremendous financial success, with an appraised value of $3,500,000. The club had also been the target of at least one group who wished to purchase it and turn it into a daily-fee private enterprise.

Although golf may have been its original and most fundamental purpose, it was the clubhouse that made Olympia Fields famous. As the massive structure was built, members camped in tents on the grounds. They watched a truly massive and distinctive building come into being. Whereas the members of Oak Hill made do with a converted barn, Olympia Fields built from scratch and built big. The structure was designed by George C. Nimmons, of Chicago, and the total cost including the furnishings was over $1 million. The club boasted that it was the largest and most complete clubhouse in the world. The general style was Gothic; the architect claimed that he sought to imitate "the large country houses of England during the Tudor period, when some of the best country homes there were built by craftsmen who were themselves, or descendants of, the great cathedral builders of England." The building was clearly meant to create instant prestige by inspiring thoughts of the English aristocracy and European churches. The central room, or "great hall," was designed to evoke the "principal room in an old baronial hall"; it featured giant timber trusses, oak-paneled walls, a fireplace, and a musician's gallery. There was also a dining room that could seat 600 and a "cafe" with room for 300. The front porch may have been disappearing from the upper-class American home, but it was dramatically reappearing at the country club in the form of huge verandas. The Olympia Fields clubhouse featured a 500-foot veranda on which the club's informal social life centered. There were huge locker rooms for each gender with a swimming pool between them. The men's locker room contained 1,200 lockers and offered every possible service. Men took their laundry to the club and could have clothing repaired there as well. The women's locker room offered similar valet service. Services once done in the home were now available at the club.

Aside from the building, the most compelling aspect of Olympia Fields was its completeness and near self-sufficiency. The club included a hospital, its own ice-making plant, a complete playground for children, an outdoor dancing pavilion, and a dormitory for 300 employees. The club composted its garbage and sold it to neighboring farmers. There was an enormous building to house the 1,400 registered caddies who carried the members' bags. There were eighty rooms for rent in the clubhouse and a number of cottages for members who wished to stay for an extended period. Interestingly, the club abandoned the old chauffeur-based system, in which members were delivered to the front door. Instead the club built a parking lot in the rear, and members entered from the back. Members could also reach the club by suburban railway; the club maintained its own station on club property. All in all, Olympia Fields was one of the most noteworthy building projects completed in the 1920s.

It was not, however, built with a mindless outlay of money. The planners clearly sought to provide an aristocratic experience on a budget. During the war, for example, they grew wheat in the roughs and other land, and the club profited. The annual budget of approximately $250,000 was defrayed by income from visitors' greens fees, the profit from the restaurant, and whatever profit the club made by selling its compost. Most important, after the building was complete, the club retained more than eighty acres of vacant land that it sold to remove their bonded indebtedness. This land had risen dramatically in value because of the club. Unlike the early clubs, Olympia Fields was the product of much planning and calculation. The club planners saw it as an investment and sought to maximize efficiency and the benefits to the membership by judicious spending early in the club's history. Country clubs had ceased being modest, quickly planned upper-class ventures. In cases such as that of Olympia Fields, they were well-planned, long-term investments.[14]

Another club that illustrates this theme is the Westwood Country Club, in St. Louis. Founded in 1907, the club occupied a small site just outside the city limits. The automobile had caused rapid development of the area around the club grounds, which precluded expansion. The members voted to abandon the site and in the mid-1920s set out to create "an entirely new country club plant, as complete as modern ingenuity could make it and produced as quickly and as economically as possible." A committee was formed to select a new site for the club; it eventually selected a 300-acre tract fourteen miles west of St. Louis. A major factor was the land's value for real estate development. From the beginning planners expected to use a good portion of the site for real estate development around the club. The club formed a design board comprising various experts, including a consulting engineer, a golf architect, a drainage and irrigation engineer, building architects, and a land-scape designer. There was also a special consultant on sewers.

The design board had to convert the 300 acres into a modern country club that would serve the needs of 400 regular members and a "club popula-tion" of 1,500, all of whom demanded the very best. This meant several things to the planners. First, they had to create "a sporty and non-crowded golf course." The course architect was given great freedom to produce twenty-seven challenging and beautiful holes. The members did place one restric-tion on the golf architect: he had to leave "the edges of the property" alone so they could be used for real estate development. Second, the board had to plan "a clubhouse suitable for social use throughout the entire year with accommodations for summer use equal to the very best resort,—swimming pool, tennis courts and handball courts, children's playgrounds, baseball dia-mond, parking spaces, garages, formal gardens, pleasant and shady terraces, possible aviation and polo fields,—with all surplus space reserved for resi-dential sites."

Workers began clearing the grounds and building the golf course in the spring of 1927. The site was altered considerably as the course developed. Beyond requiring the grading necessary for fairways, tees, and greens, the plan called for the construction of a 750-foot earthen dam that created a 4½-acre lake. The plan also called for a great deal of pipe: 80,000 feet of drain tile, 4,500 feet of sewer pipe, 25,000 feet of irrigation pipe, and 8,500 feet of pipe for drinking fountains on the course. The course cost approximately $125,000 to prepare.

The clubhouse cost estimate was approximately $250,000, not includ-ing the furnishings. Given all the modern technology and planning that went into the club, it is interesting that they selected an "English Baronial design" for the clubhouse. The building occupied 45,000 square feet and was con-structed of stone and rubble. The men of the club seem to have had their way in the design of the structure. The building was 400 feet long along its major axis, but there was a 350-foot ell that contained "the men's department," which was completely segregated from the rest of the building. The grounds around the clubhouse received great attention. Over 18,000 cubic yards of earth were moved to prepare the site. The tennis and handball courts enclosed a parking lot for 200 cars. The courts, pool, and playgrounds added $83,000 to the total cost. Since the site was virtually treeless, the club created a nursery and purchased small plants that would eventually be moved to their permanent places.

The real estate development was part of the total plan, which called for four subdivisions with "varying types of restrictions necessary on each." The club reserved forty-two lots for sale. The smallest lot was approximately one acre, and the largest was two and one-quarter acres. The planners concluded that the club represented an investment of one million dollars, but that by the act of building their club it would "have appreciated itself at least a quarter million dollars." More important, by building the club they would raise the value of "its contiguous neighborhood upwards of two and a half million dollars in value, due to its stabilization of the character of the territory." Of course, the club owned a good piece of the "contiguous neighborhood" and had a vested interest in its stabilization and exclusive nature.[15]

The membership of this club was overwhelmingly Jewish. In many ways Westwood was typical of the Jewish clubs that prospered in the 1920s. By one count in the Jewish weekly magazine *American Hebrew*, there were fifty-eight such clubs in the United States by 1926, seventeen of them in the New York City area. This number included two of the first Jewish clubs in the country: Inwood, established in 1901, and the Century Club, founded in 1898. Almost every city with a considerable Jewish population boasted at least one such club. The largest club was Philadelphia's Philmont Club, with 938 members. The only group to proclaim its Jewishness openly was the Jewish Progressive Club, in Atlanta. The list in *American Hebrew* showed that most of the organizations were established after 1910. Fragmentary membership numbers suggest that the number of Jewish country club members stood at nearly 17,500. Of the total, 13,352 were men and 4,164 were women. Twenty-two Jewish clubs banned women completely. The membership in Jewish country clubs was almost certainly overwhelmingly held by Jews of German descent.

The German Jewish population was in a position to respond to anti-Semitic exclusion by employing its economic muscle to create clubs as lavish as any of those from which they were excluded. One historian, Peter Levine, has suggested that their "goals were undeniably clear—to demonstrate their own credentials for acceptance by a dominant upper-class, white, Anglo-Saxon, Protestant elite and to distance themselves from the waves of East European Jewish immigrants living and toiling in urban ghettoes." Some of the clubs created by Jews were among the most beautiful in America, as was the Lake Shore Country Club, near Chicago, which was the product of immense economic might, including the resources of Julius Rosenwald, the president of Sears, Roebuck and Chicago's wealthiest man.

Although any analysis of the Jewish clubs must focus on the issues of exclusion and bias by Jews and Gentiles, it is also clear that golf was in some small way a democratic force. A writer in *American Hebrew* suggested that Jewish clubs had become places where "Jews and Gentiles [met] on a ground of sportsmanlike equality." Gene Sarazen, who worked at the Jewish Fresh Meadow Country Club as a professional, was a fervid proponent of golf as a means of removing barriers between Jews and Gentiles. In an article published in *American Hebrew* Sarazen called golf "one of the most potent forces in breaking down the age-old prejudices of race between the Jew and the non-Jew." These barriers were breached as well when important tournaments came to Jewish clubs (although this did not happen often enough). The 1923 USGA Open and the 1921 PGA Championship were played at the Inwood club. The Fresh Meadow club hosted the 1930 PGA and the 1932 U.S. Open Championships. The Fresh Meadow course was legendary among golfers. Designed by A. W. Tillinghast, the course drew raves from all who played it. Built just south of the point where the Long Island Expressway crosses 183d Street, the course was dead in the sights of the remorseless advance of "urban civilization." In 1946 the club moved to a new location; one of America's truly great courses is now a housing development.

The Jewish clubs of the 1920s reflect the generally mixed nature of the country club movement. No one can doubt that the clubs furthered exclusion and the separation of people of different races and faiths. Golf, the dominant sport at the clubs, in significant ways worked against this exclusion by bringing people together to play a sport with a strong tradition of being open to all.[16]

These brief portraits of Oak Hill, Olympia Fields, and the Jewish clubs such as Westwood illustrate a number of themes in the evolution of the country club idea.

Country clubs, or some of them at least, were becoming larger and more complex. Members tended to think of their clubs as investments while never abandoning the notion that they were joining a club to extend their homes and to add to the scope of family activities. Memberships also were employing experts to a much greater degree than before the war. Although the golf course architect had emerged before the war as an important factor in club construction, and clubhouse designers had also become important, it was not until the postwar years that architects fully took up the subject of clubhouse design and developed a clear set of values that deeply influenced the country club movement. The writings of these clubhouse architects offer us a crucial set of insights into what the country club became in its golden age.

Before America entered the war a few designers had begun to discuss clubhouse architecture. Most noted that early clubs either converted existing buildings into clubhouses or built simple structures to suit their purposes. By 1905 designers realized that the country club movement was no fad and that clubs had special needs calling for architectural innovation. By 1915 this process was well underway. For example, in an essay in the *Architectural Record* Harold D. Eberlein noted that the country club had become so common "that it [had] occasioned a distinct architectural need." To begin to address this need, Eberlein offered a definition of a country club that is worth citing in full: "A country club is an organization for the encouragement and convenient pursuit, whether individually, collectively or in teams of sundry forms of outdoor recreation. This definition is sufficiently comprehensive to include fox-hunting clubs, polo clubs, tennis clubs, golf clubs—or any of the other clubs definitely organized to facilitate the following of one special form of recreation."[17] Although this is helpful, it misses the direction of club development. Most crucially, Eberlein fails to note the growing dominance of golf. He also fails to see the club as a family resource or an extension of the home.

Eberlein did understand that clubs were essentially an antidote to the city and the increased pressures of modern life. For him, "the modern conditions of city life," "the tireless insistency of the machinery of civilization grinding in our ears[,] and the thronging pressure of humanity from all sides" had made some place of relaxation a necessity. Relaxation was a central purpose of the country club, and it could best be achieved "for a number of people by co-operation through the medium of the country club." Another way of looking at this, Eberlein concludes, is to see the country club as the direct descendent of the summer resort hotel.[18]

By 1925 architects had developed a more focused and complete philosophy of clubhouse design. The March 1925 issue of *Architectural Forum* devoted itself to country club architecture. Both professional architects and others contributed to the publication. J. Lewis Brown, the editor of *Golf Illustrated*, wrote the lead article, which put the topic of country clubhouses into context. He notes that the early structures were modest and designed to meet the needs of golfers only. Over the years the nongolfing demands on clubs grew steadily; clubs began to compete with one another to have the most complete and luxurious facilities. The buildings kept getting larger and larger, especially when "the demands of the women members began to receive as much attention as those of the men." Brown makes no distinction between golf and country clubs, viewing them all as substitutes for the multipurpose summer hotel and assuming that all clubs must have a golf course. Grantland Rice's essay in the same issue runs clearly counter to Brown's view. Rice claims that the golfer wants a first-rate course, maintained as well as possible. As for the clubhouse, Rice advises that simple is best and that clubs should avoid adding amenities that compete with having first-rate golf.[19]

Among architects Rice's view was becoming anachronistic. Designers were homing in on a new general conception of the country club. Although most nodded politely to the importance of golf, they were beginning to understand country clubhouses as residences. This was both a decided shift from seeing such structures as similar to hotels and a move away from conceptualizing them as the base of operation for a sporting venture. Architects understood, of course, that locker rooms were necessary and that you had to get golfers conveniently out of the clubhouse, onto the course, and back in again. Overlaying these realities, however, was the understanding that the best-designed clubhouses were extensions of the home and should be thought of as residences. In 1925 Ayman Embury II argued that under no circumstances should the modern clubhouse be thought of as a hotel. Instead, Embury asserts, "a clubhouse is the temporary residence of a group of people who do or should constitute a single family[,] the clubhouse, must, therefore be considered as if it were a residence."[20]

By 1929 the architectural community had fully adopted the view that the country club should be designed and sold to the memberships as essentially a home. The fullest expression of this view was produced by Clifford C. Wendehack, a noted country club architect. Wendehack had designed and supervised the construction of many clubhouses; perhaps his most notable achievements were Winged Foot Golf Club, in Mamaroneck, New York, and the North Jersey Country Club, in Paterson, New Jersey. His book *Golf and Country Clubs: A Survey of Requirements of Planning, Construction and Equipment of the Modern Clubhouse* (1929) remains one of the most complete guides to conceptualizing and building a country club.

Wendehack's opinions are clearly the product of much experience. By 1929 he had consulted and struggled with numerous club-building committees. In the process he had learned a great deal about the nature of clubs, what makes them work, and what makes them fail. As an architect he was also in the business of advancing his profession; he was particularly critical of attempts to alter and repair existing structures. He claims that this almost never produces the ideal clubhouse, which requires a new architect-designed building. Thus his book is intensely practical, offering detailed advice on everything from sewers to lockers to pro shops.

Wendehack also developed a clear philosophy of clubhouses. Although they should function well in practical terms, they should also be surrogate homes. He openly rejects the distinction between golf clubs and country clubs, using the terms interchangeably. In so doing, he implicitly rejects the simple golf clubhouses of Scotland and England as models. For him, the club- house should be much more than a simple golf-oriented building; it is the members' collective home. He implies that this identification was forced on architects over the previous decade (1919–29) by the memberships' escalat- ing demands for more elaborate buildings.

Wendehack asserts that one key to producing a superior and well-used clubhouse is color, citing research that in his view proves color to be "a posi- tive force which affects our nervous systems, probably by electro-chemical activity." He argues that Gothic architecture, with its "rich hued stained-glass windows," was used in European cathedrals "to inspire spiritual feelings." In time Gothic forms and colors "became the symbol of men's striving for spiri- tual perfection." Wendehack claims that country clubs have become Amer- ica's cathedrals, but the goal of "physical perfection" has replaced the quest for spiritual perfection. None of this slightly wacky theorizing about color makes much sense until Wendehack comes to the point: the real purpose of color in architecture and furnishings "is to produce a home-like and inspir- ing atmosphere." A club should make the average man and woman uncon- sciously relax and feel at home. The club should produce "a happy mood" and "a contented frame of mind" that cause members to linger at the club "so that in time they will enjoy the club as much if not more than their homes."

On issue after issue Wendehack states his preference for a homelike at- mosphere. For example, the dining room is the heart of a clubhouse and should remind the members of home, not of "the formality of a hotel dining room." In this regard Wendehack's theory of the grill room is instructive. He notes that the modern club grill room is modeled on the old English inn or chop house colorfully depicted by Dickens. He notes that grill rooms are popular features in American hotels, giving them "an informal dining room provided with a spirit of freedom and used at times for dancing." The Ameri- can country club, however, has given the grill room a new definition. While retaining its informality, the grill has become "the masculine domain exclu- sively." Its traditional place—connected to the men's locker room—proves its link to the male world. Its purpose is to produce "good fellowship and intimate acquaintance among men[,] and women are rigidly excluded from its use." It seems reasonable to suggest that the country club grill room was a substitute for separate male-domain rooms such as libraries, studies, and smoking rooms, which had slowly disappeared from the shrinking American home.

Wendehack's emphasis on creating homelike country clubs extends to fireplaces or hearths. He notes that "the family hearth" is the symbol that gives a building character and provides members with fond associations and memories. Without such symbols, a building is little more than "a mass of brick and mortar." Through the ages the hearthstone has been "a simple stone upon which the eternal fires of communal needs and interests burn." Even if modern heating systems have made fireplaces merely decorative and symbolic, country clubs should have them as a communal center intended to create the warmth of home. Wendehack is practical enough to know that this is also a "balance sheet" issue. A warm hearth that creates wintertime traffic increases the building's usefulness in the months when the usual sporting activities do not draw members to the club. Members should be encouraged to feed the fire themselves. The club should keep an ample supply of wood so that they can do so, for the activity will help them to "feel at home" and have a sense "they are taking part in the club's hospitality."

By the end of the 1920s architects such as Wendehack understood that their clients were most satisfied when their country club provided comforts and associations that were not generally available at their simpler and more modern homes. Huge dining rooms, grill rooms, servants, valet service, and recreation were part of an image many affluent Americans had of the country house, especially the English country house. As the realities of modern America became clearer, affluent Americans realized that they could have such a home only collectively, at the country club. In fact, many Americans realized that their ample but still limited affluence could never buy them a home. By 1930 one club architect argued that the growth in the number of clubs was linked to growth in the number of apartment dwellers. He viewed the country club as a way for such people to maintain the traditions of home life that were slowly being eliminated by urban and suburban realities. Thus the country club was not really "a sport club" but rather "a sort of community house."[21]

In reality, of course, it was both. The country golf club for the most part had two purposes: to provide golf and to provide a high-status surrogate home to the members. In his 1922 novel *Babbitt* Sinclair Lewis provides an example of this double nature characterizing most clubs. George Babbitt belongs to the Outing Golf and Country Club, "a pleasant gray-shingled building with a broad porch, on a daisy starred cliff above Lake Kennepoose." He plays golf with his friend Paul Riesling and truly relaxes. This is important, because "week by week he accumulated nervousness." After he has played a few holes, however, his heart beats "more and more normally and his voice slows to the drawling of his hundred generations of peasant ancestors." Babbitt is not a member of the Tonawanda Club, where the town's elite play golf and socialize. Clearly this issue galls Babbitt, who spends much effort denying his profound desire to join the elite. He characterizes the people at Tonawanda as "would-be's in New York get ups, drinking tea." Lewis suggests the subtle nature of Babbitt's frustration when Babbitt exclaims, "I wouldn't join the Tonawanda even if they—I wouldn't join it on a bet." Of course, the elite will not invite him to join, and Babbitt knows it. We can assume that Babbitt would advocate enlarging his country clubhouse to make it equal or superior to the facilities at Tonawanda.[22]

Babbitt in this sense represents many Americans who sought status in a world where the roads to it were crowded and confused. As Warren Susman has pointed out, by the 1920s Americans lived in "crowds" that made it impossible for them to differentiate themselves from others. It became increasingly important for Americans to feel that they were "somebody" and to have others think so, too. For the vast majority of Americans, the sense that they were "somebody" increasingly came by purchasing the consumer goods (autos, clothing, and appliances) that promised to give the buyer a sense of uniqueness. This was largely a self-defeating process. As mass production came to dominate American life, consumer products took on a dreary sameness, and Americans began to look and live more and more alike. At least one method remained to separate oneself from the masses: going into the countryside and commandeering a piece of land.[23]

Those who could commandeer such pieces of land and the privacy that went with them did not constitute a homogeneous group. Country clubs were seen as one way of understanding and stabilizing the class hierarchy in larger towns where more than one club was created. In small towns membership in the only club the town could support usually symbolized having made it into the elite. Babbitt's sense of social exclusion arises when he realizes that he will probably never gain access to Zenith's top-ranked club. He is apparently unaware that he practices exactly the same sort of exclusion by denying membership in his club to those beneath him in the town's social hierarchy. Such discourse on the social invidiousness of country clubs has been common coin in America since World War I. This discourse is based on solid fact: class, religion, and ethnicity have been central in the construction of country club life.[24]

Americans are unusually fond of social markers such as country clubs, probably because the class system in the United States is fluid and inexact. Club membership can nail down one's social status with a degree of exactness absent from other measures of such status. But does it? C. Wright Mills, certainly no friend of exclusive clubs, suggests that country club membership "is not of decisive importance to the upper levels, for country clubs have spread downward into the middle and even into the lower-middle classes." Mills asserts that country clubs might be significant in "smaller cities" but "in the metropolitan status market" they count for little. It is "the gentleman's club, an exclusive male organization, that is most important."[25]

Furthermore, by the mid-1920s it was apparent that clubs did not compete solely on a local level for status. Golf, and particularly national golf events, could impart to a club a prominence that no amount of local prestige could match. Clubs could gain "golf status" by hosting a major event, by creating a unique course designed by a notable architect (e.g., Donald Ross or Alistar Mackenzie ), or by employing a notable professional who won national tournaments or possessed a solid reputation as a teacher. Finally, many clubs were in no sense local institutions and were disconnected from the local status hierarchy. Pine Valley, for one, quickly developed a national and international membership. Beginning in the 1930s, Augusta National was nurtured to have national prestige (and a national membership) based solely on its golf course, the Masters Tournament, and the role the club played in the international golf community. Located in the Augusta, Georgia, area, the club derived virtually none of its status from its position on the local social hierarchy. Most commentators on country club life have not taken seriously the fact that golf is in many ways the crux of a club. Most commentators forget that beneath almost every country club is a golf club.

One important example of this tendency comes from Vance Packard and his widely read book *The Status Seekers* (1959). Packard includes the views of "Mr. Dunlap," one of his informants, on the country clubs in the city Packard used as a prototype. Dunlap listed seven clubs according to his appraisal of their prestige in the community. Packard claims that others provided substantially identical lists. The first two on the list are described as "sort of shabby" but clearly the most prestigious socially. The third club "lacks the prestige of the other two," but it "might fool you because it has the best golf course." This club holds "national tournaments" and is clearly superior as a golf club but falls short of the top rung socially. The ranking is based on a local perspective, however, not a national one. After all, which club might tourists or other outsiders wish to visit?

This portrait of club status rankings in *The Status Seekers* presents another problem with a simple class analysis of country clubs. The seventh club listed is the Jewish club. The informant placed it last because, he said, "I just don't know where to place it." Jews may rise to the highest levels of community prestige and status, but they cannot use this status to gain admittance to the "best" clubs. Jewish country clubs were anomalies and thus hard to rank on the social hierarchy. Exacerbating the difficulty in ranking them is the fact that many Jewish clubs actively discriminated against members of other religions and against certain types of Jews.[26]

Finally, it is important to remember that country clubs always create a fundamental division in the social life of the towns or cities with which they are associated, namely, the distinction between country club members and those who could not afford the country club experience. Those with country club memberships, no matter how lowly the club, share in a private realm that excludes many of their fellow citizens. The privacy that comes with land, fences, and guarded gates is one way to separate oneself from the masses huddled in apartments and cookie-cutter houses.

Who can truly do this? The very rich can. These are the lucky few whom E. L. Doctorow calls the "utmost class." The years between 1880 and 1930 saw the very wealthy create notable country houses surrounded by landscaped acres, gardens, and on occasion, private golf courses and other recreational facilities. The construction at Newport, Rhode Island, of the Marble House and the Breakers by Alva Vanderbilt and Cornelius Vanderbilt II may well have started the movement. During the fifty years after 1880, Americans avidly followed the slowly growing collection of fabulous country estates assembled by the superrich. Andrew Carnegie established himself at Skibo, in Scotland, which ironically was recently converted into an exclusive golf club. No one collected estates with more passion than did John D. Rockefeller. During his retirement Rockefeller kept busy and moved from estate to estate according to the season. Much of his retirement was given over to the management of his homes; he planted trees, built roads, and cared for golf courses. He passionately loved golf and believed that the game was good for his health. Rockefeller gathered his family about him at his estates and took special delight in supervising the training of his grandchildren. In a certain light, Rockefeller had created a series of country clubs for his own pleasure and that of his family and friends. In 1914, in fact, he acquired his very own country club. He purchased the Lakewood Country Club when it moved to a new location. Dubbing it "Golf House," Rockefeller and his entourage would tune up their games on the refurbished course during visits that usually began in late March. If country clubs were landed estates established by collective action, then Rockefeller had established a country club in reverse. Rockefeller became "somebody" not only through his immense wealth but because he used that wealth to establish a series of "homes" that separated him from all but the most affluent. Nothing created envy and a desire to emulate more than the possession of land and homes of unique character and absolute privacy.

Journalistic accounts provided the public its knowledge of Rockefeller's privileged existence at places such as Lakewood. Such accounts emphasized the fact that Rockefeller's "purpose in having a country estate at Lakewood was to have a place of rest—a place to which he might quietly go at any time and . . . be assured that he would be free from annoyance." Journalists detailed the measures Rockefeller had taken to create privacy. They noted the high fence, the guarded gate, and the thickly wooded perimeter: "He is as much lost to the outer world as though he were on a desert island." It was, however, an island on which Rockefeller had imposed his own will. Lakewood was, the *New York Times* asserted, "a little world—a little Rockefeller world that reflects in its every part the personality of its owner."[27]

In this way two great figures of the early twentieth century tend to blend. Babbitt and Rockefeller both sought in their own ways to achieve status, a sense of differentiation, in a world that was growing more corporate and homogenized by the day. By joining a country club or by helping to organize one, affluent Americans could within limits participate in the wonderful world of landed estates and separate themselves from stinking cities, summer heat, and streets full of strangers. Among the generally affluent the gradual rise in stock prices, the feeling that all investments would inflate, and the rhetoric of endless prosperity all supported the country club movement. Even if you could not be as rich as Rockefeller, the wave of prosperity could still carry you to the country club and a sense of the control and privacy the superrich must have felt as they patrolled their estates.

The stock market crash of 1929 and the depression that slowly settled over the country had a deep and abiding impact on the country club movement. Between 1919 and 1932, fueled by rising and widespread prosperity, the country club was refined as an idea, and Americans built more notable clubs than in any other period. The club idea reached its full geographical reach; from Cypress Point (1928) in California, to Oak Hill (1926) in New York, to Seminole (1929) in Florida, all parts of the nation took part in the building boom. The process brought together a number of related factors and influences to create the traditional member-owned American country club. Fueled by growth in golf as a participant and spectator sport, country clubs employed course architects, turf specialists, and golf professionals. Golf was an important aspect of a revolution in the attitude toward play. Victorian attitudes that inhibited play and leisure relaxed but did not disappear. Golf grew rapidly because affluent Americans could rationalize it as medicinal, as an antidote to lives that were increasingly nervous and anxious. The nongolf aspects of club life evolved during the 1920s as the product of the dramatic transformation of the homes of the affluent. The clubhouse began to take over functions that once were traditional in the home. Members also sought status and a sense of worth by joining clubs that, in essence, provided them with a sense of having access to their own country estate. The stock crash and Great Depression put a halt to the proliferation of country clubs, but more important, they dramatically highlighted the fact that the country club was essentially two entities: a golf course and a country estate/ resort hotel. The inherent differences between the two functions now became clear.

In its early years the depression spawned a rash of attempts to understand golf and the country club in new ways. For more than forty years the country club had been evolving and growing, and it had always avoided serious criticism in the mainstream press. Golf had suffered ridicule early on, but by the early 1920s the game had shed its image as the sport of "dudes" and "swells." It was arguably the fastest-growing participant sport in the United States. As America entered a period of intense self-examination, however, commentators of various sorts made it clear that golf and the country club were minor but compelling examples of what was wrong with the country.

The game of golf suddenly became an example of American excess. As one postcrash critic put it, during the boom in the 1920s, "the simple pastime fostered by the thrifty inhabitants of the seacoast of Scotland was converted into a luxurious game garnished with gorgeous appointments and surroundings." The 1920s were characterized as a time when "the money seemed to be showering down from the blue skies . . . [and] golf came in for its share which was lavish." The *New York Times* asked: "But what of the golfer that was tied up to the country club idea with bands of gold?" The golfer was portrayed as carrying the luxuries of the club (e.g., pool, gardens, social programs, and clubhouse) on his back. By 1933 this image and the economic downturn had led to large numbers of resignations and many club bankruptcies. Golfers themselves had capitulated to the heady atmosphere of limitless prosperity. The utilitarian golf bag had grown into "collapsible trunks." From these gigantic bags "the proud owners would drag out almost anything except a suite of Louis Quinze furniture or a concert grand piano." Of course, the owners of these bags lured small boys to carry the burden. But these days were over. Clubs that had rigorously screened new members were offering memberships to anyone who could pay. The clubs were also offering limited memberships (golf only) and opening their courses to the public to collect greens fees.[28]

Like much of the literature on golf, the post-1929 commentary attempted to use humor to make its point. Gregory Mason, writing in *American Mercury*, claims that the depression fortuitously led to "a general elevation of the national mental health because of the decline in golf playing." Remarkably Mason reverses the old rationale that golf is an antidote to nervousness; he claims that golf actually causes morbid nervous disorders. Golf, which he calls "pasture pool" and "the Scottish curse," has spawned two groups, or "psychological types." The first group, which is made up of dull, humorless sorts, produces most of the game's champions. The second and much larger group or type comprises "irritable, nervous, twitchy chaps" who are "the boobs who make a religion of golf . . . and mortgage their homes to buy up cow pastures to be converted into golf courses, to the great detriment of the nation's milk supply."

Mason's essay is clearly an attempt at satire. He turns all the virtues claimed for golf into vices. This trick could work only against the depression background. With unemployment skyrocketing and people rightly concerned about incomes, jobs, and feeding their families, golf and the country club became an easy target. Yet Mason reveals another bias against golf that lurks beneath most critical views of the game. He clearly suggests that the depression led "American males" to a crusade "against the deplorable feminization of their sex, of which golf-addiction was considered a major symptom." The outset of the depression seems to have strengthened the sense that golf, which allowed men to play a game with women, had undercut true manhood.[29]

Golf suffered a barrage of ridicule. In the *Saturday Evening Post* H. I. Phillips, a confessed golfer, asks whether golf is justifiable and answers no. Phillips, again in a humorous way, lists and rejects the various reasons to play the game. He notes that defenders of the game claim that it is an excellent way to get out into nature and that it helps to keep the city dweller in good physical condition. To this Phillips replies: "This is the bunk. Any man who can't find all the open air and good scenery he wants without a club and a golf ball is too lazy to deserve these benefactions. And so far as keeping in condition is concerned, the most distorted human figures anywhere are to be seen on any golf course. Nine of ten golf players are physically a libel on the human race, and the more they play the funnier they look."[30]

For the most part, the post-1929 discussion of golf tended to conflate the game and the country club. In this way both could be condemned as luxuries, the unique products of a callous and immoral upper class. If one looks hard enough, however, it becomes clear that some commentators in the public press understood that golf and the private country club are not inseparable. For example, a *New York Times* survey of the condition of golf and the country club in the greater New York area concluded that the club budget carried two quite different burdens. Clubs had the task "of keeping up a country estate for two or three hundred persons" while maintaining a golf course "in the pink of condition at all times." The *Times* reported a survey done of Westchester County country clubs in which it was revealed that the average club budget was $100,000. The average cost of course maintenance was $38,000. Given this figure, the commentator, Charles Puckette, concludes that "golf is a royal game." Yet Puckette cannot avoid the fact that much of the average budget was devoted to nongolf activities at the clubs. Operating the "house" and its management and upkeep cost $47,500. Obviously the club was more than a golf course. It also served as "the highest class community social rendezvous." In this guise the clubs had evolved into superluxurious second homes with "liveried flunkeys everywhere and a general air of expensiveness."[31]

In 1931 the *Times* reported on another survey of club life that explicitly pitted golf and social life against each other. Conducted by John W. Fulton, a broker of golf memberships, the survey discovered that the high cost of golf was due not to golf but to the expenses of social life at the club. The survey concluded that golf had begun in the United States as a simple affair. The early clubs were devoted to the game, and clubhouses were simple. Fulton's canvass also discovered that clubs that had instituted social, nongolf memberships had driven the cost of golf down to an average of $100 for golf-only members.[32]

One essay from 1933 states the situation with absolute clarity. Kenneth P. Kempton tells the story of a club ("White Brook") in an unnamed city from its founding in 1899 to 1933. In the beginning the "fathers" of the club took over a few acres of pasture, put up a "shack" for a clubhouse, and began playing golf, "to the vast amusement of everyone else." Over the years the club grew slowly, and the members welcomed every addition. The game took hold. You could play without ridicule, and the women joined in and began to play in increasing numbers. But everything started to cost more. This is a very American habit: "When we go into something, we like to do it in a Big Way. We began to need the money, and it came in easily enough." In the beginning people had played in rough and comfortable clothes, but this changed as well. People needed plus fours, matched sweaters and hose, chamois gloves, leather windbreakers, rubber cape coats, and sun hats. Frills became necessities "as the manufacturers began to realize the possibilities of the game, until a man could spend two or three hundred a year on his clothes alone. Many did."

Expense piled on expense. The crude clubhouse would not do, so the club purchased more land and built a grand new clubhouse. The club sold lots at the margins of its property to help "swing the deal." Everything got bigger and better. The clubhouse added a dance hall, hotel rooms on the third floor, and a restaurant that lost money every year. Soon came a "ladies ell," an enlarged pro shop, and a caddie house, because "caddies must be kept out of sight except when in use." Kempton tells an amazing story of ambition and addition; the club, once a simple golf course, added any "novelty" that anyone could suggest. In time the club boasted of its skating rink, toboggan run, tennis courts, putting green, and practice tee. Much of this was done to ease the family into the club; all the nongolf additions were designed to lure the whole family. The club's overhead "swelled like a tidal wave," and taxes skyrocketed because the club had "raised property values over half a township."

Kempton vividly describes a money-driven process: "The money rolled in and the money rolled out, and we were all of us happy as larks." In the spring of 1929, gently at first, "the axe fell." There were a few more resignations than normal. Soon membership drives that had been leisurely became more vigorous, even desperate. The club began offering bargain memberships, with no bonds to buy and no initiation fee. By 1932 the club was in serious trouble; any applicant with twenty-five dollars in earnest money was admitted. Collecting past-due bills from members became a major task.

Kempton concludes with an account of the club's annual meeting in 1933. Forty members are present from a membership of 300. There are 150 resignations and applications for leaves of absence. People slip out of the meeting "into the night." At this point a member who joined in 1900 rises and explains the situation to the loyal remnant. The Old Member argues "that golf is not a rich man's game" but claims that it has become so at White Brook. He then outlines a radical program for getting the club back to sanity and solvency. He recommends shutting up the clubhouse ("this damned château") and firing all but ten caddies, who will be reserved for players over seventy. The members should maintain the course with only a minimal crew and do some of the work themselves. The idea is to cut expenses to the bone and put the emphasis on golf. As the Old Member put it: "The game of golf has been wrapped in so much cellophane that you can't see it any more. And it costs more money than any game is worth."[33]

Kempton's essay is the best single analysis of the relationship between golf and the country club. He illustrates that within the vast majority of clubs, there was a simple, Spartan purpose: to provide a playing field for an ancient game. As time passed, the clubs responded to other desires, most notably the prosperity-driven need to elevate one's status by turning the golf clubs into country estates. People discovered that through their collective action and wealth they could possess a baronial country seat and enjoy, after a fashion, an Americanized version of what passed for aristocratic status.

## ❧ 7 ❧

# AN ENDANGERED SPECIES

I N HIS 1966 NOVEL *The Embezzler* Louis Auchincloss creates the memorable figure of Guy Prime. Prime is a Wall Street stalwart, what many call a tycoon. For half a century before 1932, Americans had looked at men like Guy Prime with envy and respect. Such men were the heroes of the age; they understood finance capitalism and the stock market. Their lives seemed demonstrably better than that of the common person; wealth gave them the power to enhance their existence, to raise it up out of the dreary round of work and financial anxiety. The Guy Primes of the world had not only embraced the new financial environment, however; they had also embraced the new world of leisure. In fact, Prime founded a country club, The Glenville Golf and Tennis Club.

Prime himself tells us about the club and the role it played in his life. For him it was a "working hobby"; he was involved in every detail. He did not just play the course; he inspected it. He readily confesses the true motive behind his efforts at the club: "My real motive was to make Glenville my home." It played another role in his life, however, for Prime's downfall in the mid-1930s was intimately connected to the club. He attempted to use club assets to bail himself out of financial trouble. Prime's life spiraled out of control, and he went to jail, publicly revealed as an embezzler. Looking back on these events from the perspective of 1960, Prime concludes that he and his club have oddly merged. They have both survived, but only "as shells": "We belonged too entirely to the era that made us."[1] Indeed, all the evidence supports Prime's claim. Nearly twenty years of depression and war did not kill the country club idea, but country club development stopped and even retreated slightly during that time, never again regaining the momentum of the 1920s. When the United States returned to a much altered normalcy in the 1950s, the era that had produced the country club (and Guy Prime as hero) was buried under a glacier of change and transformation.

As I showed in the previous chapter, after the crash of 1929 clubs such as "White Brook," which Kenneth P. Kempton described as typical, offered cheaper memberships and dropped initiation fees in response to steadily declining memberships. It is probably impossible to know the exact number of clubs that collapsed completely. Geoffrey Cornish estimates that between 1932 and 1952 approximately one thousand new courses opened while six hundred or more closed permanently. It is fair to suggest that most of the latter were private clubs.[2] For the courses and clubs that did not close during the depression, the name of the game was shrinkage. Clubs cut back on virtually everything; a favorite tactic was to keep open only one nine of an eighteen-hole course. In 1936 Pittsburgh's *Bulletin Index* put the matter clearly: "The US Depression drubbed the Country Club hard, shrank its membership, forced many a club to cut all possible corners, forced many another to the wall. To be posted on the club bulletin board for non-payment of dues became not a disgrace but the fashion. New trends have set in, with hard pressed families falling back on their own homes for weddings, debuts and swank parties."[3]

A 1936 *Business Week* survey of country clubs found evidence of a serious decline and an emphasis on new ways of delivering golf to Americans who wanted it. The survey concluded that the clubs "have been through the wringer." Basing its conclusions on the answers to a questionnaire distributed to "social professional, yacht and country clubs," the magazine reported a 14 percent drop in membership between 1929 and 1936. Country clubs were reluctant to report complete membership numbers; they often reported only the total membership for 1936, thus avoiding comparison with 1929 figures. The USGA, however, provided dramatic evidence of the decline at country and golf clubs. In 1930 over 1,100 clubs belonged to the organization; by 1936 the number had dropped to 763. The drop in the number of country club memberships was even more dramatic. *Business Week* estimated that there were 1 million fewer members in 1936 than in 1925. One aspect of the golf business, however, was doing well: the number of daily-fee courses passed the 1,000 mark in 1935. Municipal courses also increased from 184 in 1925 to 576 in 1936. The private club, which had dominated the world of American golf, was losing its leadership to public and private daily-fee courses.[4]

This amounted to an enormous change in the business of golf. Until the onset of the depression the private golf and country club had ruled the game. It is good to remember that these private clubs were nonprofit associations in which members often held some form of equity, usually stock. Public and private daily-fee courses are essentially enterprises that seek to maximize income and make a profit. Even government-controlled courses usually seek a profit to fund other recreational facilities that do not produce an income— baseball diamonds, for example. Exactly when the total number of public and daily-fee courses began to outnumber private clubs is hard to estimate, but it was probably some time in the 1950s.

The passion for country clubs and the desire to build them grew steadily from 1890 to the early 1930s. The depression simply defeated the country club idea and the people associated with it. Perhaps the most compelling example of a dedicated "country club person" who tried in vain to keep the passion alive in the 1930s was Marion Hollins.

Much of Marion Hollins's life story is lost in myth, controversy, and misplaced records, but some facts are uncontested. She was the child of affluence; her father, Harry Hollins, was one of the second-tier tycoons in the two decades before and after the turn of the century. Hollins grew up on the family's Long Island estate, Meadow Farm, where she contracted a lifelong affection for horses. Her father was one of the founders of the Westbrook Golf Club (1894), and like Glenna Collett, she played and practiced at her father's club, developing a sound golf game under the tutelage of Arthur Griffiths, a transplanted English professional. Numerous childhood trips to Europe and England allowed Hollins to play the finest golf courses and to hobnob with the English upper class.

After 1913, when her father went bankrupt, Hollins was essentially on her own. In fact, as time passed, she took more and more responsibility for her aging parents. Again and again throughout the 1920s Hollins was able to execute large, optimistic projects. After winning the USGA Women's Amateur Championship in 1921, she became the prime mover in the construction of the Women's National Golf and Country Club, located on Long Island near Glen Head. This club was financed by women and had an all-women membership; men were admitted as guests. The golf course at Women's National was an experiment that sought to adapt normal design rules to the needs of the better women players. Hollins induced the English pro Ernest Jones to become the professional at the club. Jones was a remarkable figure who remained a fine player and teacher even after losing a leg in World War I. His students at Women's National went on to win a number of national championships.

In the mid-1920s Hollins transferred her considerable energies from the East to the West Coast. While on vacation in California she met Samuel F. B. Morse III, who was developing the Monterey Peninsula into a golf mecca. Morse hired Hollins as his athletic director. The exact nature of her duties remains obscure, but she clearly played a substantial role in the creation of Cypress Point Golf Club, a private club that is inevitably ranked in the top five on lists of great courses and clubs.

Hollins's success as an agent for Morse's Del Monte Properties did not quell her own desire to create golf courses and country clubs. In 1928 she purchased a beautiful piece of land near Santa Cruz, and using contacts established in the East, she raised the money to build Pasatiempo Country Club and Estates. The course opened on September 8, 1929, with a mixed four-ball exhibition match featuring Bobby Jones, Cyril Tolley, Glenna Collett, and Marion Hollins. Opening virtually on the eve of the stock market crash, Pasatiempo symbolized the excesses of the golden age of country clubs. It had everything: an expensive course, a polo field, a steeplechase course, swimming pools, and a huge clubhouse. It also relied on real estate sales of the surrounding lots to defray costs.

Despite the cost of such facilities, Marion Hollins was well armed to meet the challenge of the depression as it deepened after 1930. While working for Morse, she had come to know the oilman Colonel Franklyn R. Kenney, who lived in Pebble Beach. Kenney convinced Hollins that there was oil beneath the barren Kettleman Hills of the San Joaquin Valley. Hollins used her eastern contacts to raise money for drilling an exploratory well. The first hole they punched in the forbidding hills was a bonanza. In May 1930 Hollins sold her share of the venture for $2.5 million.

Marion Hollins must have thought she had enough money to insulate her against anything life might present. She was wrong. In the early 1930s Pasatiempo was a center of the social life for California's elite. Athletes such as Helen Wills Moody and movie stars such as Brian Aherne and Mary Pickford were frequently seen there. The very rich (Vanderbilts and Crockers) were also regular visitors to the club. Hollins built and refined the club early in the decade. Convinced that the economic downturn was temporary, she spent as if the riotous days of the 1920s were about to return. She purchased the best of everything; she spent a fortune to water the golf course and ignored the declining membership and the drop-off in land and home sales. She was hopelessly in debt by 1937, when she was seriously injured in an automobile accident. In 1940 she sold her interests in Pasatiempo and went back to work for Del Monte Properties. She had lost $650,000 of borrowed money in addition to her own fortune in the attempt to save Pasatiempo. Ironically, in 1937 the Westbrook Golf Club, the club her father had founded and at which she had grown up, also folded for financial reasons.

Pasatiempo and most of the related properties eventually fell into the hands of a hardheaded businessman, Philip Lansdale. He fired staff and cut

costs. It was wartime, and he found himself with a golf course that was losing money. He was also confronted with a group of irate homeowners who
contended that the course must be maintained and that under no circumstances could it be developed into a housing project. This was America;
people sued. The course and club that evolved was a harbinger of things to
come. A small group of stockholders had certain exclusive rights to the
course, but in essence Pasatiempo became a hybrid. In addition to private
owners, the public played the course on a daily-fee basis. Pasatiempo sur-
vives as one of the nation's best public courses.[5]

Obviously the realities of wartime undercut all sports and especially golf.
Most Americans saw the game as frivolous and inappropriate during the dark
days of war. The absence of the many young men and women who had gone
off to war cut deeply into memberships. It was wartime rationing, however,
that hurt the most. The *New York Times* reported that gas and rubber shortages had reduced play by approximately 50 percent. People were unwilling
to use precious gasoline to travel to the club only to discover that no golf
balls were for sale. In addition, the war significantly reduced the number of
caddies available. Finally, higher personal income taxes ate into discretionary income, reducing the number of Americans with the resources to join a
club. The *Times* reported: "The unprecedented current situation [war-time
measures] hits clubs after a decade of violent readjustment. Only a minority
have recovered from the shock of the depression which began in 1929. Many
a proud course . . . is now a suburban housing development; once they had
a waiting list of members seeking to join, but the hard times of 1930–1933
put them in the hands of mortgage holders. Still other once exclusive clubs
have become semi-public."[6]

The Morris County Golf Club illustrates the combined impact of depression and war. During the early years of the depression the club steadily lost
income. Between 1932 and 1936 income from dues dropped from $58,000
to $41,000, but the club stayed open by cutting expenses and services. The
war was clearly more of a challenge; 77 members were away in the armed
forces. When gas rationing was imposed in 1943, the club considered closing. It remained open, but with severe restrictions. For three years the club

kept only two tennis courts and ten golf holes open for play. The closed holes quickly disappeared under weeds and blackberry bushes, for gas rationing severely limited the club's use of gas-powered maintenance equipment. In 1943 and 1944 the remaining members paid only half the regular annual dues. The club's finances were in a perilous state. By 1953 the club had added members, but only 38 were stockholders; moreover, 210 stockholders were not members. The club rightly feared that future control of the club could fall into the hands of individuals, trusts, and estates. The remaining members also faced $125,000 of bonded indebtedness that was due in nine years. It was only through heroic financial restructuring that the club survived in the hands of the membership.[7]

The war had much the same impact on another of the older clubs, St. Andrew's, in Westchester County. As members left to serve in the war, the membership dropped to near 100, and income plummeted 50 percent. The club's isolated location together with gas shortages made trips to the club rare. Since members were not coming, and because food shortages were a fact of life, the dining service declined, sometimes to nothing. Clubs such as Morris County and St. Andrew's survived their hardships, but many clubs simply closed up and sold out.[8]

Most of the wartime problems were temporary, but one war measure that greatly influenced country clubs lasted into the 1960s. The Revenue Act of 1943 doubled the tax on club dues and initiation fees, raising it to 20 percent. As the clubs emerged from war and sought to reestablish themselves by gathering new and old members into the fold, they were handicapped by the artificially high prices created by the continuation of the war tax. Solid numbers are hard to determine, but by any measure the private club suffered a decline in the 1950s. There were 3,049 private clubs in 1950; by 1955 this number had sunk to 2,807. By 1960 private clubs had rebounded somewhat, but only to 3,236. These figures suggest that the number of private clubs grew by approximately 200 in the 1950s. Golf course construction in general grew at a much faster pace. Daily-fee public courses more than doubled, reaching 2,254 in 1960, and municipal courses increased from 741 to 895.[9]

These numbers clearly indicate the trend in the relationship between private courses and those of the public variety. Somewhere between 1970 and 1975 the daily-fee course passed the private club course as the most common in the United States. In 1995 there were 7,491 daily-fee courses, 2,259 municipal courses, and 4,324 private courses. In 1950 the municipal and daily-fee operations together equaled 1,082 courses, while the country contained 3,049 private courses. Forty-five years later the total number of daily-fee and municipal courses stood at over 9,700, while there were only 4,324 private courses. These numbers reflect the steady decline in the importance of the private country club as an institution and particularly as an institution for delivering golf to those who wish to play.

This decline in numbers has not been accompanied by a decline in prestige. The courses built by private clubs between 1890 and 1940 dominate any list of great and prestigious courses in the United States. More dramatically, these early private courses occupy thirty-four spots on *Golf Digest's* list of the world's top 100 courses. American private club courses dominate the top of this list, taking ten of the first twenty spots.

Thus the overall situation today is rather different from that in 1930. Private clubs have retained their prestige but not their presence. Once private clubs dominated the world of golf; in 1930 there was approximately one private club for every 26,500 hundred Americans. In 1990 this ratio had changed to one club for every 52,000 Americans.

Why did this transformation occur? These are some obvious reasons. The wartime tax increase on dues and fees was a clear handicap to any group wishing to found a club. It is also clear that between 1890 and 1930 the club-building boom had taken over most of the choice locations, making it increasingly difficult for new clubs to find accessible and affordable land. In addition, many cultural and technological changes in the postwar period took Americans away from the commitment to a member-owned club. For example, the nature of travel changed; affluent Americans quickly adapted to the age of jet travel. More and more Americans took their leisure in locations far from home, often in a second home, where they wished to conduct leisure activities such as golf on a daily, ad-hoc basis. Moreover, a number of developments began to soak up time once spent at the club. Television was and is a formidable competitor for the private club. If the essential purpose of a country club is to lure an individual away from home to a surrogate home where recreation (mostly golf) is available, then television won a clear victory. Prior to the early 1950s the country club did not confront powerful alternatives such as television. Now, however, some of the hours that Americans increasingly spent in front of the television were subtracted from the time they had once spent at the club.

In fact, television was a major force in the more general process of privatizing leisure. Together with the automobile, central heating, air conditioning, and homes and yards that seemed to grow larger every year, television steadily increased the amount of leisure spent at home with family and friends. Concerns about health, stress, and anxiety that had helped fuel the country club movement before 1930 led to more private activities. Millions of Americans became solitary joggers or purchased expensive home exercise equipment. Affluent suburbanites often indulged in expensive family vacations at a growing array of resorts that catered to golfers as well as tennis players and skiers. In simple terms, affluent American families that had once made the country club a central element in their lives now adopted new patterns and habits (which they called lifestyles) that had little room for club membership.[10]

More to the point, television discovered golf. In their frantic search for product, the television networks slowly turned to golf. There were sizable problems: golf was (and still is) expensive to broadcast. Basketball courts, football fields, and baseball diamonds can be covered with only a few cameras, and the focal points of the contests take place in a relatively limited space and time. Golf is spread out over a much wider area, the key contestants in medal play may be far apart in space and time, and exciting moments may be out of camera range, if they ever materialize at all. Furthermore, golf lacked the following that other games enjoyed. Many Americans thought the game to be effete and exclusionary, the special possession of the rich and well-to-do.

As if called by the gods, Arnold Palmer strode confidently on the scene. He was the perfect antidote for golf's television imperfections. He was a working-class hero, the son of a construction worker who had slowly risen to be the club pro at the course in Latrobe, Pennsylvania, that he had helped to build. It was Palmer's style on the course, however, that made him one of the most compelling postwar sports icons. There was nothing of the dandy about him, and as if to prove it, military imagery began to grow up around him. His gallery became "Arnie's Army," and his come-from-behind victories came to be known as "charges." He was like a soldier beating the course into submission with his clubs. His victory at the Masters in 1960 was probably the most crucial event in imbuing him with iconic status and consummating the love affair between Palmer and television. Hampered by blistered feet, he shoved a score card into his shoe and marched on. He came to the last two holes a shot down to Ken Venturi, who had already finished. Palmer got his two birdies in grand style, and it was great television. The camera could focus on a compelling drama staged in a relatively small area, and the hero was a well-tanned, likable young man with whom most Americans could identify. More important, Americans could leave their clubs in the garage and get their golf on television.

The postwar private golf club faced a growing number of other competitors less significant than television. One of the most important was corporate paternalism. Corporations built golf courses and full-scale country clubs for their workers, often as part of broader recreation programs. By 1950 Firestone Tire, Sylvania Electric, DuPont, General Electric, IBM, and many other corporations had built company golf courses. In 1963 *Sports Illustrated* noted the growing number of courses subsidized by corporations, describing the company course as the perfect "antidote to the poisonous squeeze caused by the prodigious waits encountered at public courses and the staggering costs at private ones." By the early 1960s the most well-known of these corporate courses was the Firestone Country Club, in Akron, Ohio. This club functioned much as a private club would, with two important exceptions. First, it had a limited membership (six hundred), but this membership was drawn exclusively from Firestone employees in the Akron area. Second, the costs were heavily subsidized by the company. In 1963 there was no initiation fee, and a family membership cost only $144 per year. The company saw the costs of underwriting the course as good business. Officials from Firestone testified that the club was one important reason that key employees turned down job offers from other companies.

Many companies were willing to invest staggering sums to create private country clubs for their employees. DuPont maintained what *Sports Illustrated* called "the most lavish country club set up of all." Near its corporate headquarters in Delaware, the company offered its employees two eighteen-hole courses and one nine-holer, plus tennis courts, lawn bowling, and indoor and outdoor shuffleboard. The facilities included a pale rose-colored Georgian clubhouse that featured three restaurants, a ballroom, and huge locker rooms for men and women. DuPont's total investment in employee clubs was over $4 million, and the club's annual budget was over $1 million. Members paid monthly fees of $10.40 for men, $6.50 for women, and $2.60 for children.[11]

These corporate clubs pose some interesting questions. For example, were they truly country clubs or something new? Although it is clear that the corporations were trying to use the country club idea for their own largely paternalistic purposes, the clubs created were substantially different from the pre-1930 private clubs. For one thing, the early clubs were voluntary associations bringing together disparate people to achieve a common purpose: to create a private association providing golf and other recreation to its members. The early clubs were also an extension of the American family in time and space. The corporate clubs were not voluntary associations; they were a fringe benefit offered by employers. They were extensions of a person's job; the corporations offered them as a device to create loyalty and enhance employee morale. Control of the club remained firmly in the hands of corporate leaders, whereas individuals exercised something like democratic control over policy and access in the member-owned clubs.

The corporate country club was not the only golfing institution to challenge to the private country club, nor was it the most important. During the postwar decades one of the most crucial developments in both the world of golf and that of affluent Americans was the evolution of the private gated golf community. These communities are many things, but clearly they are direct extensions, refinements, and enlargements of the country club idea.

Whereas the country club was the product of a group drawing a line and establishing a private realm over which the membership held almost total control, the private gated golf community was the creation of a similar realm, with the land developer acting the part of the membership. Of course, there was a substantial difference: although both the country club and the gated communities made golf a high priority, the private developments brought real estate and housing inside the line, where it could be fully integrated with golf. If such private enterprises have a prewar precedent, it is probably Tuxedo Park, discussed in chapter 2.

Generalizing about these private communities is exceedingly difficult, for perhaps no one such site is typical. Some things, however, seem clear. Whatever they are called (e.g., condominiums, planned communities, common-interest housing, or golf communities), such entities are rapidly becoming common. In 1970 fewer than 5,000 communities were controlled by private property owners' associations; in 1995 the number had reached 125,000, and approximately 40 million Americans lived in these communities.[12] Although the number of Americans who wish to join a truly private, member-operated country club has gone down since 1950, the number of Americans who wish to live in a private gated community where power is held by a developer or residents' association has dramatically increased. The desire to seal out the problems and vexations of the public sphere has not waned; it has simply found new and more general modes of expression.

The history of these communities is illustrated by taking a brief look at the history of Hilton Head Island, South Carolina. What was once an island of cotton plantations is now divided between eleven private gated "plantations" that differ in some ways but are fundamentally similar. Some cater to tourists or "short-timers," some cater to home owners and retirees, some emphasize boating and the beach, and most invest heavily in golf courses, but in the end they are all the same thing: private enclaves where life is controlled by development companies or home-owners' associations and the normal clash of political interests is almost nonexistent. The plantations are also almost entirely devoid of commerce. Gas stations, supermarkets, and the like are concentrated in the area referred to as "off-plantation." On more than one occasion a visitor to the island has told me that Hilton Head looks more and more like America's future.

The evolution of the island as it exists today began just after World War II. Several companies began acquiring land and harvesting timber. In the early 1950s electricity and ferry service came to Hilton Head, and a few people erected vacation cottages along the remarkable beach. In 1956 the construction of a toll bridge to the island was completed, and Charles Fraser, whose family had invested in the early timber companies, came into possession of over 3,000 acres and began to develop this land into Sea Pines Plantation.

Charles Fraser did not invent the private community, but he certainly refined it to fit the postwar world. Sea Pines would become a model for developers in all parts of America. Fraser's most important tools were the restrictive covenants written into each deed. Such covenants limited the home owner in a number of ways. Landscaping and house size, design, and color were just the beginning. There was no public planning or zoning controls; the plantation would be defined by the covenants and by golf.

The importance of golf and other "amenities" (e.g., tennis, pools, and beach clubs) seemingly came as a surprise to Fraser, who grossly underestimated the need for recreation facilities. Like many developers before him, Fraser focused on the beachfront property. He developed the beachfront in a unique way, however, putting the beachside road a considerable distance from the water and arranging the lots in "rows" with walkways to the beach. At first Fraser planned only a minor role for golf, but his partner, James C. Self, and George Cobb, a course designer, changed his mind and thus the nature of Sea Pines. The golf courses (eventually there would be four at Sea Pines) did two things. First, as Cobb had argued, first-class golf draws "first-class people" willing to live in a community where the object of their passion, golf, has a dominating presence. Second, the courses allowed for the profitable development of interior land. Although not as expensive as beachfront property, lots on the golf courses sold at much more profitable rates than land with no "golf view." Fraser stated in 1962 that the first golf course "would have been financial folly except for the fact that [he] created two million dollars worth of fairway lots at the same time." Fraser noted that the land in question would have been "virtually unsaleable without the golf course in front of it." Golf made Sea Pines into a year-round affluent retiree and second-home community. Property owners who violated the restrictive covenants in their deeds were dealt with harshly. The most dreaded sanction the Sea Pines Company could impose was to suspend the violator's golf privileges. The island's historian suggests that this was "for many residents of Sea Pines . . . perhaps the severest punishment imaginable."

Sea Pines came of age in the late 1960s. In 1964 land sales reached approximately $600,000; by 1967 they had soared to $1.6 million. Sea Marsh, the development's second golf course, was begun in 1964, opening hundreds of acres of interior land to development. The most unique project during the late 1960s was the construction of Harbour Town, a yacht basin surrounded by housing and a few shops. In essence an artificial town, Harbour Town and its striped lighthouse have become the symbol of Sea Pines. Fraser built the Tennis Club and the Harbour Town Golf Links just steps from the lighthouse; both sites host important televised tournaments.

The positive response to Fraser's Sea Pines development in the late 1960s should give us pause. Was not this the time of the counterculture, when golf and all it meant were included in the vast critique of white middle-class culture? Obviously not all Americans were listening. Some were in South Carolina picking out their lot and dreaming of the day they could move in behind the security gates at Sea Pines (the first were installed in 1967).

Sea Pines Plantation has been widely influential. Affluent Americans have responded enthusiastically to what it represents. Exactly what is that? Sea Pines is a private community, structured by rules privately engendered and enforced. The people who settle in Sea Pines or similar communities are tacitly voting for private control over public politics. In this way Sea Pines is much like a voluntary association; one moves in and accepts the restrictions that define the community. To some degree residents become supporters or advocates of the "Sea Pines Way," if such a thing can be said to exist. It is clear that Sea Pines has been seen as an alternative to the public sphere in the United States, as well as a critique.

The enterprise is a critique because it values land in a novel way. For much of American history the most common method of maximizing profit from land has been to survey the parcel into a grid, leave almost nothing in the public sphere, and sell the parcels as hard and fast as you can. Almost all America's cities were developed this way—and they are paying the price for letting unbridled capitalism rule the day. Sea Pines and many communities modeled after it have taken a different route. There is no grid pattern imposed on the land; rather, housing is concentrated not on main arteries but on curving, often dead-end streets. Fraser was particularly inventive in creating open spaces and a sense that land had been wasted. He also set aside a large nature preserve. The miracle of Sea Pines is that it is very densely developed, but all the inhabitants are still directly in touch with nature and open green space. This is the result of environmentally sensitive planning, but it is also largely the product of the golf courses that wind through the plantation. Sea Pines simply does not treat land the way it is too often treated elsewhere. Where the crude desire to maximize profit rules, land is chopped up into individual parcels, and little if any space is devoted to collective pursuits and enjoyment. At Sea Pines and at most private country clubs, land is held communally, as are many of the buildings, and the use of the space is controlled by thoughtful rules instead of unrestricted capitalist speculation or highly politicized and changeable zoning ordinances. In the end, it is fair to suggest that private gated communities treat space much as private member-controlled country clubs do. The two kinds of communities are closely related. Private communities such as Sea Pines are the post–World War II manifestation of the same desire that spawned the country club between 1890 and 1930. Although it would be difficult to prove, private gated communities may have reinvigorated a sense of tribalism among upper-crust Americans. The move into such private communities often means that one accepts a new identity. The values and policies of your community slowly become your own, and they set you off from members of other, different communities. This is illustrated by a recent *New Yorker* cartoon in which a slick young woman informs her husband that "there is talk of war with another gated community."[13]

Several notable recent attempts to capture the national mood have commented on the rise of private gated communities. A common thread seems to unite the people who make often significant financial sacrifices to purchase a home in such a site. Like the country club founders of 1900, they dislike and even fear the modern city, with its masses of nameless, faceless people and its relentless emphasis on commerce and profit. In their widely read *Habits of the Heart* Robert N. Bellah and his coauthors report that many suburbanites wish to slow down or stop growth. They fear that once quiet suburban enclaves will be swallowed by the rapacious central city. One couple interviewed by Bellah was "fighting desperately" to slow down the expansion of their suburb, to "keep it from becoming like Los Angeles." Sentiments like these motivate people to move into private communities, behind gates and armed "security officers," where they believe they will have more control over their environment.

The most complete study of the growth of private communities is *Fortress America*, by Edward J. Blakely and Mary Gail Snyder, who estimate that by 1997 there were 20,000 gated communities in the United States, with that number increasing rapidly. They put the population living in these communities at 8.5 million. Like Bellah, the authors of *Fortress America* based much of their work on interviews with residents of private developments. Many of these interviews reveal a desire to escape the present and a perception of the public realm as frightening, unlivable, and hopeless. Clearly the people interviewed see this adoption of the private enclave in much the same way affluent Americans saw the creation of the private country club. Whereas the Victorian was trying to re-create the village, the modern resident of a gated community is trying to create a small town. As a resident of Blackhawk (a golf-centered community near San Francisco) put it, "It's an artificial setting here [in the development] but you're creating that environment which duplicates what Middle America used to be back when you had small towns."[14]

At the same time as these gated communities sprouted, the classic member-owned private golf or country club found itself in a new environment after the war. Taxed heavily by the authorities and forced to compete with an increasing number of municipal and private daily-fee courses, as well as corporate-sponsored clubs and courses, private clubs were in no position to duplicate the rapid growth they had experienced between 1918 and 1929. There was, however, much more to this situation; after 1945 the private golf club and the game of golf became politicized with an intensity unknown prior to 1930. This politicization built on the ageless notion that golf is less than manly and that it is a game for the rich and well born. Between 1929 and 1945 the image of the golfer and the country club had suffered a great deal. Many Americans had come to see the golfing country clubber as alien to the American spirit. After 1945 this attitude took on new energy and importance for two reasons: race relations and electoral politics.

Most Americans tend to think of school integration as the dominant racial issue during the early 1950s, as indeed it was. Nevertheless, private clubs and the opening up of golf were also explosive topics. All through the South and in some northern and western cities, African Americans pushed to open municipal courses to all races. In some instances towns and states took action before there were significant protests: In New York State in 1942 Governor Lehman signed the "Falk Bill," which added golf courses to the list of places at which racial discrimination was barred by law. The most significant action, however, took place in the South during the early 1950s. Many cities had established rules that allowed blacks to play on certain days of the week and limited play to whites only on the remaining days. This was in essence a clumsy attempt to conform to the separate but equal doctrine without incurring the heavy expense of building another course.

It was just such an arrangement in Miami that blacks challenged in 1950. When they lost in the Florida Supreme Court, they appealed to the U.S. Supreme Court, which sent the case back to Florida for "reconsideration." Florida then had to rehear the case in the light of the recent Supreme Court decision in the so-called "Sweatt case," which compelled Texas and Oklahoma to provide African American law students equal educational opportunities. The Florida court upheld the arrangement, and the case returned to the U.S. Supreme Court, which refused to hear it because the Florida court had found substantial "non-federal" grounds to support its decision. In other words, it was a state matter. Similar protests in other southern cities produced different outcomes, however. Houston lost in its attempt to keep African

Americans off the city's golf course. Some cities, such as Jacksonville, followed Miami's lead and opened their courses to blacks for a day or two each
week, closing them to whites on the selected "black-only" days.[15]

It was not until 1955 that the logic of the *Brown v. Board of Education* decision was fully applied to playgrounds, pools, parks, and golf courses. The
November 21, 1955, issue of *Time* noted without fanfare that the Supreme
Court had ordered "without comment or formal opinion" the total integration of public recreational facilities. Especially in the South, *Time* reported,
local and state politicians "fulminated against the decision and made plans
to circumvent its rulings." Georgia's governor Marion Griffin stated that race
mixing at parks and golf courses would not be tolerated and declared: "The
state will get out of the park business before allowing a breakdown in segre-
gation in the intimacy of the playground."[16]

As the pressure mounted on southern cities to integrate their golf courses
even before the November 1955 Supreme Court order, they turned to a
device that offered them a way out: the private club. Rather than integrate,
a number of cities "sold" their courses to private groups that maintained the
absolute right to discriminate. In 1957, for example, Fort Lauderdale sold its
course to the "Men's Golf Association," which ran it as a private club. This
transaction came on the heels of a court ruling requiring the city to integrate
the course. In 1959 Jacksonville's blacks went to court to stop their city from
selling two public courses. Jacksonville had shut down the courses when a
federal court had ordered them fully integrated. Most important, the Supreme
Court decided to hear a case from Greensboro, North Carolina, on cities'
rights to sell to private groups. When faced with pressure to integrate,
Greensboro sold its municipal course to the Gillespie Park Golf Club. In a
narrowly focused decision, the Court turned back the appeal to integrate the
course. In dissenting opinions Chief Justice Warren and Justices Black, Doug-
las, and Brennan outlined errors made by counsel for the blacks while clearly
showing sympathy for their cause.[17]

The role of the private club was further illustrated by events in Jefferson
City, Missouri, in the early 1960s. Prior to 1962 Jefferson City had two golf
courses, one public and one private. As blacks gained access to the public

course, white golfers attempted to flee. The existing private club refused them memberships, so the white public course players sought to form a new private club. They purchased land and, doing much of the work themselves, built "Meadow Lake Acres." It is ironic that, especially in the South, the integration of public golf courses tended to drive the creation of new private clubs in an era when the number of private clubs was in decline.[18]

Thus for more than a decade the attempt to integrate public courses and the white response remained a well-publicized issue. The idea that Americans would use the right of private association to evade the integration of public golf courses gave private clubs negative publicity. Perhaps for the first time, Americans began to think that maybe the right to private association should not be absolute. Important Americans began to express just such sentiments. In 1961 Secretary of Labor Arthur J. Goldberg issued a typical blast against what had come to be known as "private-club bias." Actually Goldberg's speech (before the American Jewish Committee) ranged widely. He attacked all forms of discrimination by private groups; he suggested that private groups of all kinds had been "a miserable source of bigotry and prejudice." Goldberg lumped country and social clubs together with trade unions and professional associations that discriminated unjustly in admitting members. The labor secretary stated that the newly installed Kennedy administration was "determined to insure that America [would] become more and more an open society, not a society closed by tacit agreement or by unconstitutional laws, against millions of Americans." The private club and all that it had meant to men like Guy Prime was by 1961 on the defensive.[19]

The country club and golf were also politicized by the ongoing postwar dispute between African Americans and the PGA. Since World War I the PGA had maintained a Caucasian-only policy. This excluded blacks not only from competition but also from club jobs and other positions that required membership in the PGA. The history of the protests against the exclusion of black professionals is long and complex. At its core, however, was the relationship between the growing PGA tour and the private clubs that were the hosts for many tournaments. If the PGA began to accredit blacks such as Bill Spiller and Ted Rhodes, it would confront the anger of private clubs, which might withdraw their support from important and lucrative tour events, particularly in the South.

While the PGA was pressured to maintain its whites-only policy by some clubs, often in the South, there was even stronger pressure to pursue a more egalitarian policy. A 1952 *New York Times* editorial noted that golf relied on the private clubs in the South and that this was a key reason behind the game's lack of social progress. The *Times* applauded the progress that had been made under the leadership of boxer Joe Louis, who pressured the PGA, but noted that "limited participation" by blacks was not good enough. The editorial called for the complete end of discrimination in the sport, where "the stu-pidity of prejudice" was still far too common. Also in 1952 the Congress of Industrial Organizations (CIO) passed a resolution condemning the PGA's exclusionary policy. The resolution claimed that such discrimination "of-fended American decency" and provided "a propaganda weapon for the com-munists to use against the United States." Golf and the central role of pri-vate clubs in promoting the game had clearly become a political issue.[20]

President Dwight D. Eisenhower contributed mightily to the growing politicization of golf and country clubs. The country, or at least the country's newspapers, took Eisenhower's golf very seriously. For eight years liberals attacked the president for his frequent golf trips and his devotion to two private clubs: Burning Tree Golf Club, near Washington, D.C., and Augusta National, in Georgia. Eisenhower sympathizers countered with the standard defense of golf—it was good for the president's mental and physical health. Golf even became an issue in the cold war. Premier Khrushchev of the USSR often criticized Eisenhower "as a man who put golf before his responsibili-ties as President." At home John F. Kennedy was more subtle when he occa-sionally paraphrased T. S. Eliot in his stump speech: "And they shall say these were a decent people; their only monument the asphalt road and a thousand lost golf balls." There was, however, a position to the left of Kennedy. In 1961 Fidel Castro criticized Kennedy for playing golf while also claiming that he could easily beat the American president at the game. Castro called golf "a game of the idle rich and exploiters of the people." Castro nationalized all the private clubs in Cuba, including the Havana Country Club, which he transformed into an academy for the arts.[21]

More important, perhaps, was the fact that Adlai Stevenson, Eisenhower's opponent in 1956, often ridiculed Ike's passion for golf. Stevenson suggested that Eisenhower had become a part-time president and a full-time golfer who escaped behind the fences of exclusive country clubs. *The Democratic Digest,* the official organ of the party's 1956 national campaign, issued a thirty-five-page indictment of Eisenhower as the "part-time President." Although much of this criticism was typical election year venom, it had a larger significance. By retreating to Augusta National, where eventually he would have his own tree and his own cabin, and to Burning Tree, Ike confirmed many Americans' belief that golf, country clubs, and conservative Republican politics go together naturally.[22]

As the country club and golf became part of the nation's political discourse, it was inevitable that the issues of bias, exclusion, and limited access would also arise. In 1959, when Dr. Ralph J. Bunche and his son were rejected for membership in the West Side Tennis Club, the nation's newspapers and magazines took the opportunity to examine the policies of private clubs in general. The *New York Times* put together a survey of area clubs and their admission policies. None of the clubs in the survey had even one African American member, and only a few clubs reported that they had admitted Jews. Attention focused on the Winged Foot Golf Club because it had just hosted the U.S. Open Championship in June 1959. Winged Foot, its manager Thomas Farley reported, had no Negro or Jewish members, but the club maintained no restrictions on membership. Farley explained the traditional membership rules: an applicant was proposed by another member and seconded by an additional member, after which followed letters of recommendation, approval by the admission committee, and finally approval by the board of directors. The implication was clear. Given these rules, no overt exclusionary rule need be written.[23]

The Jewish community was an important contributor to this discussion of bias and exclusion at private clubs. Early in the 1960s Jewish groups began to admit openly what many had assumed was the situation at the country clubs: Jews and Gentiles had their own clubs, and integration did not much interest either group. In 1962 the Anti-Defamation League (ADL) conducted a study of over 800 country clubs. The survey discovered that 72 percent practiced rigid religious discrimination or admitted few members of other religious groups. The ADL concluded that Jews practiced discrimination just as vigorously as Gentiles. Although Jews may have organized their clubs in response to their exclusion from existing clubs, the ADL suggested that Jews themselves had become a central factor in "the institutionalization of prejudice."

The ADL report clearly acknowledged the dynamics of bias at country clubs. It issued no blanket characterizations of whole memberships; the report explained that traditional admission procedures gave several groups or even individuals the ability to exclude minorities. In many clubs the majority was indifferent concerning the admission of new members, allowing the club's admissions process to be dominated "by the club's mostly rigid, unintelligent and anxiety-ridden individuals."[24]

The dynamics of the Jewish-Gentile relationship were best illustrated, however, by an experiment undertaken by the Old Westbury Golf and Country Club, in Old Westbury, New York. The posh and expensive club sits on 200 acres of land that was once part of an estate owned by William C. Whitney in the late 1880s. It includes twenty-seven holes of golf, three swimming pools, and a beautiful Georgian clubhouse. Organized in 1961 by three Gentiles, the club charged $600 for annual dues, in addition to requiring all new members to purchase a $6,500 equity certificate. From the beginning it valiantly sought to be nonsectarian. The board of governors contained six Jews, five Gentiles, and four men who came from mixed marriages (nowhere in the reports on this club's quest to eliminate bias was gender ever an issue). The club banned the method of silently and secretly blackballing prospective members. Some members saw themselves involved in an important social experiment.

The experiment quickly derailed. Supply and demand worked against the creation of a mixed club, for there were many Gentile clubs in the area but few Jewish ones, so that the number of Jews seeking membership outstripped the supply of clubs that would accept them. At Old Westbury the number of Jews reached 75 percent, very near what was called the "tipping point." Gentiles began to feel outnumbered and conspicuous and moved on to other clubs, causing the club to become even more Jewish. At this point the club's board presented a quota system that sought a club approximately two-thirds Jewish and one-third Gentile. The club would admit three Gentiles for every Jew admitted until the goal was reached. At an emotional meeting the membership rejected the plan by a vote of 130 to 120. Most Gentiles favored the quota; most Jews did not. The ADL, which had been asked for its opinion, stated that it was sympathetic to the goal of a nonsectarian club but that quotas are an inappropriate method for reaching such a worthy end. The league feared that any support for quotas even in a good cause would lend support to their use to keep Jews and other minorities out of elite colleges, good jobs, and housing developments. This story illustrates exactly what was happening to country clubs and why so few were built after the mid-1950s. The nature of political and social discourse was changing. It was not just the youthful radicals of the 1960s that began to turn their backs on an America they increasingly portrayed as racist, sexist, and devoted to the perpetuation of inequality. In such an atmosphere private clubs became rarer and rarer; golf courses were open to all, or should be. Of course, there was a catch; the new daily-fee courses discriminated by placing their fees so high that they effectively eliminated large portions of the population from playing golf. Golf remained saddled with the reputation as a rich man's game.[25]

It is difficult to give the country club issue a human face. How did individuals think about the country club? In 1977 the *New York Times* went off to the suburbs to check out attitudes toward leisure and to outline the choices facing upper-middle-class whites. The young couple whom the article prominently featured had rejected the country club, doing so because their subdivision included a recreation center that neatly substituted for a club. Moreover, the nearby recreation center and its pool were a cheaper alternative; the couple claimed that the dues to the center were only $870, much less than over $2,000 for a club. The young couple also feared discrimination.

The wife was Jewish, and they clearly did not wish to become involved in a process that they saw as closed, secretive, and discriminatory. The *Times* concluded that many young affluent whites sought an alternative to the country club and that many subdivisions were responding to this demand by installing recreation centers and daily-fee public golf courses.

The *Times* survey also unearthed another important attitude. Previously the country club had to some extent been a marker in the complex process of establishing a person's status. A young lawyer quoted in the *Times* survey suggested that using club membership to manipulate one's status had declined. He stated that "travel and a second vacation home both tended to decrease the value of a country club as a place of leisure activities." The country club idea had survived, but it was an odd, ironic kind of survival. Clearly under attack by cultural and political forces, the country club idea certainly did not flourish; new private clubs were rare. Golfers often found that the typical course was owned by "investors"; you paid your fees to the young, well-tanned, but unknown young man in the pro shop. Just as clearly, the existing private clubs grew in stature. In a world increasingly dedicated to the disposable and "the new improved version," the country clubs built prior to 1935 enjoyed a unique position. As the baby boom generation aged and the 1980s came to an end, Americans turned their hungry eyes toward these beautiful, historic places.[26]

The year 1990 was a landmark for private golf and country clubs. The controversy between the PGA and black protest groups over tour events at exclusive private clubs was the most explosive issue of the year in golf, but there was more. Tom Watson, the U.S. Open champion, resigned from his club in Kansas City when it rejected the tax-accountancy magnate Henry Block because he was Jewish. Several publications addressed the issues. *American Heritage*, the popular magazine for history buffs, published an essay on the history of private clubs that focused on social-class issues and discrimination. *Golf Digest* published a long, two-part piece entitled "A Revolution in Private Clubs," which argued that private clubs were confronted with an extraordinary number of social, economic, and legal challenges. The essay was particularly good at summarizing the legal challenges to the clubs' so-called right of privacy. Particularly important was the 1988 Supreme Court decision that upheld a New York City ordinance applying antidiscrimination laws to private groups deemed substantially "commercial." The decision encouraged cities and states to develop creative ways to force private clubs to open their membership policies, which they did by using their rights to tax, to issue liquor licenses, and to monitor businesses (one of the most controversial and well-publicized conflicts along these lines occurred in the late 1980s between the Olympic Club and the city of San Francisco). Finally, in 1990 *Sports Illustrated* published a "special report" on the boom in golf. This report, authored by E. M. Swift, was perhaps the first widely distributed statement to suggest that golf was becoming "cool." In 1990 more people were spending more time reading and talking about golf and the country club than in any other year in the twentieth century.[27]

The issue that most dramatically bonded golf and country clubs, however was the controversy at Shoal Creek Country Club. The PGA had agreed to play its 1990 championship at the club; the association had put on a successful championship there in 1984 and expected the same result in 1990. When it became apparent, however, that Shoal Creek had no black members and no plans to add any, public relations began to deteriorate. Hall Thompson, the founder and president of Shoal Creek, was amazingly honest when interviewed before the tournament. He noted that Shoal Creek admitted Jews, Italians, and Lebanese but had no blacks and would have none, not even as guests. In what was surely the most quoted statement during the controversy, Thompson stated, "The country club is our home, and we pick and choose who we want." As I tried to show earlier in this book, the country club is an extension of the home, and members tend to feel strongly that the rights an individual has at home extend to the club. The controversy at Shoal Creek clearly illustrated that country clubs were an odd coupling of a socially exclusive institution with a game that values open competition and social inclusion.

Hall's comments and the all-white membership at Shoal Creek put the PGA squarely on the spot. The tournament was quickly becoming controversial; black groups, including the Southern Christian Leadership Conference, threatened to picket the tournament site. Corporate sponsors such as IBM and Toyota pulled their support or reduced their commitment. The black mayor of Birmingham, Richard Arrington, saved the tournament by negotiating a settlement. Shoal Creek accepted Louis J. Willie, a black insurance-company executive, as an honorary member, and this seemed to satisfy the protesters. Willie was not a golfer; he joined the club to save the community embarrassment and the loss of the tournament. The club did not make Willie pay the normal $35,000 initiation fee. Following these trying events the PGA announced that it would no longer hold events at totally exclusive clubs. Clubs such Cypress Point and Butler National Golf Club refused to accept the PGA's conditions and were dropped from the list of approved courses, while others scrambled to find black applicants. At Crooked Stick Golf Club, in Indiana, the club advanced Todd Stuart to the top of the three-year waiting list, awarded him a "junior membership," and allowed him seven years to pay the $22,500 initiation fee. In California the hot property was O. J. Simpson, who accepted an invitation to join the Sherwood Country Club. Simpson told *Sports Illustrated* that Shoal Creek would be remembered as "almost like the Boston Tea Party."[28]

The "Juice" was clearly mistaken. Shoal Creek and its aftermath were tokenism at its worst. Everyone got to express vague resentments of wealth, white people, private clubs, and privilege. To my knowledge no one offered a truly serious analysis of the issue. A year later the postmortems noted the lack of progress. *Time* concluded that the private golf clubs "show few signs of more than token reform." During the entire controversy no one asked even rudimentary questions about the relationship of minorities and women to private golf clubs. No one asked, for example, why there were no eager applicants at Shoal Creek and Crooked Stick. No one asked how many among various minorities even play golf. At no point did anyone challenge the cliché that, as *Time* put it, "snobbery and exclusion have long been inseparable from golf." Most important, no one was willing to understand the issue at Shoal Creek as a complex conflict between values most Americans hold dear.[29]

This lack of analysis explains why Watson's conflict with the Kansas City Country Club was important. Watson could have portrayed his resignation as a simple act elicited by bigotry. He chose instead to express the sense of conflict behind his act. Certainly the most important thing he said was this: "Truly, as an American, I am in conflict with myself." He found that he was caught between his belief in "freedom of choice" and "equal rights for every citizen." Watson forcefully stated his support of private clubs but added a way they could be improved. Any group has the right to band together "in private association," but, Watson insisted, this right exists only "so long they *choose to admit* their own discriminatory practices." It was clearly the secrecy and the hidden machinations of a minority at the club that most distressed Watson.

For most people at the time, Watson's resignation was simply an "act of conscience," and that exhausted the issue. What most missed were the intense feelings Watson had about the Kansas City Country Club. This club was the center of his universe. His longtime teacher and friend Stan Thirsk was the club's professional, and separation from one's teacher is always painful. More important, Watson made it clear that his family was crucial in his decision. His wife, Linda, is Jewish, and Henry Block was denied admission because he was Jewish. Given its anti-Semitic membership policies, Watson could not make this institution his family's club. Finally, Watson wished in an odd way to defend his club by resigning from it. He knew that the full membership would have voted to admit Henry Block, who had been sponsored by some of Kansas City's most respected individuals. Henry Block lost his chance to join in a five-member membership committee that was dominated by bigotry. Although he never said as much, Watson resigned to force the whole membership to face the fact that a small group of bigots held the entire club hostage.[30]

Watson's opinion piece in the *New York Times* was one of only a few expressions that even suggested the events at Shoal Creek to present any kind of dilemma. For most Americans, golf and the country club were a small part of a larger problem—namely, the pervasive inequality that has characterized American life. One reaction to this problem was a massive increase in the use of "state action" to force the opening of schools, jobs, and housing to those who had been excluded. By 1990 it was clear that American courts would favor equal access over freedom of choice; country clubs would have to allow the state to judge and alter their practices or face the loss of tax exemptions or liquor licenses. Almost no one sensed that the issue involved anything more than a conflict between exclusive membership practices and equal access.

In an odd sort of way, golf and country clubs had their day in the sun in 1990 and 1991, but the public discussion was one-sided. It focused entirely on the degree to which the clubs were out of step with prevailing opinion. Any value that the clubs might have seemed to hang on their admission policies. As I have shown, the clubs have a long and complex history; they differ greatly in size, wealth, and location. In 1990 the public spotlight shone only on large, wealthy clubs (as has always been the case) that drew their members from relatively large urban or suburban areas. During the debate no one mentioned that private member-owned clubs were clearly declining in relative terms and had been doing so for a long time. Most crucially, no one generally appraised the social value of such clubs. Did they contribute anything to American social and political life? Since the clubs were so closely associated with golf, it was odd that no one asked whether the clubs had done a good job of establishing golf as an important American sport. Finally, no one asked what would result if private, member-operated courses and clubs were to disappear.

If we ask questions that go beyond the issue of admission policies, some surprising answers ensue. For example, I contend that of all the major sports, golf stands most outside the "sports establishment." Unlike the three major sports, baseball, basketball, and football, golf has had only a marginal connection to education. For instance, during most of the twentieth century, golf has had almost no support from high school athletic programs. Where it does exist, its support is dwarfed by the commitment to the big three sports. It is not just a matter of financial support, however; as any high school golfer can tell you, golf is not the path to heroic status. Compare the high school golf match with the "big" football or basketball game; indeed, scholastic golfers probably still tend to keep their participation a secret from all but their parents and a few close friends. Is this because golf is so expensive? (One wonders exactly what it costs to finance a high school football team.) No, it is not really the cost; the issues are far more complex than that. Golf as a game and the country clubs where it has been played earned an unfortunate reputation perhaps as early as World War I. For many, it was and is an effeminate game, and a young man who shows an interest in the game risks being labeled unmanly. Golf's connection with the upper classes has been another crucial negative factor. If ever there was a self-fulfilling bias, this was it. Schools and municipal sports programs kept the game from expanding for many reasons, the most important being the widespread belief that golf is somehow inherently upper class, making it dangerous to be seen supporting such a sport. With only marginal support from the schools and municipal sports programs, golf has been advanced by the private, member-owned clubs. Many clubs took it as their mission to support the game and pass it on to the younger generation. The members' sons and daughters picked up the game and its traditions, but so did the caddies. The decline in the national corps of caddies has greatly reduced the number of lower- and lower-middle-class people who come into contact with the game. It is also interesting that college golf has evolved rapidly during the years that the private clubs have declined.

Of course, golf's absence from the educational scene is not entirely unfortunate. After all, the connection between sport and education has been a disaster. Unlike any other industrialized country, America has allowed its institutions of higher education to develop a truly massive commitment to sport. This connection has harmed both sport and education. If we can even imagine a world in which sport and education never married, it might well be a world in which private clubs (voluntary associations) replace schools as the major providers of sport. Schools tend to rationalize their support of athletics on the grounds that sports build character. In this they have failed. College and pro sports are breeding grounds for fraud, violence, and immorality.

In many ways private clubs might have done a better job of providing sports than have the secondary schools, colleges, and universities. The most crucial issue involves participation versus spectatorship. Schools inevitably must emphasize spectating over participating. Schools spend vast sums providing students chances to play a sport seriously and equally vast sums introducing a wide range of sports to young men and women, but they need spectators above all. Competition at the highest levels and spectatorship by the masses has dominated high school and college athletics. There is an irresistible logic that elevates the "big football game" and championship tournaments ("the big dance") in high school and college basketball. This logic requires a vast pool of spectators willing to pay substantial sums and invest their leisure time for the right to be "a fan." These fans have to be trained to prefer watching the game as a fan to playing it. Private clubs whose members agree that participation is paramount are in a much better position to decommodify sport and advance participation.

This view of private clubs leads us to a clear understanding of what has really been wrong with golf and country clubs. In the early chapters of this book I tried to show that the clubs suffered from a split personality. They attempted to achieve two purposes. On the one hand, they sought to be pure golf clubs, essentially cooperatives that built and maintained courses and the minimal related apparatus (e.g., a clubhouse, lockers, and a restaurant). Unfortunately the clubs also sought to provide socially ambitious Americans with access to a country estate and to what passes for aristocratic status in this country. As a voluntary association for the advancement of golf, the clubs are a worthy part of American culture; as a tool in the ongoing American class war, they were clearly a negative development. The great tragedy is that the two purposes became so inextricably commingled.

The time has come to confront the key issue. We need to pit the member-owned, member-operated club against the investor-owned club and the daily-fee course. On one issue the latter two are the clear winners. They do not discriminate. Although they may call themselves country clubs, investor-owned and daily-fee "clubs" are simply businesses. During a 1991 survey of New York City clubs, the manager of the Briar Hall Country Club bluntly stated, "We're a business and we'll take anyone who'll pay." Such clubs are simple commodities available to all who have the money. At Briar Hall the initiation fee in 1991 was $2,000, and the yearly dues were $6,250. Daily-fee courses are even simpler: you purchase time on the course for the day at a rate determined by the course's prestige, location, and condition.[31]

Private member-owned clubs admit members using a variety of methods. Of course, the focus has always been on the secret, sponsor-based system that seems dedicated to keeping out all "undesirables." Nonetheless, small towns and areas where competition for members is high are often home to clubs where the membership committee accepts anyone who can pay the dues, loves golf, and shows some inclination to help run the club. Certainly there are clubs that admit minorities when they apply. In his book *The Soul of Golf* Gary Hallberg admits to having been dumbfounded when he arrived at a private Louisiana club and was paired with Ollie, an African American member with a four-stroke handicap who beat him soundly. When Ollie was asked about African Americans at his club, he offered several insights. For one thing, he said, lack of minority members is often a function of the limited number of blacks and others who are truly dedicated to golf. Ollie learned to play in the armed forces and carried the interest back into civilian life. This suggests that the Defense Department and its massive holdings in golf courses have become an important factor in the democratization of golf. In addition, Ollie stated, "If a black man has the money, he can join this club, and he'd be welcome, I assure you."[32]

Even if we grant that private clubs always engage in discriminatory admission practices, we are still obligated to assess their social value. Arguing that country clubs have some social value requires that we set aside, at least for a moment, the widespread stereotypes of "country clubbers" as vacuous, selfish social strivers and the country club as nothing more than a vehicle for social and economic advancement and social exclusion. I believe that country and golf clubs have a value that has been overlooked until recently. They have been and in many cases still are part of the "social capital" that makes democracy possible.

This view of the clubs draws its inspiration from Robert D. Putnam's controversial 1995 essay "Bowling Alone: America's Declining Social Capital."[33] Putnam argues that Tocqueville was essentially right when he asserted that American democracy was based in large measure on American's "propensity for civic association." Voluntary associations, informal networks, societies, and clubs provided Americans with habits that made them good democrats. In simple terms, clubs and voluntary associations served as training grounds for the cooperation and coordination that make democratic systems work.

Putnam argues that the level of civic engagement in America has generally declined since the end of World War II. Wherever one looks, Putnam asserts, voluntary associations are fading as part of the American scene. Churches, labor unions, parent-teacher associations, and fraternal organizations have all lost members and vitality. Perhaps the most damaged form of social capital is the family. The trend extends even to bowling; the number of bowlers is up, but the number of leagues has plummeted. Americans seem to have given up on the voluntary association and the social club, preferring to bowl alone. Choosing to deal with a corporate entity that assures "you, the customer," that you are always right is essentially a rejection of the difficult but socially valuable involvement in private associations.

What accounts for this trend? Putnam suggests that the increased number of women in the workforce and the high level of mobility among Americans are important factors. There seems little doubt that relatively affluent women were and are crucial to voluntary associations, but as employment ate into their discretionary time, they reasonably enough gave up many social groups and associations. Mobility may have been more important. As Americans move from job to job and from place to place, the habit of joining local voluntary associations makes increasingly less sense.

Putnam also suggests that the technological transformation of leisure has eaten away at voluntary associations such as bowling leagues and country clubs. Certainly television is the central factor in this regard. Today an hour or two of leisure lies no further away than one push of the remote button. The leisure experiences provided by voluntary associations are infinitely more difficult to produce. As I have shown with regard to the country clubs, providing a golf course and other activities is an intensely complex affair. A club is the product of a long process of cooperation and compromise, and its maintenance involves even more engagement. Modern technology provides time-sapping leisure with much less effort and much less opportunity to be engaged in the production of your own leisure. The rapid growth of video and computer games and the computer itself promise only to extend the trend.

Although Putnam does not specifically blame the corporation and postwar capitalism for the decline of voluntary associations, both have been crucial. The relationship between corporations and voluntary associations should be obvious. In the twentieth century corporations have increasingly pushed aside voluntary, nonprofit associations as providers of leisure. Leisure, as they say, is big business. Huge, well-financed companies such as RCA, the NFL, Paramount, Sony, CBS, and countless others are dedicated to producing profitable products that fill the growing amount of leisure time many Americans enjoy. In the world of golf the private, member-owned, member-operated country club is a nineteenth-century anachronism in an expanding universe of modern sophisticated corporations. Such corporations can provide "country clubs" on demand and maintain them without requiring the members to form committees and haggle over dues and policies. These companies can also take over existing clubs and run them more efficiently than the members ever dreamed they could be run. These corporations enjoy economies of scale that no individual club can match. They can offer management personnel vast opportunities in a corporate structure that includes hundreds of clubs. There are a number of such companies that have eaten away at the viability of private clubs. The privately owned Club Corp is probably the most well-known; its ownership of prestige properties such as Pinehurst and the Homestead have given it unusual visibility. Equally important, however, have been real estate investment trusts (REITs) that own or operate "golf properties." One such REIT is National Golf Properties (NGP), which according to its 1997 annual report owns 123 golf courses in twenty-six states. NGP's "portfolio" includes forty-five private clubs, fifty-eight daily-fee courses, and twenty resort courses. There are more than 32,000 members in NGP's private clubs, which paid slightly more than $26 million in rent to the trust. NGP does not operate courses itself, however; instead, it leases properties to operators who collect all revenues and pay a base rent to NGP. So if you play at one of the courses in the trust, you are receiving the experience courtesy of a complex, two-level corporate establishment that ultimately owes its first allegiance to its shareholders. In its annual report NGP talks easily of "the golf course industry." Apparently prospects are good; the trust expects the baby-boom generation to fuel steady expansion over the next two decades.

Does the truly private club directed solely by its members have a future, given the immense advantages of scale and financing enjoyed by corporate owners? The numbers cited earlier in this chapter suggest a slow decline for the private club. There are signs, however, that the truly private club does have a future. One of these signs is the growing place of the Augusta National Golf Club in the American imagination.[34] No other club, with the possible exception of Shoal Creek, has taken as much criticism as Augusta National. The club is almost always mentioned in stories about the traditional "whiteness" of golf and country clubs. Every spring magazines and newspapers recount the autocratic and demanding treatment the club hands out to CBS for the right to televise the Masters Tournament. The longtime head of Augusta National, Clifford C. Roberts, probably received more negative publicity than any other country clubber in the United States. Up to his suicide in 1977 and after, Roberts became a compelling public symbol of everything that was wrong with private golf and country clubs.

There is, however, a significant problem with all the negative publicity that has been heaped on Augusta National. Throughout its history and especially since World War II, the club also has slowly become an object of national respect and veneration. The reasons beneath this veneration are hard to portray clearly. For one thing, the club annually pushes a giant corporation around in a very public way. Can it be that the public enjoys watching CBS conform to the club's ideals of propriety and anticommercialism? At some level do some Americans respond to and support the club's emphasis (at all costs?) on history, tradition, and the values of the game? Maybe so, but the issues run deeper. Americans have lost their sense of place. Mobile, restless, and rootless, most Americans never live anywhere long enough to love it. Corporate America is more than willing to transform any "sacred" place if a mall or a Disney theme park will increase profits and cash flow.

One can assert that the Great Depression and World War II accelerated the rise of governmental and corporate control and the decline of interest in history, tradition, and a sense of place. In the United States, especially, Americans have accepted the generic, the mass produced, and mass distributed solely because the cost has been reduced. The modern corporation learned to produce the products that seemingly were available to all. The postwar daily-fee golf course and the clubhouse that went with it have often provided a case in point. Mass-production techniques lowered the cost of design. Ironically it was the extension of mass production to golf courses that helped to elevate the value and deepen the veneration of places such as Augusta National and Pine Valley.

The American golf and country club has had a long, convoluted, and controversial history. Although it is many things to many people, it is most fundamentally a reaction to the rise of modern, corporate, urban, and egalitarian America. There can be little doubt that over the past century the country club has served as an invidious social marker, an institution designed to stabilize and clarify the lines between classes and races. There is, however, a Quixotic quality to the clubs. In a world characterized by mass-produced suburbs, creeping urbanism, and the increasing influence of globalization, the clubs insist on preserving the values of the village. At the same time the clubs have been an important part of American social capital. As voluntary and local associations, they have fought standardization and the bleak homogenization of American life. Finally, the clubs introduced and nurtured the game of golf, which thrived under their guidance. At almost every club the social strivings of the members and the club's duty to the game met in a pleasant tension.

# CONCLUSION

IN THE BEGINNING of this book I asked a simple question: How did the country club and the game of golf take root in America? How did what is essentially a playing field become a cultural site capable of eliciting the strongest allegiance and the harshest criticism? Simply put, the answer is that from the beginning golf and the American country club constituted cultural and political expressions that openly stood as critiques and counterexamples to the modernization of American life and culture over the last one hundred and twenty-five years. They opposed nationalization and standardization by being local and unique: As the nation urbanized, golf and clubs represented the idea that men and women need rural retreats from the modern city. As the profit-oriented corporation increasingly dominated American life, golf and country clubs showed that people could create and control their own leisure, even if they could control little else. Finally, as American culture more fully committed itself to egalitarianism and open access, the clubs and golf maintained an emphasis on discrimination and exclusive access.

As a political and cultural expression, golf and country clubs enjoyed remarkable success between 1890 and 1930. Originally the invention of the upper class, golf and the country club spread downward into the vast American middle class. After 1930 both golf and private clubs suffered greatly. The

Great Depression and World War II inflicted considerable damage, but it was not until the mid-1950s that the truly formidable challenge arose. Confronted by a society deeply influenced by egalitarian reform and corporate capitalism, the country clubs lost their control—or better, their dominance—over the game of golf. Private member-controlled clubs simply were no match for the pressures that sought to destroy all racist, sexist, and otherwise exclusionist elements in American life. Equally important, the clubs were no match for the enormous power of a capitalist consumer culture that, through advertising and marketing, sought to transform every American into a passive consumer. This was especially true in the area of leisure. After World War II Americans were bedazzled by an ever-increasing array of leisure choices; the vast majority of these choices called for them to consume sport spectacles passively, either live or in broadcasts. The high level of involvement that club membership required seemed less and less attractive.

Both the egalitarian and corporate challenges to golf benefited from the close association among golf, the country clubs, and the wealthy. Golf was the great loser in this linkage, which persists to this day. Public attitudes toward wealth have increasingly soured throughout the twentieth century. This process reached some sort of climax during the depression, but the resentment and fear of wealth lived on in many guises, not the least of which was the counterculture radicalism of the 1960s. The great irony is that golf itself has suffered greatly by being connected to the country club and, through the clubs, to the amorphous and elusive group the wealthy. This is both odd and ironic because the game's heroes have often enough been lower-class, pulling-themselves-up-by-their-bootstraps, rags-to-riches sorts. Francis Ouimet, Gene Sarazen, Walter Hagen, Ben Hogan, Byron Nelson, and Arnold Palmer taken together form an unbroken chain of heroes who somehow triumphed over the dominance of wealth and the control of the game by the rich.

The crucial point is that each of these heroes confronted the game and the country club and was accepted, celebrated, and, at least in Palmer's case, crowned and canonized. Was this because they made some corrupt bargain with wealth? Were they all working-class conservatives co-opted into a servile status as "kept" athletes of the well to do? What they all did was to accept the traditions of the game as their own. Of course, in twentieth-century discourse these traditions (civility, self-policing honesty, and excessive respect for all players) have been associated with the rich and well to do. This is the core of the problem: to advocate civility and respect, to value the "style" of golf as it has been passed down, is often construed as a bias against "other" races and classes that, it is assumed, cannot authentically respond to such upper-crust values and traditions. The fact is, however, that discussing behavior and style as if they have no basis other than class, race, and gender leads to profound confusion.

Serious commentators on golf have been unable to liberate themselves from the familiar categories. The topics of rich versus poor, men versus women, and white versus black have so fruitfully dominated our public conversation that any other kind of category, any other perspective, is usually seen as counterrevolutionary. Most important for my purposes, any discussion of style and behavior is routinely seen as a cover for what is "really" a discussion of race and class. Consider, for example, a recent essay by Scott Stossel in the *New Republic*. Stossel reports that "country club pros and CEOs" told him "again and again" that "internalizing the rules and etiquette of golf . . . leads to good comportment in society at large." Stossel suggests, "One could argue that there is something implicitly racist about all this." He claims that "what no one is openly stating" is the view, widely held in these circles, that golf and its values might help "civilize" the poor and the black of the inner city. Viewed this way, golf "represents a kind of cultural imperialism."[1] Thus if golf and the country club stay isolated in the countryside, they are racist and exclusionary; if they bring their wares to town, they are cultural imperialists.

This hypocrisy is possible only if we remain historically illiterate and refuse to listen to compelling witnesses. The etiquette rules of golf evolved in Holland and Scotland centuries before the evolution of twentieth-century race, class, and gender conflicts. They are not some invention to blunt the style of newcomers to the social scene. They are organic to golf; the game is impossible without them. Commentators routinely suggest that there is something fraudulent about the civility and honesty central to the golf ethos. As Bruce McCall recently explained it, in golf "a tyrannical silence must ever prevail, the silence not of good manners so much as of ancient druidic superstition." McCall finds this ludicrous because, he says, Barry Bonds can do the "single toughest feat in sports[,] . . . poling a ninety-mile-an-hour baseball into the bleachers[,] amid forty thousand bellowing sets of lungs." Of course, McCall fails to note that the forty thousand fans are kept behind fences and in assigned seats. What would Bonds's chances be if a few hundred fans followed him out to the plate and onto the field? Let me stand right next to Bonds as he plays, and I guarantee that the players' union would soon be demanding rules far stricter than those in golf. What McCall calls "golf's sourpuss rules of decorum" are simply the normal rules of civility and a few unique injunctions given the nature of the game.[2]

Most refuse to listen to the most compelling witnesses. Commentators on golf have welcomed Tiger Woods to the game, hoping that he and his fans will bring *something* un-WASP-like to golf. McCall notes: "No wonder Wasps love golf. It must feel like church, like Choate, like their wives."[3] Tiger Woods has raised hopes among critics of golf and the country club that he can make the game less churchlike, de-WASPify it. These hopes are bound to be disappointed. Take as an example the Buick Invitational at Torrey Pines in February 1999. Woods and Billy Ray Brown were playing the back nine for the championship. Everyone else had fallen back. On the sixteenth tee a camera clicked softly during Woods's downswing. He was incensed. Brown's caddy was incensed as well, and pretty much everyone was demanding the camera wielder's expulsion from the course, if not from the world of golf. The point? Woods wants the game itself to stay just as it is; he wants minority youngsters to have more access, but it will be access to the churchlike, Choate-like game. With all the words written about Tiger Woods, no one to my knowledge has understood that he loves the game as it is reflected in its codes and traditions. What he hates is the bigoted exclusion of minorities and especially the cruel limitations placed on the early black professionals, such as Lee Elder and others. Nowhere in all his interviews has he even suggested that the game's etiquette should be changed to accommodate those who would like a less churchlike atmosphere.

In important ways Tiger Woods symbolizes the historical changes that began influencing golf after 1930. Although he was certainly the victim of racism as he learned his craft, Woods was also the product of subtle but important changes. His father learned his (pretty good) golf in the integrated armed forces and was thus in a position to pass the game to his prodigy son. Woods's high school provided an excellent program. A country club provided a free membership. In fact, there were many people ready to encourage his development. He rose to his present exalted position without, as far as the record indicates, caddying for money. This was not true of Hagen, Sarazen, Hogan, Nelson, or Palmer. If Woods has true forebears in the game, they are the white upper-middle-class prodigies Bobby Jones and Jack Nicklaus.

This consideration of Tiger Woods seems to suggest that the game will survive. It will survive because enough Americans understand that a sport that teaches honesty and civility, one that you can play with the whole family and that you can play your whole life, is too precious to tamper with. The private country club may be less secure, however. The private member-controlled club is certainly an endangered species. It competes with corporation-subsidized clubs, private daily-fee courses, municipal courses, and private gated golf communities such as the one Tiger Woods calls home. The older owner-controlled clubs, especially the more affluent ones, are usually included in the general critique of "golf-culture." Bruce McCall claims that the country club house is an important part of golf's attempt to preserve "a sense of its own stuffy Anglo-Saxon elitism." He claims that the typical architecture of "the ideal American country club" is a "sort of heavy, stone, mock-Tudor pile that could be called early Robber-Baronial." In these clubs, McCall claims, people are "probably still getting *blackballed* by the sergeant-at-arms for not eating the crust on the white-bread chicken-and-mayo sandwiches." The club thus condemns the game: "Who wants to snuggle up to a game—a culture—that exudes at its loftiest and most exalted levels all the gaudy human panache of the 1909 summer picnic of Boston's biggest Wasp law firm?"[4]

Apparently the country club in its classic form would find few defenders in the 1990s. In odd ways, however, the country club has found a new place in American culture, an ironic and ambivalent place. The private clubs have adjusted to the legal challenges to their exclusionary admission policies and internal rules (almost always limitations on women). The vast majority of clubs easily adopted the exacting standards imposed by the courts and federal law. There can be little doubt that for many clubs, if not most, a full membership roster and the avoidance of legal costs have been much more important than protecting any exclusionary policy. There remain a few clubs that have paid heavily for maintaining their "purity." Clubs now exist in a legal framework that forces them to conform to antidiscrimination policies if they wish to operate in any way as a business or enjoy any sort of tax break offered by local, state, or federal government. Burning Tree Golf Club, near Washington, D.C., is perhaps the highest-profile example of such a club. Following a long court fight it gave up a substantial tax break from Maryland to maintain its status as an all-male club (see the epilogue). Remaining a truly private voluntary association has become extraordinarily difficult; corporate America produces cheaper, more efficient substitutes, while the government imposes a growing list of rules the clubs must obey. At some point the clubs stop being truly voluntary associations shaped by the members and become simply corporate endeavors driven not by the initial purpose (golf) but by considerations of efficiency and profit and loss. Truly local member-controlled clubs are being replaced by clubs that are often inexplicable combinations of private membership, public daily-fee players, and corporate calculation.

Yet something ironic is happening. The "pure" private clubs are beginning to occupy a unique position in American sporting life, if not in American life as a whole. They are becoming like historical sites to which Americans respond in complex and ambivalent ways. I was in the middle of a tour of Drayton Hall, a southern plantation house near Charleston, when it struck me that I was seeing something importantly similar to the American country club. The forty or fifty Americans touring Drayton Hall clearly had ambivalent feelings. This was a place profoundly associated with slavery and a culture that no American would affirm, yet the site was also positive in a sense that is difficult to portray. Even in its present state, Drayton Hall reflects an ordered serenity that clashes sharply with the chaos of modern American life. Drayton Hall also reminds us of a time when Americans had a commitment to places, buildings, and land as more than an investment to be abandoned when the profits peter out. As we moved through the plantation house and grounds, several comments and questions manifested a deep ambivalence about what we were seeing. More important, it occurred to me that the private golf communities on Hilton Head and elsewhere had done well to take the names they had: Sea Pines Plantation, Hilton Head Plantation, and Palmetto Hall, among others. The tendency to give private golf communities names that suggest the plantations of the Old South is unusually common.

Ambivalence about golf and private clubs is also clear in the work of David Owen, one of the best contemporary golf writers. Owen fully understands the negative side of golf. He confesses that for Americans "of a certain age, cultural outlook and political inclination, a love of golf is more than faintly embarrassing." Owen freely admits that in one compartment of his mind he is "seventeen years old and smoking hashish at a Janis Joplin concert," while in another compartment he is a middle-aged man telling jokes about women golfers at a member-guest tournament. He understands that golf in the United States "carries a heavy freight of ugliness" based on the fact that golf "is conceptually inseparable from the country club, one of our most repellent native institutions." Yet given all this, no one to my knowledge has produced a more compelling and entertaining defense of golf and all that goes with it. Owen confesses to being a "GDP" (golf-dependent personality) and knows that golf can make anyone crazy: before a big match he cleans his clubs with steel wool, a toothbrush, and toothpicks and assembles his equipment "like an Apache warrior straightening the feathers on his arrows." Owens is also honest about golf courses; he likes them all, but the best are private clubs. He writes about Cypress Point as if it were holy ground. A round of golf at Pine Valley "has a theological dimension." His perfect club would blend features from Cypress Point, Pine Valley, Shinnecock, Brookline, Merion, and Muirfield Village. He would be a member of this club just as he is a member of a club in Connecticut. Always the democrat, however, he would let us all join too.[5]

When network television broadcasts certain tournaments, the event is more than an opportunity to see the players. The networks also understand that they are visiting historical sites. This is most obvious in the spring when CBS goes to Augusta National for the Masters Tournament. This is becoming a complex cultural moment that has much to do with the public's ambivalent feelings toward the club. Millions of golfers and nongolfers tune in to experience spring's return to America. By now the scene has become comfortably familiar as America takes in the riot of emerald green and blazing dogwoods. America checks up on the progress of the club; the network routinely reports on new members and the deaths of old ones. We applauded the recent admission of the first African American as we glumly pondered the suicide of the longtime president of the club, Clifford Roberts. Tiger Woods's victory was more than a mere win because, of course, all the winners are granted membership. Perhaps the ultimate irony is that television, which has done much to destroy the sense of place, has, in the case of Augusta and the Masters, helped to re-create it.

The crucial question is whether the government will let these clubs occupy this unusual status as historical sites while remaining essentially private voluntary associations. The major result of the politicization of golf and the country club has been to increase corporate control of golf, pressuring private clubs to give up their autonomy and knuckle under to corporate ownership and government supervision. Should this process continue until all truly independent voluntary associations have surrendered to government control? In 1930 the legal scholar Zechariah Chaffee Jr. answered this question with a comment to which I fully subscribe: "The value of autonomy is a final reason which may incline the courts to leave the [voluntary] associations alone. The health of society will usually be promoted if groups within it which serve the industrial, mental and spiritual needs of citizens are *genuinely alive*. Like individuals, they will usually do most for the community if they are free to determine their own lives for the present and the future."[6]

Chaffee's words compel us to understand that the American golf country club has been and still is a cultural and political expression. During the last forty-five years that expression has been severely criticized for its exclusionary practices, its racism and sexism. The private member-controlled club has quietly fought this criticism and just as quietly adjusted to it. For many private clubs the criticism was irrelevant and off the mark, but they bore the unwarranted stigma with quiet dignity. The country club does not openly "speak" its message; it is "genuinely alive" not as another voice in the increasingly chaotic public discourse but as an example of the way values might be incorporated in a real institution. At its best the American country club has incorporated and lived principles that ultimately stand as a critique of the larger culture. These principles are as follows:

1. It is better to play a sport than to watch one.
2. Leisure should bring families together, not drive them apart.
3. Sports should be nonviolent, not thinly disguised substitutes for combat.
4. Sport should teach self-control, honesty, and civility.
5. Sport should help people retain a sense of place.
6. Individuals acting together may create and control their own lives.

This code, with its deep Victorian roots, clearly has a place in modern American society. That this code became entangled with exclusive, aristocratic practices and principles is a great tragedy, but that should not give us reason to condemn the game and those clubs that truly support its values.

# EPILOGUE: THE FAMILY DRAMA
# SURGES ONWARD

THE COUNTRY CLUB is an odd American institution. During the twentieth century American families have increasingly stopped enjoying their leisure together, fragmenting into groups defined by gender and age. Movies, once a form of family entertainment, have clearly fragmented into age- and gender-specific forms of leisure. As I argued in chapter 4, the country club remains an almost lone exception to this trend. Although a few all-male clubs exist, the most common country club experience is a family one. Reflecting the male dominance of the Victorian era, country clubs traditionally admitted women (wives and daughters) as subordinate members, usually as part of a family package. Again, it was not uncommon for sons to receive special consideration, usually leading eventually to full memberships. Daughters, although allowed into the club, were considered to be nothing more than future wives and therefore not suitable for full equity-owning membership. That was a male preserve. In essence, the traditional power arrangements of the generally affluent, white Victorian home made an easy transfer to the country club.

As this transfer was occurring, however, there was significant resistance to those Victorian power relations. Affluent, upper- and middle-class women were shedding their submissive roles and challenging culturally sanctioned rules about the sports and play appropriate for women. Family country clubs were ruled by a subtle code that blended informal and formal powers. Men certainly possessed the vast majority of the formal power. They held the elected offices, controlled the finances, and established the bylaws. Women, however, possessed considerable informal power. They probably spent more time at the club than did their working husbands, who dominated the weekend. The women may well have controlled the weekday workings of the club, and they no doubt had considerable say concerning the social calendar. Nonetheless, these speculations should not obscure the fact that as early as 1900 there were serious conflicts between men and women over access to the course. Women wanted to play, and not just on "ladies' day."

Over the previous twenty years this long-smoldering conflict between men and women has become the most serious legal and institutional issue facing the private country club. Shoal Creek's troubles, which were essentially a racial issue, were high profile and attracted a great deal of media attention, but the challenge by women was steadier and in the end more fundamental.

Women have launched a variety of legal challenges to the status quo at the clubs. In one high-profile case a woman and her husband challenged the right of the Burning Tree Golf Club to remain an all-male club and yet retain a tax break from the state of Maryland. The club had entered into a contract with the state in which it agreed to keep the club grounds undeveloped, an "open space," in exchange for a reduction in taxes. In 1983 Steward Bainum, a Maryland state senator, and his wife, Barbara Renschler, who sought membership at Burning Tree, brought suit against the club seeking to have the club's tax exemption revoked because the club engaged in discrimination against women. In an intensely complex case, the club eventually lost and is now paying a much higher tax rate for the privilege of remaining an all-male club.[1] The Burning Tree case illustrates the method whereby women have challenged what they see as unjust and unequal treatment. Turning to state laws (and in a few cases local statutes) that grant clubs some benefit or license, they have challenged the appropriateness of allowing such benefit to flow to discriminatory institutions.

By far the most common actors in these legal dramas have been not non-members seeking access but rather female members who already have some kind of club membership. Their complaints generally concern two sorts of club rules that discriminate against women. First, many clubs ban women from the course on weekend mornings and Friday afternoons, although every club seems to have slightly different rules. Women also seek access to that most sacred of country club spaces, the men's grill. Second, many clubs still lodge memberships in the hands of men, even for family membership. The ever-increasing divorce rate poses a serious problem for this arrangement. In the past a divorce effectively drove the woman from the club. Even when the male wished his spouse to have the membership, and the equity rights that went with it, the club often refused to go along. This was the issue at the core of the suit Mary Ann Warfield filed against the Peninsula Golf and Country Club, in California. Warfield was often the club's women's golf champion and a generally popular and active member. She and her husband divorced in 1981, and the settlement stipulated that she would retain the membership, since it meant more to her. Nevertheless, the club told her that the membership could not pass to her because she was not the equity holder of record. The membership purchased for $7,200 in 1970 was worth nearly $50,000 by then. The case ground on until 1995, when the California Supreme Court decided in favor of the Warfields.[2]

For every Mary Ann Warfield there seem to be four or five women who are challenging their clubs over tee times or access to the men's grill. These challenges are clearly rooted in dramatic transformations in the workforce and the egalitarian rhetoric of the feminist movement. Many women work five days a week and can play only on weekends but are shut out by rules that reserve the first tee for men. Working women increasingly need to take clients to their clubs, and they are rightly frustrated when they cannot reserve a Saturday or Sunday tee time. As women come to value their clubs in the same ways men have, they come into direct conflict with the rules that treat the genders differently.

The number of states that have responded to the complaints of women has grown steadily. Minnesota and Maryland led the way, but most states have been touched by tee-time controversies or some other aspect of the conflict between male and female club members. *The Unplayable Lie* (1995), by Marcia Chambers, does a good job of presenting the various cases, both formal and informal, that have cropped up regularly over the previous twenty years. *The Unplayable Lie* shows how amazingly common such intraclub controversies have become.[3]

The question is, why? Some reasons are obvious. More women work and want their clubs to meet the needs of career women, not the needs of a woman who sees herself solely as a wife and mother. To some extent the feminist crusade against the club draws its strength and inspiration from the general civil rights movement. Marcia Chambers, for one, claims that country club male leadership has less difficulty accommodating the inclusion of African American men than it does meeting the demands of women.[4] The number of women golfers has grown slowly but steadily, especially over the last decade. Such numbers are notoriously unreliable, but among the groups tracked by the National Golf Foundation, women clearly show one of the largest increases in interest. There are simply more women who want a tee time at their club.[5]

Other reasons for the growing contention between clubs and women are not so obvious. Politically, from the point of view of a state representative or senator, attacking private golf clubs is a sure winner. Even granting the power of male club members, most constituencies are such that private golf clubs make safe targets. The long process that over the previous half-century created a decidedly negative image of the clubs has created state legislatures that can attack the clubs without much risk, and such attacks create the impression that the legislature is taking a stand against privilege. The female crusade against the clubs is also rooted in the notion that clubs are essentially a tool for businessmen. In the various controversies one inevitably hears the argument that clubs and weekend tee times are crucial to business success, a view that I have often heard asserted but have never seen proved.

As the situation stands today, several private clubs are waging intramural war with some of their female members. When the conflict cannot be

resolved internally, the women have found local and state law to be a helpful ally. These members pressure the clubs to change their rules by threatening that a tax break or a liquor license may be revoked if they do not in-
troduce antidiscriminatory practices. Of course, almost all the commentators
on this battle agree that most clubs have adjusted to the demands of their
female members without undue conflict or legal action—but the clubs that
silently amend their rules are not so interesting as the ones that end up in
court.[6]

On the surface this conflict between women transformed by social and
economic change and clubs that refuse to respond seems simple. Is it not just
a conflict between the idea of equal treatment and clubs that insist on maintaining male privilege? To a great extent it is, but the trials and controversies have raised two issues that are at the very least disturbing.

The first of these issues involves a problem that arose in the course of
the Burning Tree litigation. The purpose of the action by Maryland was
apparently straightforward. Maryland wished to deprive clubs such as Burning Tree access to tax relief because they discriminate. All the legislation in
question, however, took account of the fact that all clubs discriminate because they are traditionally bound to programs that feature single-gender
events. Most clubs, for example, have separate men's and women's championships. Almost all clubs put on regular events such as member-member and
member-guest functions that are limited to a single gender. Finally, many
clubs have weekly schedules that reserve the course for women or men. Traditionally men have had control of the weekend mornings, whereas the
course has been open to women on one or two weekdays. In the Maryland
statutes these practices were referred to as "periodic discrimination." Although the opinion had little bearing on Burning Tree's eventual defeat, the
Maryland court found this exemption for periodic discrimination to be unconstitutional since it clearly violated the equal rights amendment of the
Maryland Constitution.[7]

Thus, while women have been battling to wrest control of the first tee
from the men, there has developed a nagging sub rosa conflict over the extent to which one should push antidiscrimination rhetoric. Such rhetoric

proves to be a crude instrument that can produce unintended consequences. Once the state becomes involved, fine distinctions become harder and harder to make. It seems apparent that any victory by working women seeking weekend access will also cost clubs the right to stage golf programs that discriminate between the genders in any way.

Marcia Chambers, for one, has recognized this problem. In *The Unplayable Lie* she asks how can state law be written "to end gender discrimination without also destroying gender-specific sport competitions—men's tournaments and women's tournaments—that are a staple of country club life."[8] Her solution to this problem is unconvincing. Using Minnesota and Maryland as examples, she in effect shows that Minnesota has ignored the problems inherent in gender legislation aimed at the clubs. In Maryland we get a glimpse of the future. The State Department of Assessment and Taxation assigned Kaye Brooks Bushel to monitor the programs at private country clubs. Bushel admitted that "once you get government involved, then they've got to draw these lines and everything has to fit into a category." She was unhappy with the results, which she called "sort of ridiculous": "We got rid of harmless things, like ladies' and men's days."[9] According to Chambers, the Minnesota case suggests that things did not have to work out as they did in Maryland. Surely she is shortsighted here, for Minnesota is only one litigant away from changing its approach.

In a larger sense the tee-time controversy and its legal outcome so far offer us a view into life at country clubs today. The women who pushed for equal access on the weekends were, as described by Marcia Chambers, all spunky heroines, successful executives, and devoted and often accomplished golfers. At the same time, the accounts suggest, other women in the clubs fought change, often shunning and threatening the "radicals." Chambers uncharitably uses the term *WORMS* (Wives of Regular Members) to describe this group. At many clubs the conflict was not merely men versus women but also working WORMS versus nonworking WORMS. There can be little doubt that retired women and nonworking women who run homes and care for children as their primary labor have an interest in this conflict. Such a woman might care little about weekend tee times but cherish "Ladies Day" on Thursday and the annual member-guest tournament, when her sister comes up from Baltimore. Kaye Brooks Bushel, who implemented gender-neutral policies in Maryland, testifies: "We met a lot of resistance from very angry, older, often widowed or retired females who really thought we had rocked the boat to their disadvantage, because they liked their Ladies' Days, they liked their ladies' tournaments; whereas the younger group of working women were pressing to have some ladies' tournaments on weekends so they could play."[10]

Clearly the crusade to undercut male privilege at the country clubs backfired to some extent. The state in many cases stepped in and adminis- tered a not very discriminating remedy; in the long run the most important but least noticed casualty was club independence. Moreover, events in the state of Maryland are a harbinger of things to come. It increasingly seems inevitable that the practices of private country clubs will be monitored and approved by public officials enforcing a one-size-fits-all code of conduct.

The women who protested discriminatory tee times and sought access to the sacred ground of the men's grill have in many cases misperceived the nature and value of a truly private member-controlled club. Their demands have been consistent; they want the club to which they pay dues to respond to their needs. To put the matter another way, they want the club to act like a merchant who sells the same product under the same conditions to all. Private clubs, however, are voluntary associations that seek to satisfy the needs of all their members, who value their clubs in different ways. The officers of a club are unpaid volunteers trying to negotiate compromises with groups of members who want very different things from their interest in a single piece of property. They find it particularly difficult to satisfy the needs of members who value tradition *and* the needs of those who want rapid change in response to social and economic transformation.

California also is another sign of things to come. The decision in the Warfield case has at least one disturbing element. The core issue in the long- running dispute was whether the Peninsula Golf and Country Club should be construed as a business. If the club was a business, it then would fall un- der the antidiscrimination provisions of the state's Unruh Civil Rights Act. If the club was deemed to be a truly private club, it would be entitled to an exemption from the law, and its rights to act freely would be protected by the general freedom of association doctrine. When the California Supreme Court ruled that the club was a business and a public accommodation, it seemed to ignore precedent and put in doubt the existence in law of any private voluntary association protected from state action. In essence the court was asked to balance the right to free association against the right to freedom from discrimination. By defining the Peninsula Club as a business and thus subject to antidiscrimination laws, the court drastically narrowed the ground on which a truly free private voluntary association could stand.

The court's conclusions seem amazingly contrary to fact. For one thing, the justices argued that by applying the Unruh act to the club, they did not infringe on the club's freedom as an expressive association or the members' general freedom of association. Essentially the court stated that an association remains free even if the state exercises substantial control over admission policies. The implications of this decision are unclear, but if the state gains some control over membership policy, where will it stop? Can a club establish a membership limit if members of a protected group (women, African Americans, etc.) are seeking to join?

Perhaps most disturbing was the finding that the club was a business. The court based its conclusion on the facts that the club engaged in regular business transactions with nonmembers and that the club sponsored events attended by nonmembers. The justices acknowledged that the club was honestly nonprofit and that the business transactions served only to reduce the dues paid by members. As a business, then, the club had illegally discriminated against women by refusing to allow them to hold full equity memberships.

A critic of the decision, Sharon Swaim, has suggested that "the court should have given more deference to the club member's freedom of association."[11] The court did not fully consider the club's purpose, which was clearly social and recreational. It also ignored testimony from members who said that they did not view the club as an adjunct to the business world. Members were chosen not for any business-related reason. They were chosen to enhance the recreational and social purposes of the club. By applying the

Unruh Civil Rights Act to the club, the court was forcing the members to associate with people they would otherwise have rejected. Both federal and state courts have consistently cited membership selectivity as one of the basic features of a group protected by the right to free association. It is hard to imagine the association that could have been deemed truly private by this court.

Swaim wonders what impact this decision will have. She claims that groups such as the Girl Scouts and Boy Scouts or fraternities and sororities might lose their status as private groups if the court's criteria become generally employed. Any organization that engages in regular business transactions may in the future lose the protection accorded private groups. The decision in the Warfield case has the potential seriously to erode the freedom of expressive association established in several U.S. Supreme Court decisions.[12]

The legal analysis of both the Warfield and the Burning Tree cases will no doubt go on for some time. I have put this discussion of the legal conflicts between women and country clubs in an epilogue because the issues are unsettled and the outcome is far from clear. Yet some preliminary cultural analysis is possible.

Certainly the conflict is understandable as a continuation of the long war between liberty and equality. On the one side, you have the clubs asserting their members' rights to associate with whomever they choose and to create voluntary associations as they see fit. On the other side, you have women seeking equal treatment and freedom from discrimination.[13] Given the Warfield and Burning Tree decisions, the state courts have clearly become the champions of equality at the expense of liberty. A closer look at the issue, however, shows it to be messier than a simple dispute between the advocates of equality and the defenders of liberty. For one thing, the general nature of the dispute clearly pits women against women: businesswomen who seek equality with their male counterparts stand in conflict with women who work in the home and seek to have their interests recognized.

The dispute between women and the clubs also signals another, quite different cultural development. Although equality has certainly been the central issue, an unintended result has been the further erosion of the local, the unique, and the traditional in favor of the standardized and government controlled. Maryland's decision to have a state official monitor the programs of local clubs is an astonishing development. As I have argued, country clubs were established in part in response to the growing nationalization and standardization of American life. In the 1980s and 1990s the local and unique nature of the clubs came under sustained attack. This attack has employed an important new tactic, namely, the attempt to undermine the very idea that clubs are voluntary associations. The courts have insisted on seeing them as businesses and therefore as falling in a category that over the previous century has clearly come under the state's regulatory gaze and power. The idea of private, voluntary associations is on the defensive.

Golf and the country club have had a long and interesting history, a history that reflects an obdurate desire to retain some power and control at the local level. The clubs were like nineteenth-century villages. They were local sites of production; they produced recreation and a society of understandable proportions. They still mean something to Americans, even as they slip away, even as they succumb to forces that we do not yet fully understand.

# NOTES

## INTRODUCTION

1. Dan Jenkins, *"You Call It Sports, but I Say It's a Jungle out There"* (New York, 1989), 129.

## CHAPTER 1: THE COUNTRY CLUB IDEA AND AMERICAN EXPERIENCE

1. For the number of golf courses and country clubs in the late 1920s, see Robert B. Weaver, *Amusements and Sports in American Life* (Washington, D.C., 1939); H. B. Martin, *Fifty Years of American Golf* (New York, 1936); Jesse F. Steiner, *Americans at Play: Recent Trends in Recreation and Leisure Time Activities* (New York, 1933); and Francis Powers, "Our National Golf Bill," *Literary Digest*, Mar. 5, 1932, p. 35. Counting and categorizing golf courses and clubs is difficult. Courses are constantly being constructed and destroyed. Their status as private, public, or municipal is in constant flux. The number 4,000 is a conservative estimate. The number of truly private golf clubs in 1930 may have been as high as 5,000.

2. Alexis de Tocqueville, *Democracy in America*, trans. George Lawrence, ed. J. P. Mayer, 2 vols. in 1 (Garden City, N.Y., 1969), 2:513–14.

3. Sidney E. Ahlstrom, *A Religious History of the American People* (New Haven, Conn., 1972), 382–83.

4. Letters between the Morses quoted in Richard J. Moss, *The Life of Jedidiah Morse: A Station of Peculiar Exposure* (Knoxville, Tenn., 1995), 123–24.

5. Daniel T. Rogers, *The Work Ethic in Industrial America 1850–1920* (Chicago, 1974); Robert H. Wiebe, *The Search for Order 1877–1920* (New York, 1967); Daniel W. Howe, ed., *Victorian America* (Philadelphia, 1976). I have been especially influenced by Howe's introduction to *Victorian America*.

6. Thomas Bailey Aldrich, "Unguarded Gates," *Works*, 2 vols. (Boston, 1905), 2:75.

7. Brandeis quoted in Stephen Hardy, *How Boston Played: Sport, Recreation, and Community 1865–1915* (Boston, 1982), 145.

8. Wiebe, *Search for Order*, chap. 1; Frederick Jaher, *The Urban Establishment: The Upper Strata in Boston, New York, Charleston, Chicago, and Los Angeles* (Urbana, Ill., 1982), 70–74.

9. Edith Wharton, *Age of Innocence* (New York, 1920), 219, 356.

10. Wiebe, *Search for Order*, 12.

11. Rogers, *Work Ethic*, 99.

12. T. J. Jackson Lears, *No Place of Grace: Anti-Modernism and the Transformation of American Culture 1880–1920* (New York, 1981), chap. 1.

13. This view of religious thought is fully developed in James Turner, *Without God, without Creed: The Origin of Unbelief in America* (Baltimore, Md., 1985).

14. Daniel W. Howe, "Victorianism in America," in *Victorian America*, ed. Howe, 13.

15. This portrait of early Myopia is based on Allan Forbes, *Early Myopia* (Boston, 1942), 1–65.

16. The document is discussed in two club histories: Frederic H. Curtiss and John Heard, *The Country Club: 1882–1932* (Brookline, Mass., 1932), 29–30; and Elmer O. Cappers, *Centennial History of The Country Club 1882–1982* (Boston, 1983), 2–3.

17. Hardy, *How Boston Played*, esp. chap. 7, "The Fellowship of the Sporting Club," 127–46. Hardy fundamentally agrees with Benjamin G. Rader in "The Quest for Sub-Communities and the Rise of American Sport," *American Quarterly* 29 (Fall 1977): 355–69. In thinking about American golf and country clubs I have found these two works indispensable.

18. David Paine, "Prominent Country Clubs," *New England Magazine* 32 (1905): 337.

19. In attempting to understand the middle- and upper-class American search for a more strenuous and vivid life, I have been most influenced by Lears, *No Place of Grace*; John F. Kasson, *Amusing the Million: Coney Island at the Turn of the Century* (New York, 1978); Gunther Barth, *City People: The Rise of Modern City Culture in Nineteenth-Century America* (New York, 1980); and J. A. Mangan and James Walvin, eds., *Manliness and Morality: Middle-Class Masculinity in Britain and America, 1800–1940* (Manchester, 1987).

## CHAPTER 2: GOLF AND THE EARLY CLUBS

1. Edward S. Martin, "Country Clubs and Hunt Clubs in America," *Scribner's* 18 (July-Dec., 1895): 306.

2. Ibid., 303. See also Casper W. Whitney, "Evolution of the Country Club," *Harper's Magazine*, Dec. 1894, pp. 16–33.

3. This portrait of St. Andrew's is based on Desmond Tolhurst, *St. Andrew's Golf Club: The Birthplace of American Golf* (Rye Brook, N.Y., 1989); and John Reid, "The St. Andrew's Golf Club of America," *Outing* 32 (July 1898): 399–406.

4. The portrait of Shinnecock is based on Samuel L. Parrish, *Some Facts, Reflections, and Personal Reminiscences . . . as Associated with the Formation of the Shinnecock Hills Golf Club* (printed by club, 1923); Charles B. Macdonald, *Scotland's Gift: Golf* (New York, 1928), 81–85; and *New York Times*, Mar. 8, 1896.

5. Macdonald, *Scotland's Gift*, 75–90.

6. Alexis J. Colman, "The Golf Clubs of Chicago," *Outing* 32 (July 1899): 111. A work that describes the evolution of Chicago's northern suburbs and addresses the role of golf and country clubs in that evolution is Michael H. Ebner's *Creating Chicago's North Shore* (Chicago, 1988). See also H. C. Chatfield Taylor, "Country-Club Life in Chicago," *Harper's Weekly* 40 (Aug. 1, 1896): 761–62.

7. This description of Onwentsia is drawn from the club's rules and bylaws, *Onwentsia Club* (Chicago, 1910); Chatfield-Taylor, "Country-Club Life," 761–62; and Arthur Meeker, *Chicago with Love: A Polite and Personal History* (New York, 1955), 86, 91–93.

8. Carlyle E. Anderson, *Glen View Club* (Chicago, 1987), 6–10.

9. For the early days at Tuxedo Park, see Judson N. Smith, "The Tuxedo Club," *Munsey's Magazine* (Nov. 1891): 161–69; and Cleveland Amory, "Tuxedo Park—Black Tie," in *Mass Leisure*, ed. Eric Larrabee and Rolf Meyersohn (Glencoe, Ill., 1958), 238–49.

10. Chatfield-Taylor, "Country-Club Life," 762.

11. Chatfield-Taylor, "The Middle West Discovers Outdoors," *Outing* 45 (1904): 446.

12. Gustav Kobbé, "The Country Club and Its Influence upon American Social Life," *The Outlook* 68 (June 1, 1901): 253–66.

13. Macdonald, *Scotland's Gift*, 99–117; John Strawn, "One Hundred Years of the USGA," in *Golf: The Greatest Game* (New York, 1994), 34–71 (this amounts to the "approved" USGA history).

14. Macdonald, *Scotland's Gift*, 113–14. A violent discussion of this membership issue erupted in 1909; see *The American Golfer*, Jan. 1909, p. 110.

15. For these complex discussions of amateurism, see Macdonald, *Scotland's Gift*, 115–17.

16. For a good discussion of the process whereby traditions are invented and the conditions that call for such inventions, see Eric Hobsbawm and Terence Ranger, *The Invention of Tradition* (Cambridge, 1983), esp. Hobsbawm's introduction, 1–14.

## CHAPTER 3: GOLF TAKES ROOT

1. The numbers for 1900 are based on USGA estimates and appear in Martin, *Fifty Years*, 135–37; "Golf on the Seaboard," *Outing* 32 (Aug. 1898): 500.

2. Charles Turner, "Golf in Gotham," *Outing* 33 (Nov. 1899): 290; *Golfing*, Nov. 21, 1896, p. 211, Oct. 31, 1896, p. 391.

3. *Philadelphia Times*, Feb. 24, 1889, cited in Macdonald, *Scotland's Gift*, 76. See a similar piece in the *Philadelphia Dispatch*, Mar. 21, 1889.

4. The early history cited is Jerome D. Travers and James R. Corwell, *The Fifth Estate: Thirty Years of Golf* (New York, 1936); other information is from Robert Hunter, *The Links* (New York, 1926), vi–vii.

5. Henry E. Howland, "Golf," *Scribner's Magazine* 42 (May 1895): 531–33.

6. W. L. Watson, "Special Attraction of Golf," *Living Age* 3 (Sept. 1898): 680–85; Howland, "Golf," 537; Price Collier, "Golfers in Action," *Outing* 31 (Aug. 1897): 252. Almost every article on golf before 1900 mentions its Scottish origins.

7. Lears, *No Place of Grace*, 4–47.

8. "Year's Golf," *Outing* 31 (Dec. 1897): 271.

9. "A Golfing Experience," *Golfing*, Dec. 9, 1897, p. 165.

10. Andrew Carnegie, "Dr. Golf," *The Independent* 70 (June 1, 1911): 1181–92.

11. Arthur Ruhl, "What Golf Means to the Big City" (1903), in *Golf: A Turn-of-the-Century Treasure*, ed. Mel Shapiro, Warren Dohn, and Leonard Berger (Secaucus, N.J., 1986), 259–67. This hard-to-find collection is the best source of early journalism about golf and country clubs.

12. Kobbé, "The Country Club," 253–55.

13. Chatfield-Taylor, "Middle West Discovers," 449.

14. Mr. Dooley [pseud.], "Golf," *Mr. Dooley at His Best* (New York, 1938), 175–81.

15. Howland, "Golf," 546; *New York Times*, "Golf is Growing in Favor," Oct. 4, 1891; *New York Times*, Feb. 13, 1896 (Dr. Rainsford interview).

16. Price Collier, "The Rise of Golf in America," *American Monthly Review of Reviews* 22:460; Charles B. Macdonald, "Golf: The Ethical and Physical Aspects of the Game," *Golf*, Jan. 1898, p. 20.

17. Macdonald, *Scotland's Gift*, 321–22.

18. Kobbé, "The Country Club," 253–56.

19. *New York Times*, Apr. 27, 1897, June 10; 1897.

20. *Golfing*, July 16, 1897.

21. *Golfing*, Dec. 5, 19, 1896.

22. The official version of the 1896 dispute is in Strawn, "One Hundred Years." For a fuller account, see Calvin H. Sinnette, *Forbidden Fairways: African Americans and the Game of Golf* (Chelsea, Mich., 1998), 17–21.

23. Arnold Haultain, *The Mystery of Golf: A Brief Account of its Origin, Antiquity and Romance; its Uniqueness; its Curiousness; and its Difficulty; its anatomical, philosophical, and moral Properties; together with diverse Concepts on other Matters to it appertaining* (Cambridge, 1986 [1908]).

24. Arnold Haultain, "Secret of Golf," *Atlantic* 10 (June 10, 1910): 753–61; see also Arnold Haultain, "Charms of Golf," *American Golf*, Oct. 1901.

25. Haultain, *Mystery*, 8–9.

26. Ibid., 13–14.

27. Ibid., 17–20.

28. Ibid., 26.

29. Ibid., 147.

30. Ibid., 151.

31. Ibid., 26.

32. Kenneth T. Jackson, *Crabgrass Frontier: The Suburbanization of the United States* (New York, 1985), 97–99.

## CHAPTER 4: GOLF, THE COUNTRY CLUB, AND THE AMERICAN FAMILY

1. E. S. Martin, "The Rise of the Country Clubs," *Harper's Weekly* 44–45 (Sept. 8, 1900): 843.

2. Lears, *No Place of Grace*, 15–17.

3. See Daniel J. Singal, ed., *Modernist Culture in America* (Belmont, Calif., 1991), esp. Daniel S. Singal, "Towards a Definition of American Modernism," 1–27.

4. Quotations from "Golf Widows at Newport," *Golf*, Sept. 1897, p. 62. See also "The Golf Widow," *American Golf*, Mar. 1902, p. 26.

5. Paine, "Prominent Country Clubs," 342–45.

6. Candace M. Volz, "The Modern Look of the Early Twentieth-Century House: A Mirror of Changing Lifestyles," in *American Home Life 1880–1930: A Social History of Spaces and Services*, ed. Jessica H. Foy and Thomas J. Schlereth (Knoxville, Tenn., 1992), 25–48. The nature of the home was changing for all classes. As city life slowly became a norm, Americans grew accustomed to apartment life. To some extent all Americans responded to the small, less accommodating home by transferring energy and vital functions (entertainment mostly) to the saloon, the lodge hall, the movie

theater, and the city streetcorner. See Barth, *City People*, and David Nasaw, *Going Out: The Rise and Fall of Public Amusements* (New York, 1993).

7. David L. Lewis and Laurence Goldstein, eds, *The Automobile and American Culture* (Ann Arbor, Mich., 1983), esp. the essays in part 2, "The Transformation of America," 89–178.

8. The "new woman" is introduced in Carroll Smith-Rosenberg, "The New Woman as Androgyne: Social Disorder and Gender Crisis, 1870–1936" *Disorderly Conduct: Visions of Gender in Victorian America* (New York, 1985), 245–96.

9. Jeannette A. Marks, "Outdoor Life at Wellesley College," *Outing* 32 (May 1898): 119–20.

10. Mrs. Reginald De Koven, "The New Woman and Golf Playing," *Cosmopolitan* 21 (May 21, 1896): 355–58.

11. Lillian Brooks, "Woman's Game of Golf," *New York Times*, June 10, 1900.

12. William Patten, ed., *The Book of Sport* (New York, 1901), 39–40.

13. William L. Quinn, *Morris County Golf Club* (Virginia Beach, Va., 1995), 8–34. The *New York Times* closely followed the development of the clubs; see esp. *New York Times*, July 4, 1894.

14. In recent years scholars of all sorts have produced a number of fine works on women and sport. The upper-class women who took up tennis and golf at private clubs played a crucial role in this history. For a study that emphasizes the differences between upper- and lower-class styles of leisure, see Susan K. Cahn, *Coming on Strong: Gender and Sexuality in Twentieth-Century Women's Sport* (New York, 1994), esp. chap. 1. Also see Cindy Himes, "The Female Athlete in American Society: 1860–1940" (Ph.D. diss. University of Pennsylvania, 1986). I also profited from Allen Guttmann, *Women's Sports: A History* (New York, 1991).

15. Frank A. Spearman, "The Duffer," *Munsey's Magazine* 19 (Sept. 1898): 895–901.

16. Glenna Collett, *Ladies in the Rough* (New York, 1928), esp. 3–32.

17. *New York Times*, July 30, 1916.

## CHAPTER 5: FROM SIMPLE TO COMPLEX

1. Curtiss and Heard, *The Country Club*, 31–46.

2. Ibid., 67–73.

3. For a good analysis of middle-class spending habits, see Daniel Horowitz, *The Morality of Spending* (Baltimore, 1985), esp. 65–70.

4. C. O. Morris, "Country Clubs for Everyone," *Country Life*, July 1909, p. 295.

5. Ibid., 296.

6. Ibid., 296–97, 330–31.

7. Edward L. Fox, "Country Clubs for Everyone," *Outing* 47 (Oct. 1912): 108–18.

8. Morris, "Country Clubs for Everyone," 331.

9. Al Laney, *Following the Leaders* (Classics of Golf, 1991), 6–21.

10. Curtiss and Heard, *The Country Club*, 50–56.

11. Macdonald, *Scotland's Gift*, 170.

12. Ibid., 296.

13. Thomas H. Uzzell, "Pine Valley—He-Man Course," *American Golfer*, Apr. 1927, p. 22. See also J. LaCerda, "Valley of Despair, Pine Valley Golf Club," *Saturday Evening Post*, Aug. 18, 1945; and Robert Sidorsky, "Eighteen Holes of Sweet Agony," *Town and Country*, July 1991, pp. 38–41.

14. Macdonald, *Scotland's Gift*, 240–48.

15. Donald J. Ross, *Golf Has Never Failed Me: The Lost Commentaries of Legendary Golf Architect Donald J. Ross* (Chelsea, Mich., 1996), 1–13; W. Pete Jones, compiler, *A Directory of Golf Courses Designed by Donald J. Ross* (Raleigh, N.C., 1998). The number of courses "touched" by Ross has been the source of constant dispute, and the number will probably never be set to the agreement of all golf historians.

16. Virginia Scott Jenkins, *The Lawn: A History of an American Obsession* (Washington, D.C., 1994), 53, 35, 54–57.

17. The literature on the park movement, Frederick Law Olmsted, and related matters has grown rapidly in the previous few years. I have found William Cronon, ed., *Uncommon Ground: Toward Reinventing Nature* (New York, 1995) particularly helpful. Let me add a personal reflection that might help tighten the connection between park and golf course design. When you play a Donald Ross course, it is easy to become engrossed in golf-related issues such as his treatment of the bunkers and his habit of rounding off the edges of greens. I have always been impressed, however, by the parklike quality of many of his courses. My favorite in this regard is Mid-Pines Golf Course in Southern Pines, North Carolina. Unlike modern courses, in which the holes are separated by relatively great distances, Mid-Pines sets players in separate groups often very near one another. Tees and greens are quite close, and the paths from green to tee intersect as if they were designed to throw groups together for a moment of socializing. More generally, Mid-Pines looks like a park designed for strolling, the shape of the holes serving as subtle guidance to the walker.

Perhaps more to the point, most golf courses (public and private) serve the surrounding area as a park of sorts. In my experience golf courses serve a number of functions, and people (members and nonmembers) use them in many of ways. People hunt, fish, bird-watch, have "romantic encounters," cross-country ski, paint, take photographs, garden, collect firewood, and walk their dogs. At the club at which I play, an old gentleman ("the dog walker") and his beagle are as much a part of the course as are the ninth green or the pro shop.

18. *New York Times*, Mar. 13, 1913.

19. *New York Times*, June 8, 10, 1901.

20. Benjamin G. Rader, *American Sports: From the Age of Folk Games to the Age of Tele-vised Sports* (Upper Saddle River, N.J., 1999) 119–20.

21. *New York Times*, May 8, 9, 26 (quotation), Aug. 2, 1911.

22. Arthur S. Link and Bruce B. Catton, *American Epoch* (New York, 1973).

23. Ellis P. Butler, "Why I Live in a Suburb," in *The American Dream: A Half-Century View from American Magazine*, ed. John K. M. McCaffery (Garden City, N.Y., 1964), 36–46. Butler's essay originally appeared in 1927.

24. *New York Times*, Apr. 9, 1917.

25. *New York Times*, Dec. 2, 1921, Oct. 31, 1925, Aug. 29, 1926, Jan. 9, 1927, May 18, 1928.

26. *New York Times*, Jan. 9, 1927. Over time several incensed golfers took the IRS to court over the tax. In 1932 Frank J. Foran, a member of San Francisco's Olympic Club, went to federal court over $5.20 in tax payments. He lost. See *New York Times*, Aug. 30, 1932.

## CHAPTER 6: THE GOLDEN AGE

1. Rader, "Quest for Sub-Communities," 355–60.

2. Hunter, *The Links*, vii.

3. "$1,000 Course," *Golfers Magazine*, Aug. 30, 1926, p. 30.

4. Price Collier, "Golf," *Outing* 36 (Nov. 1900): 201.

5. Country clubs as institutions have shown a considerable interest in helping the caddies who work at their courses. The most notable example is the Chick Evans Scholarship Program, a project the Western Golf Association adopted after the USGA had rejected the idea. Beginning slowly in the 1920s, the program, funded by the association's clubs, has provided college scholarships for thousands of cad-dies and has also built housing (chapter houses) on many campuses. For a history of the program see Tim Cronin, *A Century of Golf: Western Golf Association 1899–1999* (Chelsea, Mich., 1998), 81–120.

6. Grantland Rice, "Golf vs. Baseball as a Paying Profession," *Literary Digest*, Apr. 9, 1921, pp. 68–69 (quoting at length Rice's essay in the *New York Tribune*).

7. Bernard Darwin, "Mr. Ouimet Makes History," in *Mostly Golf: A Bernard Dar-win Anthology*, ed. Peter Ryde (London, 1976), 68.

8. Gene Sarazen, *Thirty Years of Championship Golf: The Life and Times of Gene Sarazen* (New York, 1950), 1–95.

9. Alistair Cooke, *Fun and Games with Alistair Cooke* (New York, 1994), 76.

10. Sinnette, *Forbidden Fairways*, 30–33.

11. "Municipal Golf Pays in Grand Rapids," *American City*, Oct. 1929, p. 15; Joe

Kelly, "Municipal Golf in Indianapolis," *Golfer's Magazine*, Feb. 1920, p. 14. Many municipal courses were influenced by "clubs" that were formed to enforce rules, run tournaments, and in general direct the affairs of the course. Rebecca Rankin, who surveyed municipal courses in 1924, concluded: "In a good many cities it has been found advantageous to have clubs, even on public golf courses." She claims that such clubs make the courses more popular and that "they are also a means of securing for players reciprocal privileges with private clubs" (Rankin, "Municipal Golf in a Hundred Cities," *American City*, June 1924, pp. 599–600).

12. Steiner, *Americans at Play*, 70–76.

13. Earl Chapin May, "Neighborhood Golf in Iowa," *American Golfer*, July 28, 1923, pp. 10–13.

14. This portrait of Olympia Fields is based on Dick Smith's "World's Largest Golf Club," *American Golfer*, Aug. 1929, p. 63.

15. H. J. Elson and John Noyes, "A Modern Country Club Development: The New Westwood Country Club Grounds," *Landscape Architecture* 18 (1927): 267–76.

16. Peter Levine, "The *American Hebrew* Looks at 'Our Crowd': The Jewish Country Club in the 1920s," *American Jewish History* 83 (1995): 27–49.

17. Harold D. Eberlein, "Country Club Houses," *Architectural Record* 38, no. 2 (1915): 207–8.

18. Ibid., 208.

19. J. Lewis Brown, "The Evolution of the Golf Club House in America," *Architectural Forum* 42 (Mar. 1925); Grantland Rice, "What the Golfer Wants in His Club," *Architectural Forum* 42 (Mar. 1925).

20. Ayman Embury II, "The Small Country Club," *Architectural Forum* 42 (Mar. 1925): 176.

21. Roger H. Bullard, "The Architecture of the Country Club," *Architectural Forum* 52 (Mar. 1930): 315.

22. Sinclair Lewis, *Babbitt* (New York, 1922), 204, 155–56.

23. Warren I. Susman, *Culture as History* (New York, 1984), 277.

24. The role of class and other social factors in the world of private clubs has been treated in a number of places; see, for example, Vance Packard, *The Status Seekers* (New York, 1959), esp. chap. 13; Richard P. Coleman and Lee Rainwater, *Social Standing in America: New Dimensions in Class* (New York, 1978); and James M. Mayo, *The American Country Club: Its Origins and Development* (New Brunswick, N.J., 1998). Mayo's fine study, from which I have learned a great deal, takes a different approach to the country club. His work is more an institutional study of the country club over time that makes little attempt to explain the connection of golf to the clubs. For Mayo's discussion of class as a factor in club life, see especially pp. 190–97. In this analysis

of class and the country club, Mayo and others have drawn on two works particularly: Coleman and Rainwater, *Social Standing in America*, and Richard P. Coleman and Bernice L. Neugarten, *Social Status in the City* (San Francisco, 1971).

25. C. Wright Mills, *The Power Elite* (New York, 1956), 61.

26. Packard, *The Status Seekers*, 181.

27. *New York Times*, Aug. 2, 1915. Also see Ron Chernow, *Titan: The Life of John D. Rockefeller* (New York, 1998), 410–12.

28. John Kieran, "Golf: A Case Study in Economic Trends," *New York Times*, July 30, 1933.

29. Gregory Mason, "Golf Is Happily Disappearing," *American Mercury* 32 (Aug. 1934): 485–88.

30. H. I. Phillips, "Is Golf Justifiable," *Saturday Evening Post*, June 23, 1934, p. 23.

31. Charles Puckette, "The Biggest Hazard: The Cost of Golf," *New York Times*, May 24, 1931.

32. *New York Times*, Sept. 13, 1931.

33. Kenneth P. Kempton, "Golf Is a Poor Man's Game," *American Mercury* 28 (Feb. 1933): 158–65.

## CHAPTER 7: AN ENDANGERED SPECIES

1. Louis Auchincloss, *The Embezzler* (Boston, 1966), 15–16.

2. Geoffrey S. Cornish and Ronald E. Whitten, *The Golf Course* (New York, 1981), 88. Getting an accurate count of golf courses and country clubs during the 1930s and 1940s has proven difficult. Accurate numbers may never be available. However, the trend was clear—private clubs closed at a rapid rate and new courses were almost always public.

3. *Pittsburgh Bulletin Index*, Oct. 17, 1936.

4. "Club Comeback," *Business Week*, June 27, 1936, pp. 20–21.

5. This portrait of Hollins is based on *New York Times*, Aug. 29, 1944; Betty Hicks, "Marion Hollins," *Women Sport*, Oct. 1977, pp. 15–19; Margaret Goss, "Mistress of Court and Course," *Woman Citizen* 8 (Aug. 1925). David E. Outerbridge's *Champion in a Man's World* (Chelsea, Mich., 1998) is helpful on some issues.

6. *New York Times*, June 8, 1942.

7. Quinn, *Morris County Club*, 85–88.

8. Tolhurst, *St. Andrew's Golf Club*, 72–74.

9. *Statistical Abstract of the United States* (Washington, D.C., 1970), 204–5; ibid. (1997), 258–59.

10. Rader, *American Sports*, 227–30. Rader believes that country clubs grew after World War II, but at a slower rate than in the 1920s, and that the clubs did not grow as quickly as incomes or population. I believe that clubs absolutely declined in the

1950s and 1960s and that daily-fee courses came to dominate. Rader is surely right when he suggests that recreational facilities (golf courses, tennis courts, pools) built into suburban developments served as "a partial substitute for the country club."

11. Gwilyn S. Brown, "Where Is the Golf Course of the Workers?" *Sports Illustrated,* Aug. 26, 1963, pp. 42–44. See also John Budd, "Golf Goes Industrial," *Recreation,* Aug. 1949, pp. 260–62.

12. For my understanding of Sea Pines I am much indebted to Michael N. Danielson's *Profits and Politics in Paradise: The Development of Hilton Head Island* (Columbia, S.C., 1995), esp. 41–57. See also Margaret Greer, ed., *Three Decades of Hilton Head Architecture, 1965–1995* (Hilton Head, S.C., 1995); and the wonderful essay on Charles Fraser and Sea Pines in John McPhee, *Encounters with the Archdruid* (New York, 1971).

13. *New York Times,* Apr. 9, 1998.

14. Robert N. Bellah, et al., *Habits of the Heart: Individualism and Commitment in American Life* (Berkeley, Calif., 1985), 179–181; Edward J. Blakely and Mary Gail Snyder, *Fortress America: Gated Communities in the United States* (Washington, D.C., 1999), esp. 55–63.

15. *New York Times,* Oct. 17, 1950, Mar. 4, 1952, Dec. 21, 1951.

16. "A Chance to Play," *Time;* Nov. 21, 1955, p. 21.

17. *New York Times,* Nov. 25, 1959, Jan. 13, 1959, June 28, 1960.

18. Burk Uzzle, "The Country Club: An American Idyl," *Life Magazine,* Aug. 3, 1962, pp. 59–65.

19. *New York Times,* Apr. 30, 1961.

20. *New York Times,* Jan. 19, 20, 1952.

21. The coverage of Eisenhower's golf and his activities at Burning Tree and Augusta National was constant and often bordered on the silly. See *New York Times,* May 10, Aug. 6, 1953, Mar. 7, 27, 29, July 3, Sept. 19, Aug. 18, 1955, Apr. 17, Oct. 16, 1958, May 29, 30, 1960; and "A Long Line of Golfing Presidents," *U.S. News and World Report,* Apr. 24, 1953. Although childhood memories are usually unreliable, I am sure I remember that television news shows closely followed Eisenhower's golf game and his critics' regular attacks on his "part-time" presidency. For the Kennedy and Castro remarks, see *New York Times,* Nov. 7, 1960, and Mar. 31, 1961.

22. *New York Times,* Apr. 14, 1956.

23. *New York Times,* July 9, 13, 16, 1959.

24. The ADL report on private club discrimination appeared in Jan. 1962. It proved useful to many who sought solid numbers on the extent of discrimination. For a full analysis of the report, see Benjamin Epstein and Arnold Foster, *Some of My Best Friends* (New York, 1962), 21–25.

25. "Golf—Anyone?" *Newsweek,* Mar. 25, 1963, pp. 104–5.

26. *New York Times,* Feb. 13, 1977.

27. John Steele Gordon, "The Country Club," *American Heritage*, Sept.–Oct. 1990, pp. 75–84; Marcia Chambers, "A Revolution in Private Clubs," *Golf Digest*, May–June 1990; E. M. Swift, "Boom Sport USA," *Sports Illustrated*, July 2, 1990, pp. 46–52.

28. Coverage of the Shoal Creek crisis was dominated by television. For editorial opinion and the basic facts, see Diane McWhorter, "The White Man's Last Stand," *The Nation*, Oct. 8, 1990, pp. 379–80; William A. Henry III, "The Last Bastions of Bigotry," *Time*, July 22, 1990, pp. 66–67; Tom Callahan, "Golf's Country Club Dilemma," *U.S. News and World Report*, Aug. 20, 1990, pp. 60; and Peter Fuich, "Racism: Golf's Intolerable Handicap," *Business Week*, Aug. 13, 1990, p. 112. The Simpson quotation is from William O. Johnson, "The Gates Open," *Sports Illustrated*, Aug. 13, 1990, p. 59.

29. Henry, "Last Bastions of Bigotry," 67.

30. Tom Watson, "The American Way of Golf," *New York Times*, June 17, 1991; John Garrity, "An Act of Conscience," *Sports Illustrated*, Dec. 10, 1990, p. 110.

31. *New York Times*, June 6, 1991.

32. William Hallberg, *The Soul of Golf* (New York, 1997), 64–65.

33. Robert D. Putnam, "Bowling Alone: America's Declining Social Capital," *Journal of Democracy* 6 (Jan. 1995): 65–79.

34. The literature on Augusta National and the Masters is larger than that for any other club by a considerable margin. See, for example, Curt Sampson, *The Masters: Golf, Money, and Power in Augusta, Georgia* (New York, 1998); Steve Eubanks, *Augusta: Home of the Masters Tournament* (Nashville, Tenn., 1997); and David Owen, *The Making of the Masters: Clifford Roberts, Augusta National, and Golf's Most Prestigious Tournament* (New York, 1999). Owen's book shows conclusively that previous writers, animated by desires to bring Augusta National down a peg or two, have believed and spread myths and outright lies about the club and the people who have run it.

## CONCLUSION

1. Scott Stossel, "The Golf of America: Class, Culture and a Little White Ball," *The New Republic*, Aug. 3, 1998, p. 19.

2. Bruce McCall, "The Case against Golf," in *1998: The Best American Sports Writing*, ed. Bill Littlefield (Boston, 1998), 190.

3. Ibid., 189.

4. Ibid., 186.

5. David Owen, *My Usual Game: Adventures in Golf* (New York, 1995), 5, 9, 234–67.

6. Zechariah Chaffee Jr., "The International Affairs of Associations," *Harvard Law Review* 43 (May 1930): 1027 (emphasis added).

## EPILOGUE

1. *State of Maryland et al. v. Burning Tree Club Inc. et al.*, no. 106, Sept. term, 1987, Court of Appeals of Maryland. All cases and law review articles are available on Lexis-Nexis.

2. *Warfield v. Peninsula Golf and Country Club*, Supreme Court of California, June 29, 1995.

3. Marcia Chambers, *The Unplayable Lie: The Untold Story of Women and Discrimination in American Golf* (New York, 1995), esp. sect. 2, "Disadvantaged in the Land of Privilege."

4. Marcia Chambers, "Driving away Sex Bias at Private Clubs," *National Law Journal*, June 17, 1991, p. 14.

5. The growth in numbers of female golfers has not been very dramatic. Indeed, growth in the number of players in any group is hard to measure because many people try the game, quit, and return in a pattern that no one understands. The on-again, off-again passion is generally common among most groups, but some commentators suggest that women do not continue as players because they feel uncomfortable at male-dominated courses; see Sue Adam Barr, "Golf, Women and the Turn of the Century," *Golf Market Today*, Sept.–Oct. 1998, pp. 1, 3–5.

6. Chambers, *The Unplayable Lie*, 3–9; Rhonda Hillbery, "Restriction at Private Clubs," *Los Angeles Times*, Jan. 6, 1994.

7. The exemption for periodic discrimination was originally part of the legislation aimed at private clubs and groups that sought guidance on what was allowable. This language is referred to as "Chapter 334 of the Acts of 1986."

8. Chambers, *The Unplayable Lie*, 1999. One of the plain answers to her question is that laws mandating equality cannot apply only on Saturday and Sunday.

9. Quoted in Chambers, *The Unplayable Lie*, 202.

10. Quoted in ibid.

11. Sharon Swaim, "Forcing Open the Doors of Private Clubs: Warfield v. Peninsula Golf and Country Club—Did the Court Go Too Far?" *University of California Law Review* 30 (Spring 1997): 925.

12. Ibid., 934. See also the concurring dissenting opinion by J. Mosk and especially the dissenting opinion of C. J. Lucas in *Warfield v. Peninsula Golf and Country Club*.

13. The multifaceted debate between proponents of equality and advocates of liberty is fundamental to any understanding of contemporary political discourse and conflict. For a particularly interesting view of this issue, see Benjamin Barber, "An Epitaph for Marxism," *Society*, Nov.-Dec. 1995, 22–25; Richard J. Ellis, *The Dark Side of the Left: Illiberal Egalitarianism in America* (Lawrence, Kans., 1998), offers a balanced critique of the egalitarian movement.

# INDEX

RICHARD J. MOSS is the John J. and Cornelia V. Gibson Professor of History at Colby College. He is working on a history of golf in America. His handicap is three.

## SPORT AND SOCIETY

Big-Time Football at Harvard, 1905: The Diary of Coach Bill Reid
  Edited by Ronald A. Smith

Leftist Theories of Sport: A Critique and Reconstruction
  William J. Morgan

Babe: The Life and Legend of Babe Didrikson Zaharias   Susan E. Cayleff

Stagg's University: The Rise, Decline, and Fall of Big-Time Football
  at Chicago   Robin Lester

Muhammad Ali, the People's Champ   Edited by Elliott J. Gorn

People of Prowess: Sport, Leisure, and Labor in Early Anglo-America
  Nancy L. Struna

The New American Sport History: Recent Approaches and
  Perspectives   Edited by S. W. Pope

Making the Team: The Cultural Work of Baseball Fiction   Timothy Morris

Making the American Team: Sport, Culture, and the Olympic
  Experience   Mark Dyreson

Viva Baseball! Latin Major Leaguers and Their Special Hunger
  Samuel O. Regalado

Touching Base: Professional Baseball and American Culture in the
  Progressive Era (rev. ed.)   Steven A. Riess

Red Grange and the Rise of Modern Football   John M. Carroll

Golf and the American Country Club   Richard J. Moss

REPRINT EDITIONS

The Nazi Olympics   Richard D. Mandell

Sports in the Western World (2d ed.)   William J. Baker

University of Illinois Press
1325 South Oak Street
Champaign, IL 61820-6903
www.press.uillinois.edu